The Complete Book
of Horses & Ponies

Also by Margaret Cabell Self

A WORLD OF HORSES

RIDING WITH MARILES

The Complete Book
of Horses & Ponies

Margaret Cabell Self

ILLUSTRATED BY R. W. MUTCH

McGRAW-HILL BOOK COMPANY, INC.

New York   Toronto   London

The Complete Book of Horses & Ponies

Library of Congress Catalog Card Number: 62-22203

56109

Second Printing

Credits for Photographs (*following page 62*)
Page one (top) Alexander; (bottom) Maryland Jockey Club. Page two (top)
Mrs. Sylvia Linkhart; (middle) Mary B. Beever; (bottom) Lounspach, courtesy
American Saddlehorse Breeders Association. Page three (top) Sargent, courtesy
American Saddlehorse Breeders Association; (bottom) Les Nelson, courtesy Tennessee
Walking Horse Breeders and Exhibitors Association of America. Page
four (top) Hellbusch, courtesy Leon H. Harms; (bottom) Darol Dickinson,
courtesy Carl Miles. Page five (top) Fort Worth Photo Lab; (bottom) Ewing
Galloway. Page six (top left) Sunset Hill Pony Farm; (top right) Mrs. E. I.
Culver; (bottom) Freudy Photos, courtesy Mrs. J. Macy Willets. Page seven
(top) Freudy Photos, courtesy Sally Cogie; (bottom) R. Earl Finley. Page eight
(top) Werner Wolf, Black Star; (bottom) Morgan Horse Club, Inc.

Contents

The Complete Book
of Horses & Ponies

I

Horses Through the Ages

Have you ever stopped to think how different the world of today would be were it not for the horse? For thousands of years, mankind depended entirely on the horse for transportation and communication, for exploration, and as a war machine. Even the wearing of trousers can be traced back to the advent of the saddle with stirrups, for the stirrup leathers irritated unprotected legs, and necessitated some form of garment which would provide protection.

Without the horse, many countries, and sections of countries, which today are heavily populated, would still be primeval jungles and deserts. Without the horse, only cities that were situated on rivers or seacoasts would have been able to exchange knowledge. Without this exchange, such modern inventions as electricity, motors, and airplanes might have been much later in appearing.

The Prehistoric Horse

The horse is one of the oldest mammals whose descendants still inhabit the earth. He is far older than mankind. The earliest horses roamed the Rocky Mountain regions of our West forty-five million years ago. The first traces of prehistoric man go back only seven million years, and the first evidence of what one might call civilized man did not appear until about ten thousand years ago.

Do not think, however, that this primitive prehistoric horse, which we now call Eohippus, or Dawn Horse, looked like the noble Thoroughbred or Arabian horse of today. Indeed not. Eohippus was about the size of a large cat. He had four toes on his front feet and three on his back feet. His teeth were small and not well developed. He had no horns or other weapons of defense, but he did have speed.

For eons of time, Eohippus and his descendants ran away from their enemies. We know now that when bodies of living beings are used consistently, they become stronger and better adapted to the demands made on them. So the descendants of Eohippus grew longer legs. This made them taller. They developed bigger lungs and more efficient breathing systems, and this changed their body construction. Their feet changed the most, for they ran on the tips of their toes. Very, very gradually, the nail of the longest toe became harder and harder, and longer and longer, for it was needed to protect the other toes from injury. As a result, the smaller toes gradually disappeared—they were not used, for now they did not reach the ground at all. It took forty million years for the soft-toed feet of Eohippus to become the hard hoof of the present-day horse.

While Eohippus was skipping about on our western plains, and his descendants were developing into quite different-looking animals, a similar breed of horses, descended from the same common ancestor as their American cousins, was gradually overrunning Europe. This period, between thirty-five and forty million years ago, might be called the Horse Age.

Either climate or natural enemies, however, changed conditions in Europe to such an extent that these prehistoric horses ceased to exist. For the next fifteen million years or so, there were no horses whatsoever in Europe or Asia.

Eohippus and his descendants were nomads. They liked to wander in search of greener pastures. One of these descendants, Mesohippus (the "middle horse"), was about the size of a sheep and looked much more like a modern horse than did his ancestor the Dawn Horse. About twenty million years ago, Mesohippus found his way through Alaska and across what is now the Bering Sea, into Asia and on into Europe.

For the next several million years, there were prehistoric horses in both Europe and America. Then the glaciers came and the American branch disappeared. Long before these glaciers reached down into our northern states, there was a cold period lasting hundreds of thousands of years, and the vegetation disappeared. Hyponippus, the descendant of Eohippus, who lived in North America at that time, could not live on stones or sand, and was forced to migrate. So for over seven million years, there were no horses of any kind in North or Central America.

The history of primitive man began seven million years ago. The last ice age was one million years ago. At that time, in Europe, there was a small horse with hard hooves that looked like a modern pony, which we now call Equus. Because of the glaciers, Equus wandered all over Europe and Asia. It is from him that all the types of horses we know today are descended.

The Horse as Servant

Although we know that the cave men probably hunted horses as a source of food, it is hard to say exactly when mankind began taming the horse and making him into a servant. The earliest written record of it was engraved on stone tablets by Kikkulis, a member of the Hittites, a people who lived in Asia Minor hundreds of years before the birth of Christ. Kikkulis was in charge of the stables of a king in the Hittite capital of Hattusas. The five stone tablets describe in great detail the stable routine judged at that time to be best for conditioning horses for sport and warfare. They discuss the value of hay, grass, and grain. They recommend bathing the horse at frequent intervals, and rubbing him down with sand to stimulate his circulation. They state exactly how far he should walk, trot, and canter each day. All this proves that the Hittites were by no means the first people to utilize the horse as a servant. It must have taken hundreds, and perhaps thousands of years, for man to have learned so much about the needs and characteristics of the horse.

The Horse in Battle

The Assyrian war chariots of about 500 B.C. were much better designed than the Greek chariots of the same time. The Assyrians used their heavy war chariots in battle. Great numbers of these lined up and then charged the enemy with tremendous impact. This "heavy cavalry," as it was called, formed one of the earliest effective war machines.

Alexander the Great, the Macedonian Emperor, perfected the use of the mounted horse in warfare. Alexander, who from birth had loved horses, received as a gift from his father a supposedly untameable stallion, named Bucephalus. Alexander was only thirteen at the time, but understood horses so well that he soon mastered the fiery animal and made him a good companion and servant.

In 326 B.C., at the famous battle of Hydaspes, Alexander, with only 9,000 foot soldiers and 5,000 mounted men (light cavalry), was faced with the tremendous force of the East Indian potentate, Porus.

Porus had his army already lined up in battle formation. It consisted of four miles of elephants, 150 chariots, each pulled by six horses, 30,000 foot soldiers, and about 4,000 light cavalry. Porus expected Alexander to meet him in an open plain, but Alexander had different ideas. He split up his light cavalry into two divisions. The larger one he sent around Porus' left flank to attack the foot soldiers behind the chariots and elephants. As Porus' mounted men rushed in to help the infantry, Alexander bore in from the other side with the remainder of his cavalry, and attacked from behind. Porus' chariots were too closely packed and could not turn around. For the same reason the elephants were also unable to turn. All they could do was to charge forward into the now empty plain! The battle took eight hours and Alexander won. But Bucephalus was killed and buried, with the honors of war, on the spot. Thus, a new weapon of warfare, the flying squadron of light cavalry, came into being.

From that day, light cavalry played a major role in organized warfare until the latter part of World War I, when it was replaced by the armored tank.

In the days of chivalry, the horse was the knight's most important asset. Indeed, without steeds, there would have been no knights-errant to win honor and protect the weak. Due to the extreme weight of his armor, the knight could not have moved about at all without his horse.

The Horse in Sport

The early Assyrians drove their horses harnessed to chariots when they went hunting. They also rode them and, like the American Indian, had them completely trained to obey the shift of weight so that the hunter could use both hands on his bow and arrow.

The sport of hunting on horseback has continued from the hunting of lions by the ancient Assyrians, through medieval times, right down to the present. The horn of the huntsman is still heard as he urges on his hounds in pursuit of fox or stag. There are still men and women who value above any other kind of sport a day spent following hounds over wall and rail, ditch and brook, atop their favorite hunters. In addition, there is the game of polo, developed first by the Persians, and various forms of racing.

The Horse in Agriculture

As a draft animal, the horse has been, and in some countries continues to be, very valuable. He has helped to clear the forests by pulling the great logs away after they have been cut down. He has carried produce to market. Above all, hitched to the simple plough, or to the huge combines of the West, he has made the cultivation of crops easier.

The Horse in Transportation and Communication

In the history of transportation, the horse has drawn many strange vehicles. Strong coach horses pulled heavy European carriages over roads that, in winter, were veritable seas of mud. The first vehicles to run on rails, the forerunners of the railroad, were coaches pulled by horses. The first trolley cars were pulled by horses. Even the early canal boats, which traveled natural or artificial waterways, were pulled by one or more horses. Between work shifts, they were carried aboard the boat itself.

The mail in Europe was carried by post, or mail coach. In

our own West, Pony Express riders on tough little mustangs sped through rough mountain passes, across almost unfordable rivers, and through Indian country carrying light pouches of mail.

The Pony Express was preceded by many-horse teams hitched to the Conestoga Wagons that carried the pioneers across the Western deserts and plains.

No one breed or type of horse would have been suitable for all these different roles, which the horse has been called upon to play through the ages. How special aptitudes and characteristics have been developed through selective breeding, and how all these different breeds, which we know today, differ from one another, you will find in Chapter 2 of this book.

Later, we will discuss some individual traits, both physical and mental, as well as general characteristics which all horses have inherited from their common ancestor, little Eohippus.

2

---◆◆◆---

Types & Breeds
of Horses & Ponies

In this section of the book we shall read about the different types and breeds of horses and ponies, where and how they came into being, what they look like, and for what purposes they are best suited. But first let's answer one very important question.

What is the difference between a horse and a pony? Since horses and ponies have the same ancestry, they are technically one and the same animal. The horse is big, as a rule, however, and the pony is always small. For many years there was much confusion. Some animals that were mostly from pony bloodlines grew to be quite tall. And many horses that had no pony ancestors, whatsoever, stayed small and looked more like ponies than horses.

Finally it was decided that for show purposes, and for general classification, any animal over 58 inches (14 hands 2 inches) was to be called a horse. Animals that measured less than 58 inches were to be called ponies. But this rule is not always strictly adhered to, for horses of small registered breeds, such as Arabs and Morgans, are always referred to as horses no matter how little they may be; and a stock horse is usually called a "cow pony," even though he may be quite tall.

The Arabian Horse

The Arabs are a roving people to whom the horse has always been very important. Long, long ago, they began keeping track of the "bloodlines," or pedigrees, of their horses. Some of these pedigrees go back to the days of Mohammed, who was born about 570 A.D.

Even then, the Arab realized that the foals of certain stallions and mares were better for certain purposes than were those of other parents. There were five different "families," or bloodlines, each with specific strengths and weaknesses. By choosing a mate for his mare or stallion from a family line with qualities which promised to balance certain weaknesses in his own horse, the Arab tried always to produce the best possible foals. This is called "selective breeding."

Why is the Arab so dependent on his horse? Living in a sparsely settled land with miles of deserts, the Arab has often had to depend on the alertness and courage of his horse to save his life when he was attacked and pursued.

Do the Arabs usually ride stallions or mares? They ride mares, which are less apt to "nicker" and give away the presence of their masters when they smell strange animals. The Arabs also believe that the mare is more "prepotent" (able to pass her own characteristics on to her foals) than the stallion. The record of bloodlines is named for the mares, rather than the stallions, as is usual in most other countries.

What does the Arab want in his mare besides speed? He wants an alert animal that will warn him by her actions if an enemy is near. He even takes his mare into his tent at night and has her sleep beside him, knowing that she will hear the approach of marauders long before he can hope to do so himself.

What other qualities do we find in Arabian horses? Intelligence, for one thing. Because of the close association with their masters, Arabian horses have become very intelligent. They also seem to have more affection for human beings than horses of other breeds. Many Arabs teach their war mares to fetch and carry like dogs. A famous legend tells of a man wounded in battle who was captured, tied, and left in a tent. Hearing the whinny of his horse just outside, he managed to roll himself under the tent flap and chew through her tether rope, so that she might escape even though he could not. Instead of running off, the mare lifted her master in her teeth and carried him back to his sorrowing family. The great effort was too much for her, and she died of fatigue, but she is still remembered in songs and stories.

Because Arabian horses often have to travel for hours at high speed over rough ground without food or water, they have developed tremendous stamina and endurance.

What does an Arabian horse look like? The Arabian horse of today is the direct result, physically and mentally, of centuries of selective breeding. He is not very large. Large horses need more to eat than small ones and are sometimes less agile. But, since Arabs are often big men, their horses had to be strong. A horse with a short back can carry weight much more easily than one with too long a back. One of the unusual characteristics of the Arabian horse is that he has one less vertebra than other horses. This gives him a short back. His tail is set rather high, and this, too, indicates strength in the back.

The legs of Arabian horses are reputed to be stronger than those of other breeds. This is because the bone is of a more compact, "denser," material, with a smaller channel running down the center. The Arabs use a shoe that covers the whole sole of the horse's foot. This keeps the walls (outsides) of the hoof from chipping off and wearing down too close to the sensitive part. One foot is always left bare to prevent slipping. In choosing breeding stock, the Arabs were particular about selecting animals with strong hoof walls rather than brittle ones. As a result, today's Arabian horses usually have good feet.

Speed and stamina depend largely on a good supply of wind. For this the horse needs a good breathing apparatus: wide, flaring nostrils, and a big windpipe. If the head is set onto the neck at too sharp an angle, there will not be room for a wide windpipe. Compare this "hammer-headed" conformation (see Fig. 1) with that of the Arabian horse with a well-cut-out "throttle."

The Arabs reasoned that the bigger the brain the smarter the horse, and chose horses that were wide between the eyes and had bulging foreheads. This bulge is called the "jibbah." The combination of wide nostrils and the jibbah give the typical

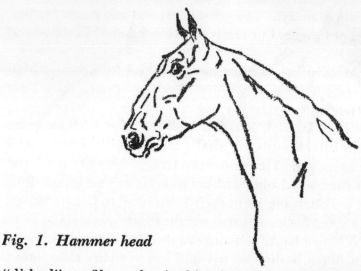

Fig. 1. Hammer head

"dished" profile to the Arabian horse, in contrast to the "ram" profile (see Fig. 2).

The Arab needed a mare with good eyesight, so he chose an animal with full bulging eyes set on the sides of her head. The ears act as semaphore flags, flapping to let the mare's master know when danger is afoot. This is why the ears are small, pointed, and alert.

The Arab wanted a horse that would obey instantly. Such a horse had to be sensitive enough to respond to the slightest touch of the rider's heel. She needed a skin so thin that the veins showed through it.

So you see that it was from having been bred for certain desirable traits that the Arabian horse came to look as he does.

What are the colors of the Arabian horse? Arabians may be any solid color, or they may be roan (a solid color with white mixed throughout). They are never spotted. They may, and often do, have white markings on the face and lower legs. The Arabs had all sorts of beliefs about the value of horses of the various colors. Horses of certain colors were said to be very swift, others especially intelligent, and others extraordinarily sturdy. The way the hair grew, the number of little whirls or cowlicks, and exactly where these occurred were all supposed to indicate particular characteristics also.

Fig. 2. Arabian with   *"Ram" profile*
"dished" profile

What are the gaits of the Arabian horse? He has a smooth free walk with a great deal of head motion, and a speedy canter. His trot is apt to be short and choppy, for this is not his natural gait. However, many can be trained to reach forward with both the front and hind legs and so develop a longer trot. Although they have a fast gallop, Arabians cannot compete successfully in races against larger breeds such as the English Thoroughbred, because of their short legs and short stride.

How big are Arabian horses? Most Arabians are from fourteen hands (56 inches) to fifteen and a half hands (62 inches).

What are Arabians most used for today? They are very popular as "pleasure horses"; that is, they are used for ordinary riding, especially trail riding, rather than for showing or hunting. Arabians are often seen in parades, and there are special classes for them in horse shows. Perhaps the most important use for the Arabian is for breeding purposes. For hundreds of years it has been known that an introduction of Arabian blood at intervals into the bloodlines of other breeds improves the resulting foals.

Is an Arabian horse suitable for a boy or girl to own and ride? Only if the boy or girl is a good rider, since the Arabian is one of the most sensitive of all breeds. The flutter of a leaf is apt to send him off in a flash. For the expert rider he is ideal, since he is so responsive; but he cannot be expected to behave well under the guidance of the beginner who has not yet learned "horse language," and who often makes his horse uncomfortable without meaning to do so.

Draft Breeds

What is a draft horse? A horse bred for the purpose of pulling heavy loads, and for farm work.

How are draft horses different from the horses we ride? They are much bigger and have a more powerful look. Their muscles are the kind that make them strong but do not give them power to run fast.

Is there more than one breed of draft horse? Yes, there are many different types all native to foreign countries. Most of these have been imported into the United States and are now bred here. They are also used to cross with Thoroughbreds to produce the popular Half-Bred hunter. They are even crossed with various pony breeds such as the Shetland and Hackney to produce a rugged calm type of pony.

What are the most popular draft breeds seen in this country? The Belgian, the Clydesdale, and the Percheron.

Where did these come from and what are they like? The Belgian is a descendent of the old Flemish horse and he has been bred for many years in Belgium. He was first imported in 1866 and the American Association of Importers and Breeders of Belgian Draft Horses was organized in 1887. The Belgian is a very large and powerful horse. He can be any solid color, although originally he was solid black. Teams of four or six glistening black Belgians wearing white harnesses and with their manes and tails braided in white and pink are popular as exhibition acts at fairs and horse shows.

What does the Clydesdale look like? The Clydesdale, which comes from Scotland, is somewhat smaller than the other draft breeds. He moves more freely and his "feathers" (the long hairs that grow on the lower legs) are so full and long that they look like trousers. He usually has a white face and four white stockings and is dark brown or black.

Where does the Percheron come from? He comes from a little section of France called Le Perche. Many people like the

Percheron best. He is very large, often weighing over 2,000 pounds. He is usually dapple-gray with a white mane and tail, and has a lovely disposition. The Percheron is the only one of the draft breeds which is said to have Arabian blood. He has been popular for many years, for it was the Percheron that was most valued by the knights as a battle horse in medieval times. The first Percheron stallions came to this country in 1839.

The Thoroughbred

In medieval times the knights rode the Great Horse. When knights charged each other the main purpose was to knock the enemy down or, better still, to upset both horse and rider. Here the weight of the horse was especially important, and speed or agility secondary. Then came the invention of the "crossbow," a weapon that could penetrate armor; later still came gunpowder, making armor obsolete, so that men no longer needed the tremendous horses. But where were suitable lighter ones to be found? The ladies had their palfreys. The Arabs had fleet mounts but these desert horses were very small. There were all kinds of other horses of no particular breed in Spain and middle Europe, but none of these was outstanding.

At about this time, in the late sixteen hundreds, kings and nobles also became very interested in racing and hunting. In the breeding of horses, therefore, speed came to be essential. A tall horse was needed, one with longer legs than the Arabian's. It was decided that the best way to produce such a horse was to mate desert-bred stallions with European mares, most of which were descended from the Great Horse line and had size but not speed.

Between 1690 and 1730, three Arabian stallions were brought into Europe for this purpose. Their names were the Darley Arabian, the Godolphin Barb, and Byerly Turk. The first word of each of these names refers to the owner or importer, and the second word to the special breed. The foals of these matings were called English Thoroughbreds.

Did people keep track of the pedigrees of these foals from the very beginning? Yes, indeed. At first each person kept track of his own, but this soon became impractical. Naturally, a colt

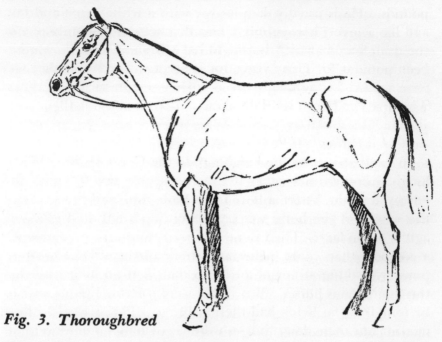

Fig. 3. Thoroughbred

that could trace his ancestry back to one of the three "foundation sires" was more valuable than one that couldn't. It was not long before dishonest people tried to claim that their animals had the desired bloodlines, whether they did or not. An association or club, known later as the Jockey Club of England, was formed for the purpose of keeping an accurate record of the pedigrees of Thoroughbred horses. The owner of a foal received a paper, called a "registration," which he could show to prove that his colt really was a Thoroughbred. Meanwhile the name and an assigned number were written in the "stud book" which the Association kept. Breeds of horses whose members are registered in stud books are called "registered" or "recognized" breeds.

Are American Thoroughbreds descended from the same three desert stallions as the English Thoroughbreds? Yes, they all trace their ancestry back to the Darley Arabian, the Byerly Turk, or the Godolphin Barb, through English Thoroughbred stallions and mares imported into this country.

Who keeps the stud book of American Thoroughbreds? The American Jockey Club keeps the registry. It approves the names of American Thoroughbred foals entered for registry, checks the pedigrees, and has certain other duties pertaining to racing and to race horses.

If the word **Thoroughbred** means a special breed, why do some people talk about "thoroughbred Morgans" and "thoroughbred Arabians"? This is because some people don't know that Thoroughbred is a distinct breed. They think the word means "purebred." They even talk about "thoroughbred collies" and "thoroughbred setters," etc. What they should be saying is "purebred collies," etc. It is easy to see how this misuse of the word came about, because in England the Thoroughbred *was* the first purebred horse.

What does the Thoroughbred look like? Since the Thoroughbred was bred primarily for racing he is not a heavily built animal. Compared with many other breeds he looks streamlined. His legs are long and his muscles long and flat. His head is never heavy, though it is not as small and delicate as that of the Arabian. Some horses, such as the Saddle Horses about which you will read later, hold their heads very, very high. The Thoroughbred does not hang his head, but if he held it too high he couldn't run as fast. For the same reason, when he gallops he takes very long strides but does not pick his feet up very high off the ground.

He has a fine, silky coat and a very thin skin and, like his Arabian ancestors, is very sensitive. Unfortunately he is more nervous and timid than they. He is more apt to lose his head and struggle senselessly when he is caught in wire, or when he lies down and gets into such a position that he cannot get up.

Can a Thoroughbred be any color? Thoroughbreds can be any solid color or they can be roans, but like Arabians, Thoroughbreds are never spotted.

What are Thoroughbreds used for besides racing? Many people like Thoroughbreds for ordinary riding, for hunting, for jumping, and for a very special kind of riding called "dressage" (see page 203), as well as for competition in various classes in horse shows. Thoroughbreds, like Arabians, are also used extensively for breeding. When they are mated with horses of other breeds, or with horses of mixed breeds, the result is better foals. When the United States still had a horse cavalry, for example, the government placed Thoroughbred stallions all around the country with farmers. These stallions were bred to local mares and the foals made splendid cavalry mounts.

Is a Thoroughbred a good kind of horse for a boy or girl to ride? Only if the boy or girl is a really good rider. And don't be fooled by the apparent quietness and gentleness of some types of Thoroughbreds. There are many that even seem slow and listless until suddenly, because a leaf has rustled, or for no reason at all, they explode like firecrackers! Unless you enjoy having a horse buck and play on a windy day, and are sure that you will never touch your horse with your heels without intending to, you had better stick to one of the quieter, less nervous breeds.

Half-Breds

What is a Half-Bred? We learned that Thoroughbreds are wonderful, though nervous, horses, bred primarily for speed, and therefore not very heavily built. We also learned that they are very sensitive and that many people don't want this kind of horse, either because they are too heavy themselves or because they don't enjoy always having to be on the alert. Yet these people like to ride and to hunt. The answer is the Half-Bred. His father (or mother) is a Thoroughbred, and his other parent an animal with a good deal of draft blood, as a rule. Sometimes one parent is all draft. The result is a good-looking, strongly built, free-going horse with a quiet disposition. This horse can carry a rider all day long over rough country in the hunting field.

Is there a Club that keeps track of the pedigrees of Half-Breds as there is for Thoroughbreds? Yes, it is called the Half-Bred Association. In show catalogues, you will sometimes see the letters HB after a horse's name. This means he is a Half-Bred. The letters TB show that the horse is a Thoroughbred. There is also an Arabian Half-Bred registry in which a horse with only one registered Arabian parent can be registered.

Standardbreds

Standardbreds are used for racing in harness. The driver sits in a tiny vehicle that weighs under thirty pounds, has bicycle-

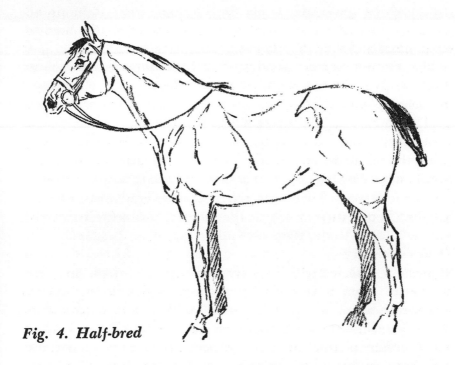

Fig. 4. Half-bred

type wheels, and is called a "sulky" (see Fig. 2-4). The horses do not gallop; they either trot or pace. The races are held on oval tracks and are sometimes a mile long, sometimes a half-mile, and sometimes two miles long. Many years ago, races at the trot were very long, sometimes extending as far as from New York to Boston, but the horses were ridden, not driven.

In Europe, and in the South and West of this country, the roads were muddy most of the year. The heavy mail coaches were pulled by big strong horses. Rich people who had more lightly built horses to pull their carriages were more interested in style than in speed, and usually drove Hackneys (pages 44–45) which held their heads very high and lifted up their feet. In winter in Canada and in the United States, the hard-packed snow was excellent for fast driving in sleighs.

Country people, who didn't care too much for the expensive, high-stepping carriage horses of the rich, began breeding "roadsters." These were horses with fast trots that could do a bit of work on the farm during the week, and then draw their masters

to church on a Sunday. If, on the way, the farmer came up behind another vehicle and couldn't pass it, the drive was not very
comfortable. In wet weather the roads were knee deep in mud;
in dry weather they became very dusty. A fast-stepping roadster
that could pass everything he met and make others "eat his dust"
was most popular.

These were not race horses, however. There was no stud book
which kept track of their breeding, and no "foundation" sire
whose blood produced fast harness horses. Perhaps there never
would have been any interest in harness racing had it not been
for the Puritans. These very religious people, who came to our
country in order to worship as they chose, made some very strict
"Blue Laws." Under these laws all racing was forbidden. Later
it was decided that a race was "a competition between two or
more horses to see which could run fastest." If horses raced
at the trot, they were not really racing, by definition, because
neither horse was going as fast as it could! At first this racing
was informal, with no tracks and no records. Then harness
races became popular at fairs. Money prizes were offered and
people made bets on the horses. There was still no stud book,
however.

In 1788, a registered Thoroughbred stallion named Messenger,
an ordinary English race horse, was brought to this country to
be used for breeding. He was a descendant of the Darley
Arabian; his sire was Mambrino, the founder of a famous strain
of coach horses in Europe. A "flea-bitten gray," Messenger was
not very good-looking, nor did he have an outstanding track
record. It was soon noticed, however, that his colts had all had
tremendous speed at the trot! Today all Standardbreds and all
"gaited" and "Saddlebreds" (which will be discussed later) trace
their ancestry back to Messenger.

A great-grandson of Messenger, called Rysdyk's Hambletonian,
even more than Messenger, is considered the "Father of the
Standardbred." Rysdyk, who owned Hambletonian, raced him
in harness for a few years and then used him for breeding. When
Hambletonian was about twelve years old, it was noticed that
his colts and fillies were winning all the races at the trotting

tracks! From then on, Hambletonian became very much in demand for breeding.

Is there a good way to tell a Standardbred from a Thoroughbred? Yes. A Standardbred is apt to have a somewhat longer back than a Thoroughbred. His head is not so fine and he seldom has the "dished" profile. His hindquarters are higher than those of the Thoroughbred, and when he is standing still his hind legs are not set as far under him as the Thoroughbred's, but are so placed that the hocks are behind the buttock points.

However, it is easiest to recognize a Standardbred by the way he travels at the trot. In trotting, a horse springs from one pair of diagonal legs to the other (the right foreleg and left hind leg move at the same time, for example, followed by the left foreleg and right hind leg). The hind legs of the Thoroughbred follow exactly in line with the front legs. The print of the back leg is almost on top of that of the front leg on that side. When a Standardbred trots, he takes tremendously long strides (the stride of a good trotter is often 22 feet, and Greyhound, the Standardbred that holds the world's record, has a stride of 23

Fig. 5. Standardbred

feet!) In order to take such long steps and still avoid hitting his front foot with his hind foot, the Standardbred spreads his hind legs wide apart and puts them down ahead of and outside of the prints made by his front feet. Fig. 6 shows tracks made by a Thoroughbred and a Standardbred.

Do all Standardbreds race at the trot? No, many of them pace. In this gait, instead of moving the diagonal legs at the same time, the horse moves the two legs that are on the same side at the same time (the two right and then the two left). These are called the "lateral" legs. This gait is sometimes slightly faster than the trot, and some Standardbreds tend to break from a fast trot into a still faster pace.

If the pace is faster than the trot, why aren't all harness races run at the pace? Many horses trot very fast but do not pace at all. Also, if a pacer breaks into a gallop in racing, he cannot be

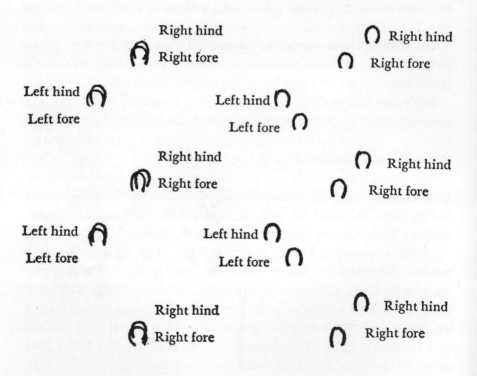

Fig. 6. Thoroughbred   *Standardbred*

pulled back into the pace, but has to come down to either a trot or a walk and start all over again. This is such a handicap that for many years no one bothered with pacers. Then in 1885, a railroad conductor named John Browning invented a kind of harness called "hopples." These were worn on the upper part of the legs, and were strapped to the two side or "lateral" legs in such a way that the horse could take long steps and go fast, but could only move these two side legs together at the same time. Later, for horses that trotted faster than they paced, but tended to go into a pace from a trot, hopples that connected the diagonal legs were developed.

Are trotters good riding horses for boys and girls? It is fun to ride a Standardbred because he can go so very fast at the trot, and he is not as nervous as the Thoroughbred. But, since he has been bred only to trot for so many generations, it is hard indeed to teach him to take a slow canter. Most people also like to canter and canter slowly. They don't want a horse that will only gallop fast.

Do trotters make good jumpers? Trotters can often jump well, but they are hard to train, for a horse jumps highest from a fairly slow canter and not from the trot or a fast gallop.

Is a pacer fun to ride? Not as a rule. A pacer throws his body from one side to the other as he travels and this is very uncomfortable. A horse cannot jump safely from a pace either, and this takes away a good deal of the fun.

Are there any classes in the horse shows for Standardbreds? Yes, these are called "roadster classes." Some are classes for horses that are shown in harness, and others for roadsters under saddle. In both, the speed of the trot counts most.

What association keeps track of the pedigrees of Standardbreds? The United States Trotting Association. To get into their stud book a horse either has to be a purebred Standardbred, or be able to trot or pace a mile at a specified speed. This speed depends on the age of the horse, and whether it is a mare or a stallion. Originally, in order to be registered, a horse had either to trot a mile in two minutes, thirty seconds (2:30) or less, or pace a mile in two minutes, twenty-five seconds (2:25). This was called the "standard" for harness horses and explains the name Standardbred.

The American Saddle Horse

This is a registered breed with its own stud book. Of all the types, he is the proudest-looking. He has a fine and delicate head which he holds very, very proudly. He lifts his feet so high and puts them to the ground so lightly that it is almost as though he hated to touch the ground at all. He holds his tail very high also, and his fine coat glistens as though it were varnished.

There are two main types of Saddle Horses. One is the highly educated "gaited" horse. Not only does he know how to walk, trot, and canter; he knows at least two other gaits. One is the "rack" or "single-foot," in which the horse travels very fast but moves each foot separately, as he does at the walk. The other is called a "slow" gait. This can be either a "running walk" (an amble), a "stepping pace," or a "broken trot." In each of these gaits, the horse moves his legs in the same order as in the ordinary form of the gait (at the trot the diagonal legs go together, for example), but not at exactly the same time. If you listen to the sound of the footsteps of the slow gait they seem to say, pat–ter, pat–ter, pat–ter, pat–ter; not plock–plock–plock–plock, as they do at the true trot or pace, or plock—plock—plock, which is the walk.

The gaited horse always has a long, fine mane. Sometimes the mane hangs almost to his knees, and in shows, the part nearest his ears is braided in pigtails. His tail is very full and bushy, as well as very long. In fact, if the horse hasn't a naturally good tail, in shows he sometimes wears a false tail added to his natural one.

The other type of Saddle Horse is called a "walk-trot." This is a little misleading, for he also knows how to canter, but he doesn't know the rack or slow gait. He wears his hair differently, too. The walk-trot horse has his mane cut off entirely. All the hair on the upper part of the tail or "dock" is pulled out until little more than a wisp is left. There is also a cruel practice, called "setting the tail," which is popular with people who breed three-gaited horses for showing. Since high-set tails are fashionable, many exhibitors operate on the tail of the horse by cutting the tendon. The tail is then kept in a sort of harness at all times except when the horse is in the show ring. As a result the horse can no longer use his tail to protect himself from flies. Many states outlaw tail setting.

Sometimes five-gaited Saddlers are driven in harness and called "Fine Harness Horses" to distinguish them from the roadsters. Sometimes also, in shows, there are "Combination Classes," in which the horses are first driven, then lined up, unhitched, saddled, and ridden.

Where did the Saddle Horse come from? In Virginia, Kentucky, and the Carolinas, plantation owners spent many hours in the saddle looking at their crops. They were fond of sports and wanted a stylish-looking horse to ride and drive. They didn't want a Hackney, such as the well-to-do people in the North drove, for the gait was too rough under the saddle. A Morgan (which breed we will discuss shortly) was too small, and a Standardbred didn't have a good canter. A nervous Thoroughbred was unwilling to stand quietly while his master surveyed his fields. The European palfreys were too small and not fancy enough. What the Southern planter wanted was a horse that had the smooth gaits of the palfrey, and the flash and fire of the Thoroughbred, with the high action of the Hackney. Where was such an animal to be found? A new type must be produced through breeding, and it wasn't many years before the proud plantation owners were riding across country on proud saddle horses.

Are Saddle Horses descended from the original Arabian foundation sires? Yes, through the Mambrinos (from whom Messenger, the famous Thoroughbred stallion, was descended), they go back to the Darley Arabian.

Do Saddle Horses have a special foundation sire of their own? Yes, a Thoroughbred horse called Denmark. He was standing at stud in Kentucky in about 1850.

What other bloodlines are there in the American Saddle Horse? Many Morgan horses were used in developing the

American Saddle Horse, as well as some Canadian horses of various lines.

Does the American Saddle Horse make a good horse for a boy or girl to own and ride? For a good rider, yes, but they are too sensitive and spirited for the beginner.

Are there any registered Saddle Horses, besides the gaited and walk-trot? Yes, there is the Tennessee Walking Horse, a breed developed from the saddle strains. Neither as showy nor as sensitive as his cousins, he has an excellent disposition. He does not trot, pace, or rack, but has only three gaits—the walk, the "slow gait," and the canter. The plantation owners who wanted comfort rather than style found him perfect. He could canter all day and travel between closely planted rows of corn without stepping on a single shoot!

The Morgan Horse

Of all the American breeds of horses, the Morgan is one of the most interesting and romantic. In the middle seventeen hundreds, at West Springfield, Massachusetts, there lived a traveling music teacher named Justin Morgan, who used to ride all over upper New England and into parts of Canada to teach singing. He was not a large man, so he didn't need a very large horse. His mount, which today we would call a pony, was a stallion that became known by his master's name, Justin Morgan.

Justin Morgan, the horse, had a tremendous trot, both under the saddle and when hitched to a cart. He was often used in the woods to drag heavy logs out. Stories are told about how he would work all day and then go into an informal jumping contest on his way home. Small as he was, he held his head high and looked proud.

But what has made him famous is not so much what he himself could do, as the fact that he passed both his talents and his looks down to his sons and daughters. So pronounced were these characteristics that he founded a distinct breed which bears his name, the only horse in history ever to do this. The United States Department of Agriculture has had a statue made of the little horse. It shows a deep-chested, very muscular animal with a high head set on a strong neck.

Who were the parents of Justin Morgan the horse? There is no written record of his parentage, though it was claimed that the sire was a Thoroughbred named Beautiful Bay (sometimes called "True Briton"), and that the dam was part Thoroughbred.

How old was Justin Morgan the horse when he died? He was twenty-nine years old, a great age for a horse, and was still perfectly healthy and strong, and still working. He was kicked by another horse and died of the injury.

Do the Morgans of today look like Justin Morgan? Not entirely, although occasionally one crops up that looks very much like his old ancestor. However, there are certain characteristics, such as the strength, stamina, and small size that still show up.

What are Morgans used for mostly today? Present-day Morgans can be divided into three types. One, the "general usage type," is used as a riding and driving horse, particularly in mountainous parts of New England where a sturdy, agile horse is needed. These horses are most apt to look like the original Morgan. The "Vermont Trail Ride," a special contest for "trail horses" of this sort, takes place each year in early September at Woodstock, Vermont. The test requires the rider to cover a hundred miles in three days: 40 miles the first, 40 miles the second, and 20 miles the third.

A second type is the more slender, stylish-looking Morgan bred for show purposes. So much Saddle Horse blood has been introduced into the bloodlines of the Saddler type of Morgan, that today old Justin would have a hard time recognizing his own children.

The third is the type bred for work on ranches as cow ponies. Rarely a purebred Morgan, it is apt to have Arabian and Quarterhorse (a breed discussed later in the chapter) blood as well.

Is the Morgan a gentle horse? Yes, the Morgan is gentle, intelligent, and not nearly as timid as some of the other breeds.

Is the Morgan a good horse for a boy or girl to own and ride? Yes, a Morgan is a splendid type of mount for a young rider. Although many are much bigger than was the original Justin Morgan, they are never enormous horses and are very tough.

Unless they are carefully trained as colts, however, they are apt to be more stubborn than the Thoroughbreds and Saddlers. But their good dispositions and lack of nervousness make up for this.

The Lipizzan Horse

Nowhere in the world is there a breed of horse so strikingly beautiful as the famous Lipizzan horse of Vienna, Austria. Born black or dark brown, as are nearly all white horses, when they mature they are a pure, dazzling white. Not very big—sixteen hands is about as big as they ever become—they are strong and muscular and carry themselves so nobly that they look bigger than they are. They are trained to do all sorts of intricate movements that you would never imagine possible for a horse, with a man on his back, to perform.

Let us watch the magical white horses at work in a hall that used to belong to the Emperors of Austria. It has crystal chandeliers, golden mirrors, and velvet hangings. Some of the horses are being ridden by men in fine costumes; some are being driven in long white reins, with the driver on foot.

In one corner is a horse balancing on his hindquarters, his front legs off the ground and curved like those of a dog that has been taught to beg. He has sunk so far back on his hind legs that his hocks are almost touching the ground. Like a statue in white marble, he holds this position until the trainer signals him to return to his feet. This movement is called the *levade*.

Just in front of us is another horse on his hind legs, but he is standing tall instead of sitting back, as did the first. His forelegs dangle in front, and he is making a series of little hops. One, two, three! Like a crow he hops, then comes back to a normal position and rests for a moment in the movement called a *courbette*.

A horse is just being driven past us. Instead of a saddle, he wears a scarlet velvet pad trimmed with gold. The horse is cantering, and the man who is driving him with white reins walks close behind him, never needing to hurry, for the gait of the horse is slow and perfectly controlled.

Fig. 7. Levade

In the very center of the hall between two pillars, is a horse that trots in place, without moving forward or backward. Like a soldier marking time, one two—one two, he lifts his legs high in a beautiful slow rhythm. This horse is practicing the *piaffe*.

Cantering slowly towards us are six horses in line. Suddenly, without breaking the rhythm of their pace, they *pirouette* like ballet dancers, three going off to the right and three to the left.

But what is that horse at the end of the hall doing? There is a man on his back, and another close behind carrying a long whip. The horse takes tiny steps, then gathers himself and

Fig. 8. Courbette

springs into the air several feet off the ground! At this instant, the man on the ground snaps his whip and the horse kicks his back legs straight out behind him! He looks exactly like Pegasus the winged horse, as he flies through the air! This movement is called the *capriole*.

Where do these beautiful horses come from? The name of the school answers this question. Although it is in Austria, it is called the "Spanish Riding School of Vienna." In Europe,

Fig. 9. Capriole

when armor was adopted for warfare, the knights rode with a straight stiff leg, and all riders copied them. But this is not the best way to ride, for you cannot use your legs to signal your horse. The Arabs, who did not wear armor, rode with a bent knee. In the eighth century, they conquered Spain and ruled there for 500 years. Naturally, they imported both their horses and their methods of riding. When they, in turn, were conquered and driven from Spain, they left their traditions behind them. In the fourteenth century, visitors to Spain from Italy carried back stories of the remarkable horsemanship of the Spaniards, and of the extraordinary training of their horses. One of the popes arranged for a group of these horsemen to come with their mounts to Italy. Soon, all over Italy, riding schools blossomed.

In 1560, the Archduke Charles of Austria set up his own stud farm in the town of Lipizza, near Trieste. It was from his Spanish horses that the Lipizzaner strain was developed. When the Emperor of Austria started a riding school in Vienna, he chose the white Lipizzan horses and the Spanish riding masters, so the school was called "The Spanish Riding School of Vienna."

Why are the horses taught such fancy movements? These movements, called *haute école,* or "high school" figures, seem to us beautiful but artificial. Actually, it was these movements which were the most important in early times, when riders depended on their horses to save their lives in battle. A skillful horseman on a well-trained horse, surrounded by a mob of foot soldiers, could signal his horse to take the position of the *levade,* which was the most favorable position from which to use the lance or sword. Then, by signaling for the *courbette,* he could raise himself still higher. With the *capriole* his horse could kick over the soldiers behind him, turn swiftly on a *pirouette,* and gallop away through the path he had cleared.

Are there any Lipizzan horses in the United States today? Yes, a number have been imported, but most of them have not learned these very advanced "off the ground" movements.

What are they used for? They are used for riding and for "dressage" work. You will learn more about *dressage* later in this book.

How old is a Lipizzaner when he starts being trained in "The Spanish Riding School of Vienna"? At the age of three and a half, young stallions worth training and fillies suitable for becoming brood mares are selected. The rest are sold.

For the first year of his training, the young stallion receives all of his schooling, or lessons, with the trainer on foot. First he is "longed," then driven on long and on short reins. He learns to walk, trot, and canter very precisely and to do the simpler of the "lateral movements" (page 193). When the horse is four and a half, his trainer begins to ride him, but not until he has had at least three years of training does he start the advanced *haute école* work. His training continues until he is retired to the stud, dies, or is sold. Neither horse nor horseman is ever considered to have learned all he can learn, nor to have reached perfection.

Can anyone go and ride at the Spanish Riding School today? Yes, instruction is open to anyone interested. It is not expensive, but is very gruelling. The pupils ride four hours a day in two two-hour stretches. Most of this work is done on the longe, without stirrups, at the trot or canter, and the rider is required to hold the "fixed leg" position (see pages 196–197).

The Quarter Horse

The English Thoroughbred was bred, as we have learned, for racing in England where flat fields were common. In the new world, the Virginia gentlemen loved racing, but there were few suitable fields, and most of the roads were winding. Sometimes, however, there would be a straight stretch of road for about a quarter of a mile. Soon, in Virginia and other Southern states, short races were being held on these stretches. The Thoroughbred horses were not very good for these races. They were bred to travel fast and far, but having long legs and being tall, they were not as handy and couldn't get started as fast as a smaller horse. Of course there were no Arabians in this country at that time. They would have made good horses for these early competitions.

In 1756, a Thoroughbred stallion named Janus was used for breeding in Virginia. He was a stocky, heavily built animal, with bulging muscles and short legs set well under him. It was soon noticed that all his colts could get away to a fast start, and keep going for about a quarter of a mile. Then they tired and could race no further. These horses came to be known as "Quarter Horses," because of the length of the races. Later, when tracks were built, they lost their popularity as race horses, but were found to be ideal for work on ranches. They were very strong, agile, speedy, and tough, and didn't need nearly as much grain or grass as the rangier horses of other breeds.

How big is a Quarter Horse? He is little more than a pony in height, usually from 57 to 60 inches tall. He weighs about 1,200 pounds, however, as much as a large Thoroughbred.

What color are Quarter Horses? All colors, including pinto, or spotted.

Does he make a good horse for boys and girls? For Western riding and trail riding, yes, but he is not a natural jumper. The strong and reliable Quarter Horse is much too heavy an animal to be good for more advanced riding and schooling.

Crossbreeds

What is the difference between a horse that is a Crossbreed and one that is a Half-Bred? We learned that a Half-Bred could be a horse whose dam or sire was a Thoroughbred and whose other parent could be any breed, and that there were also Half-Bred Arabs. A Crossbreed is a breed in which each of the parents has to be a registered horse of a specified but different breed from the other. Two of the most important Crossbreeds are the Anglo Arab and the Morab.

What is an Anglo Arab? An Anglo Arab is half Thoroughbred, half Abrabian.

What does an Anglo Arab look like? This is a little hard to say since some take more after one bloodline, and others after the other. Generally speaking, they are more delicate-looking and smaller than a Thoroughbred, but have longer legs and less choppy gaits than the purebred Arabian. They are very apt to have the Arabian-type head and rather high-set tail, but are not usually as "close-coupled" (short in the body).

Do Anglo Arabs make good horses for boys and girls? For a good rider, yes. They are smaller, gentler, and less nervous than Thoroughbreds. However, they are generally too sensitive for beginners.

What is a Morab? A Morab has one Arabian parent and one Morgan parent. The Morab usually has a very strong Morgan look, especially in the head and neck, but is more lightly built, with more slender legs than a pure Morgan. His body is usually longer and heavier than an Arabian's.

Is a Morab a good horse for a boy or girl? Yes, excellent. He generally has a nice disposition, and is very tough and hardy. He is less stubborn than the pure Morgan, but not nearly as nervous and high-strung as the Arabian. His gaits are usually comfortable and he has good stable manners.

What else are Morabs good for? Morabs are good all-around horses. They are useful for ranch work, since they are agile. They make excellent trail horses. They are not large but are very strong and do not tire easily. They take readily to driving and can be used for light farm work. Some inherit the fine roadster trot of Justin Morgan.

Color Breeds

Color Breeds are those whose members are identified solely by color.

How many Color Breeds in the United States have stud books and registries? There are three: the Palomino, the Appaloosa, and the Pinto, or Spotted Horse Breed.

What color is a Palomino? A Palomino is a pale golden color; his coat has almost a metallic glitter in the sun. His mane and tail are flaxen (pure white). He may have any bloodlines except Shetland or draft.

Where did the first Palominos come from? We don't know where the Palomino was first seen; probably this color has been common as long as any of the other solid colors. It is really a sort of dun, and dun is one of the foundation colors of the pre-historic horse. But the dun has a black stripe down his back and black on his legs, as well as having a black mane and tail. We do know who first specialized in Palominos and had a large group of them. This was Isabella of Spain, the same queen who sold her jewels and lent the money to Christopher Columbus to finance his expedition to the New World.

How did the Palominos get to this country? Some of them came with Cortes and other Spanish explorers. The horses of these explorers were descendants of the Arabian horses but they had no Thoroughbred blood. We occasionally find a Palomino Thoroughbred or Saddle Horse, but we find Palomino more often in Arabian or stock horses. This is easy to understand since we know that the wild horses of the West, the mustangs, were all descended from the horses of the early Spanish explorers.

What are Palomino horses used for? Besides being used for everything that a horse of his type but of another color might be used for, the Palomino is especially valued as a "Parade Horse." Because they can be almost any breed or any combination of breeds, Palominos aren't all the same type. Some are small, some large; some are rangy and make good jumpers; some are close-coupled and come from Quarter Horse stock. This last is the type most used on the Western ranges as a stock horse. But since the Palomino is so flashy looking, many breeders breed the Parade type. The Parade horse, which often has Thoroughbred and Saddle Horse bloodlines, must be good-sized and must carry himself proudly. He is taught a special "parade step" which is almost like a marching step. There are many groups of adults or children calling themselves "Sheriff's Posses," who specialize in formation riding for exhibition purposes, and in going into parades. Very often all members of such a group will be mounted on Parade-type Palominos.

Do a Palomino stallion and a Palomino mare always have a Palomino foal? No, unfortunately, they don't. Usually the foal of two Palominos turns out a pale cream. This is certainly not always so, however, and one of the main purposes of the Palomino Association is to try and establish the breed as a true breed, and not as just a color breed. Eventually, through mating only stallions and mares whose foals always turn out to be Palominos, this may become possible. At present, the foal of a Palomino stallion mated to a chestnut mare with Palomino ancestry is more apt to be a true Palomino than one whose parents are both Palominos.

Are there any Palomino ponies? Yes, the color is very common in all breeds of ponies, especially in the American Shetlands, harness type.

If a foal is born Palomino does he always stay that color? No, many turn either lighter or darker with age.

What is an Appaloosa? An Appaloosa is a very strangely marked horse. The main body color is either very light gray or white all over, or white over the hindquarters with a much darker gray over the front part of the body, neck, and head. Sometimes all over his body, and sometimes only over the white areas, there are many black or brown spots. Some of these spots are tiny, some as big as saucers; all are round or oval in shape. You can easily guess why, with this peculiar marking, he is often called the "raindrop" horse. The Appaloosa also has odd-looking hooves with up and down stripes of black and white. His eyes usually have a border of white edging the eyeball.

Where did the Appaloosa come from? This coloring has always been quite common in horses of middle and Southern Europe. Early paintings of horses often show Appaloosas. You learned that the Lipizzaners are usually white; in old pictures of herds of these animals we sometimes see Appaloosas running with them. Like our other horses of the West, the Appaloosas came to the New World with the Spanish Explorers. It was the Indians who called them "Appaloosas," and they valued them above horses of other markings, for they claimed that these horses were unusually hardy.

Have the Pintos or Spotted Horses had their own stud book very long? No, although this coloring, sometimes called "calico," is very common in the West, it was only recently that an association was organized with a formal stud book. Just as with Palominos and Appaloosas, any type of horse with the desired coloring may be registered.

Breeds of Ponies

There are two distinct types of small ponies: those best suited to driving, and those more suitable for riding.

The first is the "harness pony," and there are three main breeds—the English Shetland, the American Shetland, harness type, and the Hackney.

Why are the English Shetlands better for driving than for riding? They are sometimes too small to be ridden. Forty inches high at the withers is average, and many English Shetlands are 36 inches or under. (One breeding farm in England specializes in very tiny ponies which are used in theatres at Christmastime to pull the Cinderella coaches in pantomimes.)

English Shetlands are built like little draft horses with wide flat backs, very thick shoulders and necks, and flat withers. It is almost always necessary to have a strap running from the back of the saddle to the tail to keep the saddle in place, for the withers are so flat that the saddle tends to slip forward over the neck.

The English Shetland's legs are so short that he must take very quick little steps, especially at the trot, if he is to keep up with larger animals. Although the gait is smooth, the child has to post (move up and down to the trot) very fast, and this can be tiring.

This animal is extremely smart. Because it is small, people often think of the miniature Shetland as a toy and expect any child to be able to manage him, whether he knows how to ride or not. Since an adult cannot ride and train the pony himself, very often the animal gets no proper training. Though he may be gentle to start with, he soon realizes that he is free to choose what he will or will not do. It doesn't take long for him to decide that the thing he doesn't want to do is to work!

In the cart, with an adult driving, the English Shetland earns a good place for himself in the stable.

Is the American Shetland driving pony like the English one? So much Hackney blood has been introduced into the breed that he resembles the Hackney much more than he does the true Shetland. Actually, he has become a miniature "Fine Harness" horse. His hooves are allowed to grow very long and he often wears special, heavy shoes. This makes him pick his feet up very high. He is very spirited, and is kept so in order that he may look as "showy" as possible in the ring. He is never shown under the saddle, but only in breeding classes in hand (that is, he is led into the show ring, and is judged on his appearance alone), or in harness. In the harness classes, adult men or women usually do the driving, for our quiet Shetland has now become too much of a handful for a boy or girl to manage.

What is a Hackney? As a matter of fact, Hackneys were originally coach horses developed in Europe to pull mail coaches. Today, we have both large and small Hackneys, but the Hackney ponies are far more numerous than the horses. They are slightly larger than the American Shetland described above, and they always have their tails cut short to prevent their getting over the reins. They are even more fiery and hard to handle than the Shetlands. Their gaits are too rough for them to be good riding ponies, but a little mixture of Hackney blood often produces a good "hunting-type" pony. Hackneys do have good natural ability in jumping. One of the most famous jumpers of this breed was a horse named Sir Gilbert that started his career as a Hackney show stallion, was blinded in one eye in an accident, and finished as an open jumper.

What are ponies that are not used for driving called? We call these "hunting-type" ponies, or "pet" ponies, to distinguish them from the driving ponies. For small children there are "pet-pony-type" American Shetlands. These run from very small, 36 inches or so, up to 48 inches. The extremely small ones are very endearing, have extremely gentle dispositions, but must be carefully trained if young children are to handle them successfully. They are not nearly as chunky and heavy as the English Shetlands.

How can a "pet" be properly trained if he is too small for adults to ride? First he must be "voice-trained" on the longe by an adult. You will learn about longeing later in the book. Then he must be driven in a cart by someone who knows how to drive, and what to do if the pony tries to misbehave. When he has become quiet in the cart he may be ridden by a child, but only by a child who has had enough experience to know how to walk, trot, and canter well, and who does not need to squeeze with his legs or grab the saddle with his hands to keep from falling off. Only when the pony is seven or eight years old, and has had good habits well established, should beginners be allowed to ride him.

What is a Welch pony? The Welch pony, a hunting-type animal, is a native of Wales, in the British Isles. His is a very old and very popular breed. The Welch pony has some Arabian blood, and is both larger and more delicately built than the English Shetland. He is quite spirited and much more sensitive than the Shetlands and some of the other breeds. Crossing him with Shetlands, Hackneys, and Arabians often produces very fine hunting ponies for general purposes. He has a natural jump, and for a good rider makes both a good show pony and a good hunter.

What other breeds of ponies are there? In England, there are the "Moor ponies," the Exmoor, Dartmoor, etc. Often quite large, they have gentle dispositions and are easily trained. We do not see many of them in this country, but a few importers are bringing them in and raising them as general-purpose ponies, or as hunting ponies.

In Ireland there is the "Connemara," a strong, well-built pony running from 13 hands to 14 hands 2 inches. In his native country he is much in demand for hunting, for he has unusual jumping ability, and can carry a child or a fair-sized adult all day long in the hunt field without tiring. The farmer drives his milk to market in a primitive cart pulled by the same Connemara that, the day before, was leaping onto and off the high banks in the Irish hunting field.

Have there ever been any Connemara ponies in this country? Yes, one of the most famous jumpers in the history of horse-show jumping competitions was a small, 54-inch gray Connemara pony named "Little Squire." For years he won all the contests, sometimes jumping as high as 5 feet, sometimes 6 feet. He competed against horses that were twice his height, and usually outjumped even the best.

Are there any other, less well-known breeds of ponies? There are many breeds of Northern ponies, such as the Icelandic pony and the Mongolian pony. These are tough, shaggy animals. They have big heads with wide air passages, so that the icy winds are warmed before they reach the lungs. Their tails are carried tucked in tightly for warmth. They are very hardy and exist under conditions which would mean death from exposure and starvation for the more delicate animals with desert blood.

Are there any other American breeds of ponies? Yes, there are the Chincoteague ponies. The story goes that in the sixteenth century there was a shipment of small Moorish ponies sent from Africa to the Viceroy of Peru, to work in the gold mines. The ship was wrecked off the coast of Virginia, near Assateague

Island. Some of the ponies swam ashore. No one bothered about them for many years, and they ran wild like the British ponies. Since no new blood, such as Arabian or Thoroughbred, was purposely introduced to improve the breed, these ponies are not as well-built or as pretty as the British ponies.

Why are they called Chincoteague ponies? Once a year the herds are rounded up. The yearlings are separated from the others and made to swim the channel between the islands of Assateague and Chincoteague. On Chincoteague a pony auction is held, the money going to the Chincoteague Volunteer Fire Department. The ponies, never having seen man before, are very wild and not easy to train. Carefully handled by a good trainer, however, some of them make good children's mounts.

Is this the only breed of American pony? There is one other breed, though it is really valuable only as a curiosity. Some years ago, travelers in the Rocky Mountains found a herd of tiny, slenderly built ponies in a deep canyon. They were not like ponies at all, but like small horses, and were only about the size of large dogs. Evidently a pair of wild horses had fallen into the canyon many years before, and had never found their way out. All these little Canyon ponies are descended from the original pair. Because the grass is scanty, and because they are inbred (no new blood has ever been introduced), they are stunted and not nearly as strong as the ordinary pony.

Crossbred Ponies

So far we have talked only about specific breeds of ponies, but by far the largest group of ponies being ridden today by children, for ordinary purposes, are ponies which are a mixture of various breeds, with a good bit of horse thrown in. Later in the book we will learn about choosing such a pony, and see which makes the best type for a boy or girl to ride and own.

Types of Horses and Ponies Bred or Trained for Special Purposes

Earlier in this book, we learned that horses used for hunting were sometimes Thoroughbreds and sometimes Half-Breds. In fact, many people preferred the Half-Breds because they were sturdier and less nervous. Today, there are three sizes of hunters being bred: the lightweight hunter, the middleweight, and the heavyweight. This does not refer so much to the size of the horse himself, as to his ability to carry a certain weight for a day's hunting without tiring. The lightweight must carry up to 160 pounds, the middleweight up to 180, and the heavyweight up to 200. Breeders in different parts of the country specialize in breeding the different types of hunters, introducing blood from various strains such as draft, Hackney, Thoroughbred, etc., to get the animal they want.

Another special type of horse being raised for a specific purpose is the polo pony.

Is the polo pony a real pony or can he be a horse? The original polo ponies, used in India, where polo was first played as an organized sport, were real ponies. They were mostly of Mongolian stock and none could be more than 54 inches in height. Naturally, the smaller the animal, the easier it was to reach the ball with the mallet. As the game became popular in other countries, this limitation of size was eliminated, and today a polo pony can be of any size, though horses over 15 hands are not very practical as a rule.

Is there any particular breed that makes a good polo pony? Most polo ponies have a good deal of cow pony or range stock in them. Many have Quarter Horse blood, perhaps mixed with Arabian or Thoroughbred.

In South America there is a special breed of horse used both as a stock horse and for games such as polo. It is called a "Criollo." This horse is not a very beautiful animal, but is exceptionally hardy.

What is a "stock horse"? A stock horse is a horse used to work cattle or other livestock. Another name for this type is cow pony. In the West, where livestock runs loose on wide grazing lands, cowboys often have to move the herds from one part of the country to another to provide fresh pasturage. Every so often, too, they round the animals up to check for injuries or illness, to separate the foals or calves from their mothers, to brand them, or "geld" them, and take out of the herd those animals which are

48

ready to be sold or trained. A man on foot, or even a dozen men on foot, cannot control several hundred beasts. Nor can a man on foot go into a milling herd and "cut out" one particular animal, lassoo it, throw it, and then hobble it so that it can be worked on. But a man on a well-trained horse can do this. The stock horse (or cow pony) is very highly trained and very intelligent.

Where did the first cow ponies come from? They are the direct descendants of the Spanish horses which went wild after the withdrawal of the Spanish explorers. In recent years, Quarter Horse, Thoroughbred, and Arabian stallions have all been used to improve the fleetness and appearance of the common stock horse.

Does a cow pony make a good horse for a boy or girl? This depends on how the horse has been trained, and how the boy or girl is going to ride him. You must remember that most cow ponies run wild until they are three or four years old. Unfortunately, as a rule the horse breaker does not have time to handle the young colt, win his confidence, and teach him that man is his friend. So the "Western-broke" cow pony usually regards man as something to fear. When we study a little more about training colts, we will learn why this is not a good thing. Also, because the cowboy must at all times have one hand free to handle his lasso, he teaches his horse to work more or less independently and on a very loose rein. He also teaches him to dig his heels in and stop short at the slightest touch on the bridle. To do this he rides him in a rather cruel bit; or at least it would be cruel, if the rider kept constant contact with his horse's mouth through the reins as the Eastern or "English" type of riding requires. Horses that have first been broken to Western tack are sometimes very difficult to retrain for other types of riding. But for ranch work and trail work the cow pony is ideal.

Are there any other types of horses that are trained for one particular purpose? Yes, there is the police horse, for example. If you watch a mounted policeman weave his way in and out of a line of stalled automobiles, you can easily see why the police horse is still so valuable. The mounted man can see over the

49

heads of people on foot and over most automobiles. Secondly, he can even go up on the sidewalk, if necessary, in getting through a tightly packed mass of cars. In handling crowds at parades, the mounted policeman's horse—a rather fearsome animal that might kick, bite, or step on the feet of the man on foot—gives the officer more authority.

Are police horses any special breed? No, but they must be between the heights of 15 hands 2 inches and 16 hands 2 inches, and between the ages of four and seven years. They must have good conformation, of the "officer's charger" type, quiet dispositions, and be willing and apt at learning. In New York City, they must all be bay horses with black points.

Where do police horses come from and how are they trained? Dealers and breeders know what kind of horse the police need and will often save such horses for them. After he has been purchased, the future police horse goes to a police school for at least a year. There he is trained as a good riding animal, and learns how to remain absolutely motionless, when necessary, to ignore all kinds of unusual noises, and to push his way through a crowd of people without hurting them.

Do police horses wear any special kind of equipment? They wear a special type of saddle to which may be attached a night stick (for use in controlling crowds that get out of hand), and other articles such as a raincoat, or anything else the officer may have to carry. A specially trimmed and marked saddle-pad identifies them. They also wear special rubber pads under their shoes. Even slow work all day long on hard pavements is very hard on a horse's feet and legs, and these rubber pads help.

What happens to police horses when they can no longer do the work? When a police horse, either from old age or from some minor defect, is considered unsuited for the rigorous work required, he is retired. Sometimes he is put out on a farm. Children or adults who live in the country where the ground is soft are sometimes allowed to take him and use him gently. They must promise to feed him well, and never to sell him.

3

How the Horse Is Made

Like most living creatures, the horse has a bony framework called the skeleton, which gives him his shape and protects the vital organs inside. The horse has a great many bones, and you should learn the names of some of these, especially the delicate and easily injured ones. In Fig. 10, which shows the skeleton of the horse, the bones listed are the ones you should know.

You will also want to know something about how these various bones work and what their purpose is. Later, in the section on choosing your own horse, you will learn how to judge whether or not your horse is well-built. In still another part of this book, we will discuss common injuries, especially of the various bones and joints of the legs, how to prevent and how to treat them.

But first, let us take a look at the skeleton and see exactly how it is constructed. We'll start with the skull.

Is the skull all one bone? There are about twenty-two bones in the skull. As you have learned, horses of different breeds have different types of heads. Animals that eat bulky foods, such as grass which must be chewed, need large jaws. Animals that depend on speed to escape from enemies need plenty of room at the base of the head, and at the "throttle" (see Fig. 11), for the big tubes which carry air to the lungs and food to the stomach. For this reason, the head of the horse is long, and much larger in proportion to his body than is the head of a cat, for example. In the chapter which tells how to choose a horse, you will learn how the size of the horse's head affects his balance, as well as how it

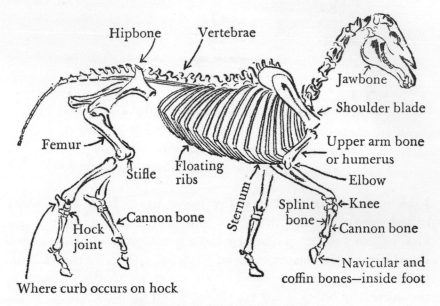

Hipbone   Vertebrae

Jawbone

Shoulder blade

Femur

Upper arm bone
or humerus

Stifle   Floating
ribs

Elbow

Splint   Knee
bone

Cannon bone

Sternum

Cannon bone

Hock
joint

Navicular and
coffin bones—inside foot

Where curb occurs on hock

Fig. 10. Skeleton of horse

should be set on his neck.   But now let us go on to the body structure and look at the "rib-cage."

How many ribs has the horse?   Most horses have eighteen
pairs of ribs, or thirty-six ribs in all.   Notice that all these ribs
are fastened to the spine which runs along the "top" of the horse
and gives him what we call his "top-line."   Notice, too, that the
front ribs are fastened also at the bottom to the breastbone, or
"sternum," but the back ones are not.   These back ribs are
called "floating ribs."

Why does a horse have floating ribs?   This is to allow his
diaphragm to expand and contract as he breathes, and to permit
him to bend his body freely.   Your ribs work the same way.   If
the ribs of human beings were all fastened down at both ends
you couldn't breathe at all well.

How is the spine put together?   The spine consists of small
bones called "vertebrae" (VERtebray).   Each vertebra is separated from and connected to the one next to it by a rubbery

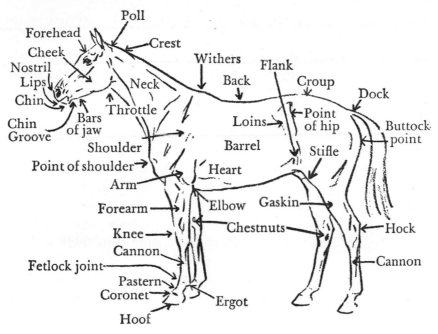

Fig. 11. Points of the horse

disk. Most of the vertebrae are so constructed that they can move slightly; this makes it possible for the horse to arch his neck, shorten his length by bringing his hind legs under him, and move his tail.

Are the vertebrae all the same size? No, the seven "cervical" (SERvical) vertebrae in the neck are much larger than the others. Then come the eighteen "thoracic" (thoRAsic) vertebrae to which the ribs are attached. Just behind these are the six "lumbar" (LUMbar) vertebrae. All these are individually jointed and the spine at these points is flexible. Then come five vertebrae which form one immovable bone, the "sacrum" (SAYcrum). The sacrum is the top of a structure of bones called the "pelvic girdle." Attached to the end of the sacrum are a series of vertebrae, called the "coccyx" (COXsix), which form the tail.

All the main organs and other working parts of the horse are suspended from the spine. The spine has a hollow canal called the "neural (NEWral) canal" running down its center. Inside this canal is the all-important "spinal cord." The center of the nervous system, the spinal cord is like a gigantic telephone exchange, transmitting messages from the brain to all parts of the body, giving orders to the muscles to act, etc. When the spinal column is injured, the horse can no longer move. This is why nature has protected it so carefully.

Do the horse's front legs work the way our arms do? The main bones of the horse's front legs correspond to bones in your bodies, which work somewhat the same way. But there is one great difference: Your upper arm bone, which runs from your shoulder to your elbow and is called the "humerus" (HUmerous), is attached to the rest of your skeleton by a bone called the "collarbone." Also, your humerus is outside your body and you can move your arm in all directions.

But the horse, the dog, and many other animals have no collarbones. Their humeri are not attached to the main skeleton, except by muscles. In fact, the humerus, as you can see by studying Fig. 10, is built right into the body. For this reason, the horse can move his legs only forward and backward; he cannot extend them sideways at all.

Notice that the elbow of the horse is the joint at the very top of the leg. The joint below, which we call the "knee" of the horse, is really the horse's wrist. There are two big bones which run from the elbow to the knee. They are fused together and are very strong. They are called the "ulna" (ULna) and the "radius" (RAdius).

The knee, like your wrist, has several small bones which help form the joint. Some horses have eight of these, some only seven.

If the horse's knee is the same as our wrist, what became of all the little bones which we have in the backs of our hands? You have five main bones in your hand, which are the beginnings of your fingers. Originally, the horse had four toes on his front feet and three on his hind feet. We know this to be true, not only because fossil bones of the original ancestor of our horse, little "Eohippus," the Dawn Horse, have been found, but also because even in today's horses we can see the remains of the original toe bones. As you see in the drawing, there is one large bone called the "cannon" bone which runs from the knee to the ankle or "fetlock joint." But on each side of this main bone is a thin little splinter of a bone which runs only a little way down and ends in a tiny knob. These little bones, called the "splint" bones, are all that are left of the prehistoric horse's two outside toes. Many horsemen wish that they would disappear altogether, for they are of no use and, as you will learn later, are the seat of a common injury called a "splint."

Are the bones of the hind legs of the horse connected directly to the frame or are they like the front ones? The big bone, marked the "femur" (FEEmur) in the picture, corresponds to the big bone in your upper leg which runs from your knee to the point where your leg joins your body. The horse's femur, like yours, is attached to the pelvic bone at the hip. But unlike yours, it is enclosed inside the body. The joint on the chart which is marked the "stifle" corresponds to your knee. Running from the stifle to the hock joint, the horse has 2 bones, a large one called the "tibia" (TIBia), and a thin little one called the "fibula" (FIBula). These correspond to the bones of your leg which go from your knee to your ankle. The hock of the horse is really his ankle joint, just as his knee is really his wrist. From the hock down, the construction of the horse's back legs is similar to that of his front legs.

What happened to the toe of the prehistoric horse? The bones of what was the horse's longest toe form what is called his "pastern" and his foot. Two of these bones are above the hoof, and are called the first and the second "phalanx" (FAYlanx). In the original toe, the first phalanx ran from the knuckle to the first joint. The second extended between the first joint and the second joint. Encased in the horny wall of the foot of the horse is the third phalanx, which is usually called the "coffin" bone. There is also a much smaller bone there called the "navicular" (naVIcular). These last two are very easily injured, as you will learn later.

The Horse's Hoof

Does it hurt the horse when the blacksmith trims the wall of the hoof before putting on the shoe? No, the wall of the hoof is very much like your fingernail and is quite insensitive, provided it isn't trimmed too short. But, as with your fingernail, we must be careful not to trim too close to the "quick," or sensitive part of the horse's foot.

How can we tell where the "quick" begins and the wall ends? Fig. 27 on page 89 shows the bottom part of the horse's foot. You will see that the wall is like a rather thin shell, and that between this shell and the sole is a line marked "white line." This line, though not actually white, is lighter in color than the wall and marks the beginning of the sensitive area. When the blacksmith drives in his nails, he is careful not to penetrate the "white line."

Is the sole of the foot hard and insensitive like the wall? The sole of the foot is insensitive, but it is somewhat different from the wall. The harder the wall is, the better we like it, but the sole can become too hard. This is caused by standing or working all the time on dry surfaces. When this happens the horse is apt to go lame, for there is no flexibility left in the sole. A healthy sole can be scraped with the point of a nail and will seem slightly chalky.

What is the purpose of the part in the picture called the "frog"? This is a sort of cushion and acts like a rubber heel. When the horse gallops or jumps, there is a tremendous strain on his front feet. If the frog is big and healthy, it is in constant contact with the ground and absorbs much of the shock of this strain. If it is dried up and diseased it becomes very hard. In this case, it no longer touches the ground, and the hoof takes the full impact of the weight when the horse jumps. This often causes lameness. Horses shed their frogs every so often and many people think this is a sign of disease, but it is perfectly normal.

What are the things called "bars"? These are strong ridges which extend out from the clefts marked "commissures" to the outer wall. They act as spreaders and help to keep the horse's feet from being pinched in and becoming too narrow. Many blacksmiths cut these bars off in shoeing because it makes the foot look neater, but this is not a good practice.

You will learn much more about the care of the horse's feet in the chapter on caring for your horse.

The Teeth

How many teeth has the horse? A mare has twenty-four teeth, called "molars" or "grinders," at the back of the jaw, and twelve teeth, called "incisors," at the front of the mouth. A male horse has four additional teeth called "tushes," located about a half-inch behind the incisors. A few mares develop very small tushes, but this is not common. Sometimes horses also have tiny teeth that appear just in front of the grinders. These are called "wolf" teeth and should be pulled out, as they are of no use. Furthermore, they are so situated that the bit rubs on them, annoying the horse and making him bad-tempered and restless.

How does the horse use his teeth? The grinders work with a rotating motion, just like a pair of millstones, and grind the horse's food up very small so that it is easy to digest. The front teeth are for biting off grass and leaves.

Do horses have toothaches? No, in this respect a horse's teeth differ from ours. Since there are no nerves in a horse's teeth, he does not have toothaches. However, if a horse gets an infection in the jawbone, where the roots of the teeth are, it can be very uncomfortable. Another way in which the horse's teeth differ from ours is that they never stop growing. As the grinders work against each other, they grind away the top surfaces of the teeth. If the teeth didn't continue to grow, the horse would soon wear them away altogether. Then he couldn't eat and would die. However, these teeth do not grind very evenly, and often on the outside edges of both top and bottom teeth, little points are left. If these points are not taken care of, they very soon rub sores in the horse's jaws. Then the horse stops chewing as he should, the food goes into his stomach before it is properly ground up, and is not digested. Before you know it, your horse becomes very thin, even though you are giving him plenty to eat.

In a later chapter on first aid, you will learn how to keep your horse's teeth in good condition.

What does the saying, "Never look a gift horse in the mouth," mean? This saying is related to the horse's teeth, for by looking at these the experienced horseman can tell just how old the horse is.

Fig. 12a shows a series of drawings of the horse's bottom incisors, as they look when you open his mouth and look down at them. Soon after the foal is born, his two first baby teeth break through. Sometimes a foal is born with two, or even four, teeth. These teeth look very large in the tiny jaw, but actually they are somewhat smaller than the permanent teeth which come in later. Two at a time, the foal's teeth come in until at a year he has all except the tushes. At three years he loses the two center incisors, which are replaced by the larger, stronger, permanent teeth; at four years he loses the next two incisors. At five years he loses the two outside incisors, and, if he is a male colt, grows in his four tushes. He is now said to have a "full mouth."

In the center of each of the permanent teeth in the drawing, the artist has put a black spot, called the "cup." This is a depression in the tooth surrounded by a slightly higher wall of enamel. As the horse chews, the walls of enamel wear away and gradually he loses these cups. At six years, the walls of the two center

a. Lower incisors

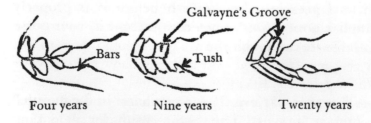

One year   Five years   Six years   Seven years   Eight years
(milk teeth)   (Smooth mouth)

b. Upper and lower incisors seen from the side

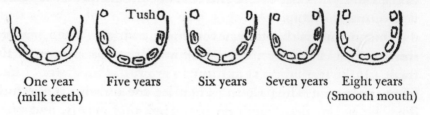

Four years   Nine years   Twenty years

Fig. 12. The teeth

teeth are gone, at seven the next two, and at eight he no longer has any cups and is said to have a "smooth" mouth.

Up to the age of eight, then, we can tell very accurately, exactly how old the horse is. The saying means, as you can see, that you may think a horse that is given to you is young, but on looking in his mouth, be disappointed!

How do we tell a horse's age after the age of eight? After the horse is eight years old, we cannot be quite so accurate, although the general appearance of the teeth still helps a great deal. A more reliable sign is called "Galvayne's Groove" (GALvayne). Look at Fig. 12b. This shows two views of a horse's upper and lower incisors as seen from the side. One is of a horse about nine or ten years old, and the other of a very old horse. You will notice at once that the older horse's teeth are much longer and protrude more. Now look at Galvayne's Groove, which appears first at the gum line of the horse's upper corner tooth when the horse is nine years old. As the years go on, this groove becomes longer until at fifteen years, it is halfway down the tooth, and at twenty years, all the way down. Then the upper portion of the Galvayne's Groove begins to fade out until, at thirty years, it has usually disappeared.

What is the space between the front and back teeth marked the "bars"? This is the area where the bit rests. Remember that there is also another part of the horse called the "bars." You learned about it when we were reading the section on the foot. The bars of the mouth are very important to us, for if the horse's teeth went all the way around his jaws, as yours do, we would not be able to use a bit in his mouth. The bars are sensitive and it is on them that the bit works. Sometimes in putting a bridle on, it is necessary to put your fingers into the horse's mouth at the bar area. This is not dangerous, for, having no teeth there, the horse cannot bite you.

The Muscles, Ligaments, and Tendons

The horse, like you, has two types of muscles—the voluntary and the involuntary muscles. The voluntary muscles, those that you can work at will, are the ones which attach to the joints throughout the body and enable you to move about. The involuntary muscles go on working all the time without your having to tell them to do so. Among these are the muscles with which you breathe, and the muscles that enlarge and contract the pupils of your eyes when you go from bright sunshine into a darkened room. The heart is your most important involuntary muscle, since it must beat without ceasing from the day you are born until the day you die. The involuntary muscles can work for years, and if the body itself is healthy and not put to too great a strain, they will not tire easily. The voluntary muscles do tire easily and have to be rested.

Fig. 13 shows the main muscular system of the horse. You may find it interesting to notice how much the muscles differ from one another in size.

How do the voluntary muscles work? Look again at the drawing and notice that the muscles extending down the upper legs

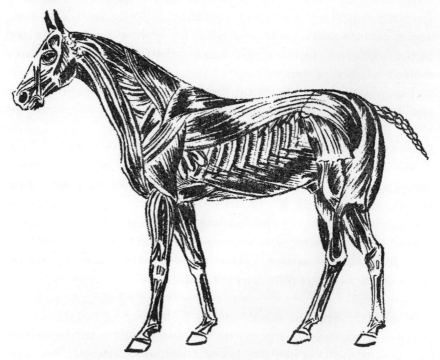

Fig. 13. Muscular system

end in points. These points are tough, stringlike tissues called "tendons." These attach to the covering of the joint, which is of similar tissue, called a "ligament," and to the bones themselves. Now make a fist with your right hand and bend your right elbow; at the same time, put your left hand around your upper arm. Did you feel something bunch up and become hard? That was your muscle. As you bent your arm, the muscle got thicker and shorter. In doing so, it pulled on the tendon which in turn worked the joint. Most voluntary muscles are in pairs, with nerves attached. In each pair, one muscle opens the joint and the other closes it; the two help each other to make the motion smooth.

Is there any difference between the horse's ligaments and ours? Generally speaking, they are alike, but there is one way in which the ligaments covering the main leg joints of the horse differ from yours. As you know, a human being cannot go to sleep without lying down or at least sitting down and leaning against something, but this is not true of the horse. The ligaments covering his hocks and other large joints are made like hammocks, and support the horse when he is asleep, even though he may be standing up. Later, in the section on the care and handling of the horse, you will see why it is so important to remember this.

The Internal Organs

Are the horse's internal organs like ours? Yes, they work pretty much the same way. The stomach digests the food. The heart pumps the blood which carries oxygen and nourishment throughout the body. The lungs exchange the poisonous wastes from the cells, which the blood brings back in the form of carbon dioxide, for fresh oxygen. The brain, which is in three parts, controls the nervous system of the horse as well as being a thinking apparatus. Fig. 14 shows the location of all these organs.

What is the organ marked "spleen"? No one knows the whole purpose of the spleen, but we do know that it is a storage place for extra blood. When the horse races, or in some other way exerts himself so much that his body needs more blood to carry

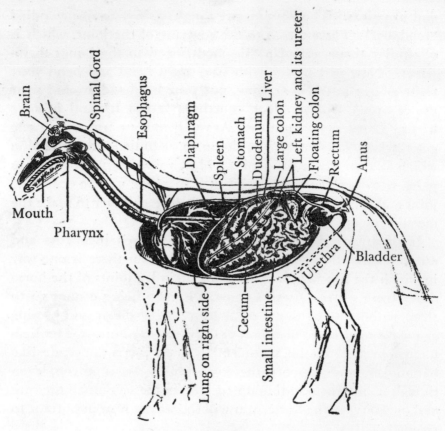

Fig. 14. Location of organs

additional oxygen to the cells, the spleen, which is a sort of blood bank, supplies it.

The Colors of the Horse

The body colors of the horse * are classified as solid, particolored, pied, and mixed. The solid colors, beginning with the darkest are black, brown, chocolate, bay, chestnut, dun, palomino, gray, and albino (pure white).

What gives the horse his color? Each hair is a hollow shaft. Inside this shaft is a black or very dark coloring matter called "pigment." This pigment is the same color for all horses, but in

* For color breeds see Chapter 2.

An Arabian horse with rider in native costume

The famous Thoroughbred Man O' War

A Half-bred gelding

The American Standardbred Greyhound, whose 1938 record of a mile in 1 minute 55¼ second has never been equalled

A prize-winning walk-trot Saddle Horse with 4 H club owner

American five-gaited Saddle-bred mare

Merry Go Boy, a famous Tennessee Walking Horse sire

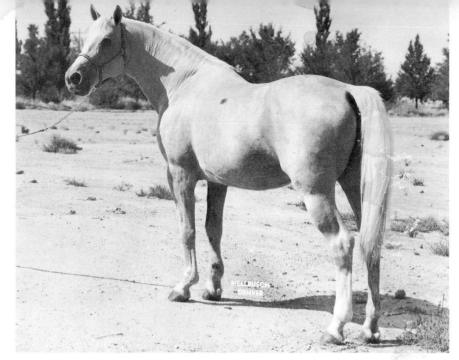

A Palomino Quarterhorse

An Appaloosa stallion. The dark spots can be felt as well as seen

"Cutting Horses," or Stock horses, used for "cutting out" or separating one animal from a herd

A Percheron mare

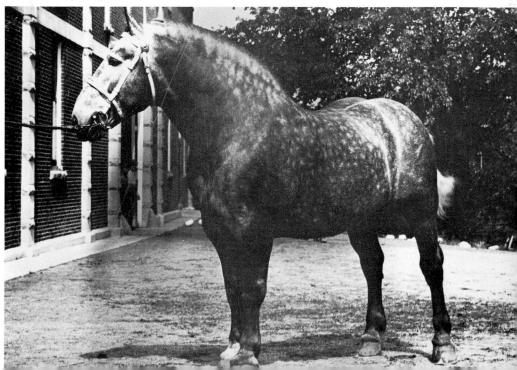

(Left) Shetland pony in a Fancy Turnout Class *(Right)* Welsh mountain pony stallion

Hackney pony of the modern show type

Large type children's Half-bred
hunting pony

A miniature Shetland pet pony
and his friend

A Lipizzan horse during a visit to the United States

A Morgan horse and his son, both splendid examples of Justin Morgan's descendants

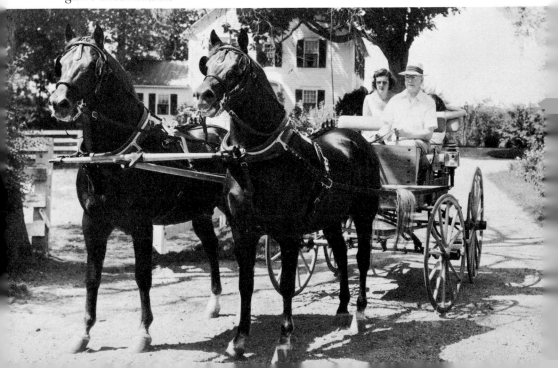

the blacks there is a great deal of it, and in the lighter colors very little. In all the solid colors, other than the palominos and the duns, the pigment is more or less evenly distributed in the shaft; in the duns and the palominos, it is not evenly distributed. Consequently, in these colors, the light is reflected differently. This, in the duns, gives a somewhat faded appearance, especially in the very light ones. In dark duns, the ends of the hairs are often lighter. In the palominos, this distribution of pigment gives an almost metallic glitter.

Are there special names for the different duns? There are many shades of dun; some are just called "dark" or "light" duns. There is also a grayish dark dun called a "mouse" dun, and a very light, almost cream-colored dun called a "clay-bank" dun. All duns have black points, like the bays, and most have dark stripes running down the spine from mane to tail. A few also have light zebra stripes on the upper legs; prehistoric horses had these. Dun was one of the colors of the prehistoric horse, and in some cases the markings have also been retained.

Some horses that look black are called brown. How do we tell the difference? A true black is a shiny, patent-leather black. There is no hint of a brownish tinge anywhere. Such horses are rare. There are two military units that specialize in black horses: the Queen's Guard in London, and the Musical Ride Team of the Royal Canadian Mounted Police. Sometimes, however, it is not possible to find enough really black horses for these units, and one sees an occasional dark bay or brown.

What is the difference between a brown and a dark bay? Both these horses have about the same color body—deep brown, almost black, with tinges of a lighter brown inside the legs. However, the dark bay horse has a reddish bay muzzle whereas the brown has not.

Are there any other kinds of bay besides the dark bay? Yes, there is the light bay and the blood bay. The latter is a real reddish color; the light bay is paler. Most bays have "black points"; that is, the lower legs, mane, and tail are black. Occasionally, we find a bay whose lower legs are very little darker than the body color.

What is a chestnut? The body color of the chestnut ranges from a rich, deep brown to a pale gold. The darkest shade is called a "liver chestnut," the lightest, a "golden chestnut." In between is a bright red chestnut.

Is there some way of telling a liver chestnut from a dark bay? Yes. The bays always have black manes and tails, and usually black lower legs, whereas the chestnuts never do. The manes and tails of the chestnut group are either the same color as the body, or lighter. Some of the chestnuts have pure white manes and tails.

What is a "chocolate" pony? A chocolate pony is a type of chestnut. It has a rich brown body generally, with darker dapples and a flaxen mane and tail. This color, which used to be very rare, has lately become extremely popular.

What is a gray horse? Nearly all the white horses you will see are really grays, for they have been born either black or very dark brown and turned white with age. Some, like the Lipizzaners, are pure white by the time they are four or five years old; others remain dappled gray or even a deep iron gray until they are much older. Most true white horses are albinos. These are white from birth.

How do we tell an albino from a gray horse that has turned white? An albino usually has pale eyes and pink skin. The skin of other solid-color horses is black, except under white markings. Remember that the true albino is born white with a pink skin. Not all have light eyes, known as "watch" eyes. On a ranch in Nebraska, Mr. and Mrs. C. R. Thompson have been trying to establish a breed of pure white horses. These horses are born white, with pink skins, and most of them have pale eyes, although the Thompsons have succeeded in producing some with dark eyes. These horses do not seem to have the same weaknesses and sensitivity to sun as albinos of the horse world and of other species. The foundation sire of the Thompson's horses was Silver King, a show horse with Saddlehorse ancestry.

Can horses with watch eyes see as well as those with dark eyes? Yes indeed, they can.

What is a mixed color? This is a solid color with white hairs mixed throughout. The other name for this classification is "roan."

Are there different kinds of roans? Yes, the black roan is black with white hairs, the red roan is bay with white, the strawberry roan has chestnut as the basic color, and the gray roan looks like an iron gray. The blue roan has black, bay, and white hairs mixed.

What is a parti-colored horse? A parti-colored horse (sometimes called "paint," "pinto," or "calico") has large or small patches of different colors on its body. The "piebald" has black and white patches. The "skewbald" has white and some color other than black. Sometimes skewbalds have black as well as the other solid color. The Appaloosa, which has already been discussed, is one of the parti-colored horses.

What color is the skin of the parti-colored horse? Under the white areas, it is pink, and under the colored areas, black. Sometimes the dark skin extends an inch or so around the dark areas. If you clip such a horse or pony closely and then give him a bath, he will have a gray border showing through under the white hair, close to the black patches, and people will think that his colors have run!

What is a "pied" horse? A pied horse is one whose body is almost entirely a solid color (generally chestnut), but with one or two very small patches of white. Thus we speak of a "pied" chestnut or, more rarely, a "pied" brown or black.

What are the markings of a horse? The white areas on the horse's face and legs; those on the head are the *star,* a small spot in the center of the forehead; the *strip,* or *race,* a narrow stripe running down the nose; the *blaze,* a wider stripe running down the nose; the *snip,* a small patch of white, generally on the nose, nostril, or lip; the *calf-face,* a wide patch of white covering most or all of the face. Calf-faced horses usually have watch eyes.

The markings on the legs include the *stocking,* which runs from hoof to hock or knee, the *half-stocking,* which goes halfway up, and the *sock,* which just covers the ankle or fetlock joint. White markings on legs and face are more common in chestnuts than in other colors.

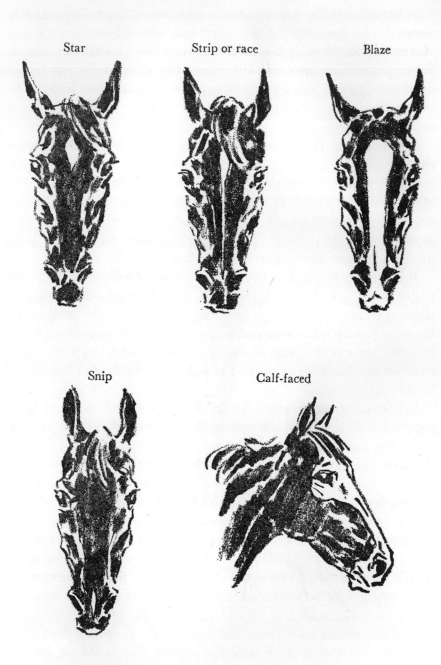

Star   Strip or race   Blaze

Snip   Calf-faced

Fig. 15. Markings on face

What color is the skin under the white markings? It is usually white. The wall of the hoof of a horse with a white stocking is also apt to be white. It is said that these white walls are not as strong as the dark ones, and there is an old adage which runs:

> *One white sock, buy him!*
> *Two white socks, try him!*
> *Three white socks, deny him!*
> *Four white socks and a white nose,*
> *Take off his hide and throw it to the crows!*

Age

It is important to know the exact age of your horse or pony, for then you will know how to feed him and how much work he should have.

One year of a horse's life is said to equal about three and a half years of a man's life. So a seven-year-old horse, like a twenty-four year-old man, is grown up. Horses that are raced, hunted,

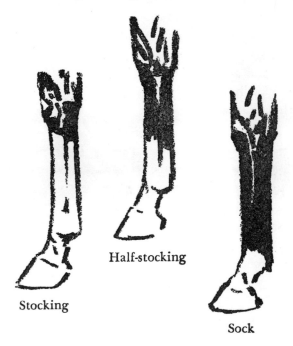

Half-stocking

Stocking

Sock

Fig. 16. Leg markings

jumped or ridden hard with too much weight on their backs when they are only two or three years old usually wear out at about the age of ten, at least as far as hard work goes. They develop all kinds of weaknesses in their legs and lungs. But the colt that is given only light work until his bones and tendons are strong (between five and seven years of age) will be able to go on working into his twenties and sometimes longer.

How long do horses and ponies live? Healthy, well-cared-for horses and ponies have been known to live to the age of fifty, and there was once a horse that was supposed to have died at the grand age of seventy-two! The average length of useful life is fifteen years. January 1 is considered the birthday of a horse or pony no matter when he is born during the year. An animal born in September or October, for instance, will be called one year old the following January.

How do we tell the age of a horse or pony? In an old horse or pony the point of the withers is higher and sharper with a deep dip in the neck in front of it. The knees buckle outward and there are deep sockets above the eyes. These are only general signs of old age, however. A well-cared-for horse of eighteen or nineteen may look far younger than a ten-year-old that has been overworked and underfed. The most accurate way of telling the age of a horse is by examining his teeth, as explained earlier in this chapter.

4

How Horses & Ponies Behave & Why

Every good horseman should know why the horse or pony behaves as he does, how much he can be expected to understand, and what his reactions will be under certain circumstances. One of the qualifications of good "horsemanship" is to know what the horse is going to do an instant before the horse himself knows, and thus be able to forestall trouble.

Since little Eohippus, the Dawn Horse, had no weapons of defense, his first instinct in the face of danger was flight. We have learned that because of this constant running, from being a mere pigmy animal, the size of a large cat, the horse has become the noble creature that he is today.

One of the greatest fears of an animal that depends on flight as a defense, is of being put in a position from which he cannot get to his feet. This sometimes happens when a horse lies down in his stall and rolls over. He may end up cramped against the wall, with his feet doubled up. Struggle though he may, he cannot get up. Such a horse is said to be "cast."

Did the lack of horns, sharp teeth, or other means of fighting enemies affect the development of the horse in other ways? It made him very timid, and also very alert, ever on the lookout for something strange, and unwilling to trust an unusual object until he was positive that it was harmless.

Are the horses of today timid? There is a great difference in the timidity of individual horses. Horses that have been handled since birth are much bolder than those that have run wild in their first years, and been broken by force. But the basic, primeval instinct to flee in the face of danger is still there. Have you ever watched a horse drinking? He doesn't drink a whole pailful without stopping, unless he is very thirsty indeed. He takes a few swallows, lifts his head and gives a snort or two. His ears waggle back and forth, then he takes another swallow or so, and again stops to look around. This habit goes back to the time when Eohippus drank at a water hole, where larger animals were most apt to wait and pounce on the defenseless creature as he quenched his thirst.

Can horses see in the dark? They can see in the dark much better than we can, but their eyes work quite differently from ours. Perhaps you have wondered why, when a horse sees a strange object, he puts his nose down to it and carefully smells it. It is true that he wants to sniff it so that he can recognize it again by smell and perhaps identify it with something he knows. But the reason he gets his head so close is also that a horse is rather far-sighted. When his head is up he can see things in the distance very well indeed, but things close to him look fuzzy. He has to put his head right down to them before they become sharply defined.

What other basic instincts does the horse have? The horse has what we call a "herd" instinct. Unless he is with other horses he feels insecure and uneasy. When the modern horse developed, nature gave him hard hooves as weapons. But even with these, a lone mare, attacked by a band of wolves, would find it hard to defend her baby foal. However, when the herd of many mares and foals is attacked from several sides at once, so that flight is impossible, the herd sticks together and fights as a unit. The foals are pushed into the center and the mares surround them, ever alert to let fly with their hind feet and shatter the skulls of the attackers.

What does the stallion do to help? Stallions attack with front feet and teeth. The stallion, running wild, learns to fight even though his band may never have been attacked. He must fight the other young stallions when he is still a colt, beat them, and earn the right to have a herd of mares of his own.

Do mares ever fight one another? Yes, and the reason is very interesting. All animals that run in herds, and birds that live in flocks, quickly set up an order of rank in their midst. In the herd of horses, besides the stallion who is the defender and the ruler, there is also a lead mare. When the herd travels, she is in the lead, while the stallion sometimes forms the rear guard. If you watch a herd of mares and foals in a field with a stallion, you will notice the stallion grazing a little away from the herd and constantly circling around it. Since, if attacked, the herd always runs away when possible, it often follows that the stallion has to stay at the back to keep off the enemy.

The little foals, who are born with very long legs and can run as fast or faster than their mothers as soon as they are a few hours old, run up front, with the mares behind them. Now, every organization needs a leader to follow, and so we find that in every herd of horses one mare acts as ruler. And she becomes the ruler by fighting her way to the top. This is one reason why mares are more apt than geldings to pick fights with other mares, even though they may never have run wild in a herd.

Is it the herd instinct that makes it so hard to teach a horse to leave others and work alone? Yes, there are many horses that have never learned to work by themselves. Of course, a properly trained horse will not put up a fuss when asked to leave the barn alone, or to leave his companions. Unless he has had this special training, however, his herd instinct takes over.

What happens when a herd has chosen its leader and a new horse comes into the stable? For the first week after a new animal, mare or gelding, is introduced into a herd which grazes in the open, there will be frequent battles. Nothing can prevent this. Every other animal will run at the newcomer with bared teeth and ready heels. Gradually things will settle down, however. In a few days it will be noted that the newcomer has picked out a pal and the two may be seen grazing peacefully together in a far corner of the pasture. Usually this buddy is the next most recent arrival in the stable.

Do horses and ponies ever graze in groups of three or more? Usually they prefer to graze in pairs, but there is one exception. Sometimes a gelding will attach himself to a mare with a young foal and help her take care of her baby. As they work their way over the pasture in search of the tastiest morsels, mother will be on one side and foster father on the other, with small fry in the middle. If the foal gallops off to play with another youngster, or just to explore on his own, immediately the two older horses will so place themselves that no matter how the foal turns, there will always be a guard on each side.

Why do horses and ponies always face all the same way when they graze? Again, we go back to Eohippus. By all facing the same way, the herd can get away as a unit, to a fast start.

Can horses communicate with one another? Yes, horses can communicate, and not just with their voices either. Watch two horses meeting for the first time in the riding hall, or old friends greeting each other in the field. The first thing they do is approach each other cautiously, heads outstretched. Then they sniff noses. Nostrils distended, they puff and sniff. Then apparently they decide whether they hate each other or whether they can be friends. If they have decided to be enemies, heads go up, impatient feet are stamped and one, or both animals, lets out a squeak of rage. If they are going to be friends, each gives the other a friendly nudge and then they trot off together.

Perhaps you think this is the limit of the horse's ability to convey ideas, but I assure you it is not. We don't know how they do it, whether with the flick of an ear, a certain position of the head, a quick snort, or what, but horses can and do communicate quite complicated ideas to each other.

Does the horse have a good memory? Yes, luckily he does. Without his memory, the horse would be virtually useless, for we should never be able to train him.

Is the horse's memory as good as a human being's? It seems far better, probably because his mind works much more simply and is not cluttered up with too many ideas.

What kinds of things does a horse remember best? He remembers places and frightening experiences best of all.

Horses rarely forget trails, roads, or places they have visited. Once they have gone over a certain road, they will always remember it. If you are lost, you can usually trust your horse to bring you home safely.

Can a horse find his way home from a strange place if he has been taken there by railroad or van? Tests have shown that horses carried at night by van to places twenty or more miles from home are still able to find their way back. Some authorities think this is explained by their highly developed sense of smell. However it may be, the ability of horses to find their way to their own barn, or even to a strange barn where their friends are, is really astounding.

Do ponies behave the same as horses? The basic instincts of ponies and horses are the same, but there are many differences in their behavior. Ponies and their prehistoric ancestors lived in parts of the world where the climate was very severe and there was not much food. Horses, on the other hand, developed in milder climates where food was more abundant. This accounts, in the main, for the different forms of behavior.

The cold weather gave the pony a much thicker skin for protection. This means that he is less sensitive, and therefore, less nervous and hysterical. The pony had to spend many hours looking for food, and for several months of the year probably went hungry most of the time. As a result, he learned a patience which the horse does not have. No matter whether everything goes just the way it should or not, the pony will plod along and make the most of what he has.

Ponies are certainly smarter than horses when it comes to getting themselves out of a pasture, field, or paddock. They like to wander and are never contented with their own property. This is probably due to the scarcity of food in the Arctic tundras, where the ancestors of most ponies roamed.

Because ponies are less sensitive and less timid, they are also more determined about what they will and will not do than are horses. This has given them a reputation for being stubborn. Once a pony finds out that *he* can be boss, you will get little work out of him. The gentler and more phlegmatic the pony, the stronger and more determined must be the rider.

A pony will often work much better for a child than he will for a grownup. Once he has accepted the child as his master, he will be servant, nurse, and inseparable playmate, all in one.

73

5

Choosing a Horse or Pony

Suitable Type

Suppose the time has finally come to choose a horse for yourself. Horses, like people, have their individual differences. This is important to remember, whether you are actually buying a horse or merely renting one. How can you tell whether the horse that is being so highly praised by the dealer, breeder, or owner, and looks just perfect to you is really the right one? Start by asking yourself the following questions:

How good a rider am I? To the person who has never ridden, anyone who can stay on a horse at the walk, trot, and canter is a good horseman. Some people think that if they can not only stay on, but make an ordinary horse do what they want it to do, then they are good riders. As an aid in deciding on a suitable type of horse, ask yourself a few additional questions:

a. Do I prefer a horse that trots quietly along minding his own business?

b. If my horse bucks or rears, do I hold on to the saddle or pull up on the reins to keep from falling off?

c. Can I ride just as well at the walk, trot, and canter with stirrups and reins as without?

If your answer is "yes" to questions a. and b. and "no" to question c., then you should look for a quiet, well-trained animal, either a pony or one of the smaller, gentler horse breeds such as the Morgan.

But if you are thoroughly at home on an active animal and don't need your stirrups and reins to keep from falling off, then you are ready for a sensitive, high-spirited animal such as an Arabian, a Thoroughbred, or a five or three-gaited Saddler.

What kind of riding am I going to do? Do you live in the country where there are plenty of dirt roads and trails? If so, and you want a pony or horse principally for trail riding and cross-country work, you need a sturdy sure-footed animal. Your horse should have easy gaits and go well either alone or in company, without needing either to be booted to make him move on, or held in to keep him from going too fast.

If you are tall and prefer a horse to a pony, look for a gentle, well-trained stock horse, one with some Quarter Horse blood in him, perhaps. Other possibilities are a Morgan, or a Tennessee Walker.

If you prefer a pony, choose one of the good sturdy breeds such as the Conemarra, Shetland, or Moor pony. Many German and Scottish types, as well as the Icelandic pony, are ideal for trail work, but are not easily found in this country. We do have what is called a Pennsylvania "Chunk." This animal, part draft and part Shetland, often makes a fine trail pony, and takes readily to driving besides.

Do I intend to ride with other children? If you do, choose an animal with good manners and average gaits, one that gets along well with other ponies and doesn't walk or trot either too fast or too slowly. Perhaps there is an open field in which you and your friends will want to play games and jump a bit. For activities like these, you need an active pony. He must be able to start, stop, and turn easily, and not mind being crashed into occasionally. He ought to be flexible and alert, but not too excitable. For this kind of work a medium-sized pony or a small horse is best. A very tall horse may be clumsy and hard to turn; a very small pony is sometimes dangerous to ride if all the other animals that are playing are big.

Do I live in a hunting country and plan to follow the hounds? Jumping ability, stamina, good manners, and sure-footedness are what you need in a hunting pony.

Is competing in shows my main interest? If so, you will have to buy not only for suitability, but for looks and showiness too. The horse or pony that catches the judge's eye has a far better chance of coming off with the blue even in an equitation class (which is supposedly judged only on the ability of the rider) than a calmer, commoner type. Smooth gaits and good manners are also essential. Of course, if you plan to show a specific breed, or to compete primarily in jumping and hunting classes, you will have to choose an animal that puts on a good performance and makes a good appearance in such classes.

Am I going to take care of my horse or pony myself? If so, don't buy an animal too tall for you to saddle, bridle, and mount easily. It must have good stable manners, and be easy to groom, shoe, and clip. Some things you can teach him, but the horse or pony must have a willing, docile disposition to start with. If he is going to be the only pony in the stable, you must make sure that he will leave the barn without putting up a fuss, and will go well alone.

Conformation

Now, let's talk a little about how the horse is made. Although every horse and every pony is different from every other, certain basic physical characteristics are considered good and others poor. Since we want our horse or pony to stay sound and strong for many years, we must remember this and not choose him only for his good looks or because he seems gentle and sweet. A horse that is built well is said to have "good conformation." General Harry D. Chamberlain, a very famous rider, trainer, and writer, used to refer to the "beauties and blemishes" of horses. First we'll look at the whole horse, and decide how he should be built, and then we'll look at different parts and discuss both the beauties and blemishes.

How can I tell if a horse is well-built? Look at Fig. 17 and see how various parts of the horse's anatomy compare with one another in size or length. First, think of the horse's body as being a perfect square. The distance from the withers, C, to the ground, is the same as the distance from the buttock point, H, to

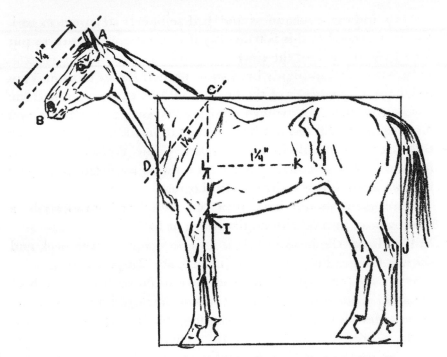

Fig. 17. Comparison of basic lines and sizes of parts

the shoulder-point, D. The distance from the poll, A, to the tip of the muzzle, B, is the same as from C to D. When the horse is holding his head naturally, the lines from A to B and from C to D are parallel. The distance from C to the horse's elbow, I, should be the same as the distance from I to the ground. The point K marks the last rib. From there to L, where a line running from K meets the line C–I, should be the same length as the C–D and the A–B lines. Notice that the hock, marked J, is right under the buttock point, H. So much for a general idea of conformation; now lets look more closely at certain parts of the horse, beginning with the head.

What are the "beauties" in the head? Although there are many different types of heads, some beauties apply to all. The horse should be wide between the eyes and the eyes themselves should be well-rounded and prominent. Some people are afraid of a horse that shows white around the dark of his eye. They say this indicates meanness and bad temper. My own experience has been that this is true only if the horse also tends to put his ears back most of the time.

In horses and in highly bred show ponies, the head should appear lean. The bones of the head should be easily seen, and the veins prominent. Northern-bred ponies, such as Icelandic and Norwegian breeds, do not have such lean heads, especially when they are wearing their winter coats. The Arabians, as you learned, highly prize the "jibbah" or bulging forehead, but many horsemen think this indicates stubbornness.

Your horse should have thin but well-flared-out nostrils, a healthy pink inside, with no discharge or bad odor.

The size of the head in relation to the length of the neck and the way the head is attached to the neck are also important.

What does the size of the head have to do with the length of the neck? One of the main functions of the head is to balance the horse as he moves. When he is going fast, he stretches out his neck and holds his head quite low. When he prances or does the "passage" (a movement in which the horse lifts his feet very high, and trots with a slow cadence but a very extended stride), he brings his head up. In jumping, his head first goes out, and then up, as the hindquarters rise over the jump. As he lands, the head goes out again.

Thoroughbreds and Arabians which have been bred for speed have long necks and rather small heads. Draft horses and Northern-bred ponies have shorter, thicker necks, and heavier heads. If you put the heavy head of a draft horse on the long, slender neck of the Thoroughbred, he would have a really dreadful time trying to hold it up. So, in judging the head of the horse, look also at his neck, and if the latter is long and willowy, be sure the head is not too large.

Why are some horses called "hammerheads"? In Fig. 18 you will see both a "hammerhead" and a horse with a head that is set on well. The difference is in the angle at the throttle, which should curve smoothly. This allows plenty of room for the windpipe and gullet, the tubes through which the horse breathes and swallows. In the hammerhead type the angle is abrupt, so the

Well-proportioned head
well-set on neck

Hammerhead
Head too large for neck

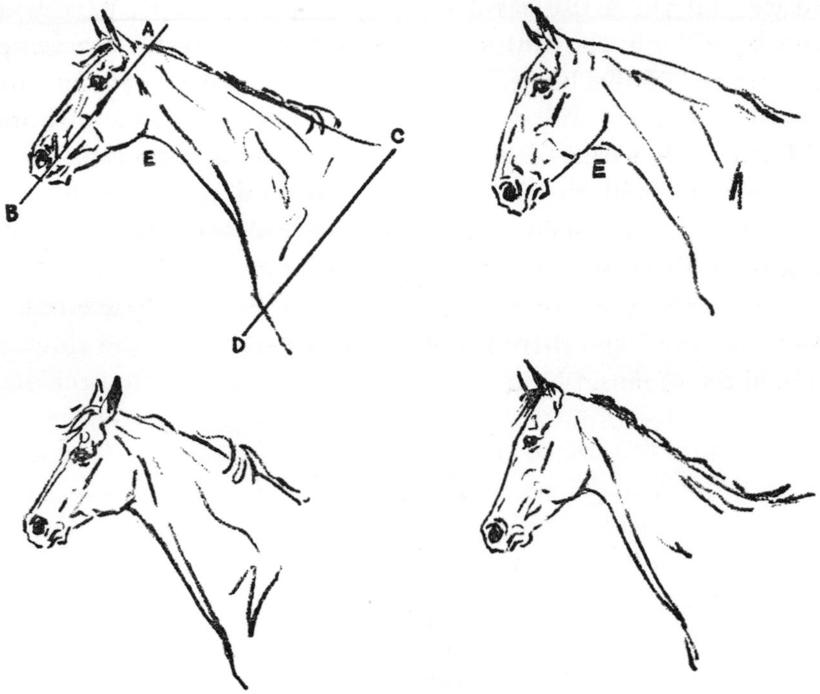

Head too small for neck

Ewe neck

Fig. 18.

gullet and throttle are smaller. A horse of this kind will be prone to weaknesses of the respiratory (breathing) system.

Is there anything else I need to know about the neck? One of the beauties in the horse is a good "crest" (see Fig. 11). The curve begins just behind the first vertebra. Without a good crest, a horse will be hard-mouthed, for he must relax and bend at the poll and crest when he slows down or stops. The opposite of a good crest, and a real "blemish" in a horse of any breed, is the "upside-down" or "ewe" neck shown in Fig. 18. Although this can sometimes be corrected, the correction is not easy, so steer clear of such horses.

Do we look at the horse from the side in judging his chest and rib cage? No, as shown in Fig. 19, we look at him from the front. Notice that the artist has drawn an elliptical shape, narrow at the top, wider at the bottom. This is the ideal conformation of the "front" of the horse. The withers, which are at the top, should be narrow and well-defined, not flat and wide. A horse with flat, wide withers is referred to as "mutton-withered."

Below the withers, the front widens to allow room for the heart, lungs, etc. Too wide or square-looking a front is bad, because in this case, the legs are set too far apart. A front that is too narrow is even worse. The front legs seem to "come out of the same hole," and there is not room enough inside the rib cage to hold the organs.

Fig. 19. Chest and rib cage seen from front

Should the rib cage be the same width all the way back? No, at the shoulders it is narrower than immediately behind the girth. From that point, in a well-conformed horse, the ribs spring out and the rib cage becomes rounder and wider. This is important for the health and stamina of the horse. It provides enough room for the vital organs, and forms a correctly designed structure to which well-placed legs are attached. It is also important from the rider's point of view. The springing out of the ribs just behind the girth area makes it easy to keep the saddle in place. Horses with flat ribs have to wear a special piece of tack called a "breast-plate." Otherwise the saddle is continually sliding back too far towards the rump.

Ponies with chests that are too round and with mutton withers present the opposite problem. Such ponies (many otherwise good ponies have poor withers) have to wear a "cropper" (CRUpper) strap. This fastens to a ring at the back of the saddle and then goes back and under the pony's tail. It prevents the saddle from sliding forward over the withers.

Are there different kinds of "top lines"? Yes. There is a "sway-back," as in Fig. 20, and there is a "roach back." A sway-back indicates weakness or old age. Horses that are made to carry too much weight when they are under three years of age often develop sway-backs before they are twelve. Roach backs are associated with mutton shoulders and withers. Don't confuse a roach back with the back of a horse that has a straight top line and well-developed muscles in the loin area. The latter is very desirable. It's easy to tell the difference. In the roach back, the spine itself curves upward, and there is no muscular development on each side. In the well-developed horse, the muscles, which do not feel at all like bone, rise on each side of the spine.

Next we come to the hindquarters. The size and position of the big bones of the haunch determine the shape of the hindquarters. Some breeds, such as the Saddle and Arabian, have a very level line from croup to tail. The Thoroughbred has hindquarters that are shaped slightly differently. Fig. 20 shows what is called a "goose rump." This is ugly, weak, and highly undesirable.

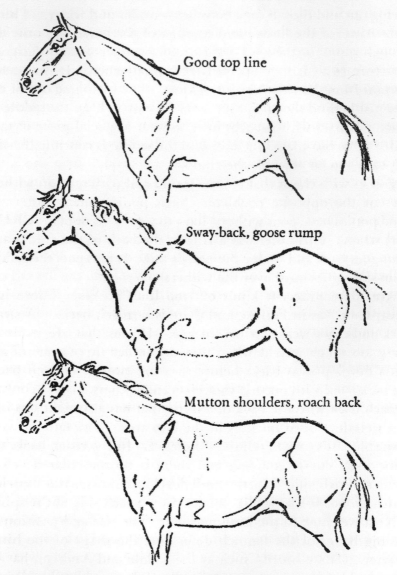

Good top line

Sway-back, goose rump

Mutton shoulders, roach back

Fig. 20.

What are the best kinds of legs in a horse? There is more variation in the shape and type of legs in horses than in any other part of his anatomy. In Fig. 21 *a* shows what the horse's front legs should look like seen from the front. They are set at the corners of the chest, and are perfectly straight. In *b*, the legs come together too much at the top, then bulge out again, making the horse slightly bowlegged; *c* is very bad indeed. The horse's toes point so far out and the legs are set on so badly, that the knees almost touch each other. Such a horse will be continuously cutting the inside of one leg with the foot of the opposite leg.

In *d* we have the opposite fault; the horse toes in. This is better than toeing out, but is still not good. In *e* the horse stands and travels with his feet too close together, and in *f* with the feet too wide apart.

Fig. 22 shows the legs from the side; *a* shows the correct type and setting of the leg. In 22*b* the horse pushes his feet out in front of him as he stands. Some horses are taught to do this. It is called "stretching" or "camping." It derives from the days of carriages. Knowing that a horse standing in this position was unable to move out without first bringing his legs under him, coachmen taught the horses used in ladies' vehicles to "stretch" while the owner was getting into the phaeton or victoria. Thus there was little chance of a nervous animal taking a step forward at the wrong time, and precipitating the Victorian lady on her nose into the gutter. You can tell the horse that has been taught to "stretch" from the one with a naturally bad stance. The trained Saddler stretches his back feet out behind him, as well as stretching his forefeet in front of him, and then poses. The badly conformed horse just pushes his forelegs a few inches forward. This stance usually indicates a weakness of some sort.

The next drawing, 22*c*, shows a horse that is what we call "over at the knees." This, too, is an indication of weakness and is common in very old horses. In 22*d* the horse is standing with his front feet too far under him, another common fault of conformation, not as serious as the opposite position, shown in *b*, but not desirable either. Another thing to notice, in regard to the legs, is the development of the tendons in the lower region, or can-

a. Good legs   b. Bowlegged   c. Knock-kneed
                                                 and toeing out

Fig. 21.

non. In Fig. 23, *a* is a good lower leg and cannon bone; *b* shows a horse with weak tendons. The leg is "tied in" below the knee and the tendons not well separated at that point. The horse in *c* has strained his tendons at some time and been left with a "bowed tendon."

Seen from the front, the knee should be broad. From the side, the cannon should appear wide, with the tendons well-defined. The elbow should not be too closely pinned to the horse's body, nor should it push out away from it.

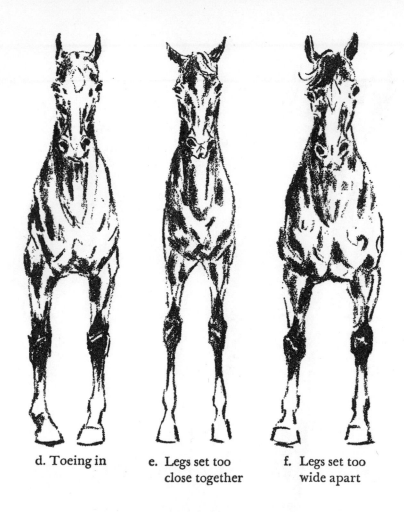

d. Toeing in   e. Legs set too   f. Legs set too
                 close together   wide apart

What about the hind legs? Fig. 24 shows good and bad hind legs as seen from the side, and Fig. 25 shows you how the horse should and should not look from behind.

How can you tell whether the horse has good feet? Notice the slope of the wall in relationship to the pastern and cannon bone; the type of horn or "wall"; and the shape of the foot. Be sure that the sole and the frog are healthy, too. Fig. 26a shows the type of foot and pastern we like to see. In 26b the horse has pasterns that are too long and weak. Notice that there is no

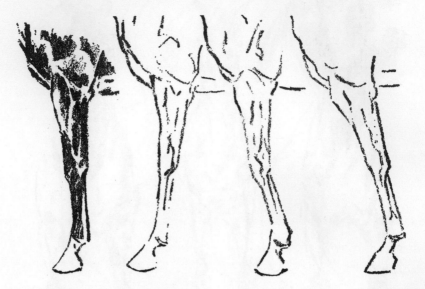

a. Good front legs   b. Feet pushed too   c. Over at the knees   d. Feet too far
far to the front   under horse

Fig. 22.

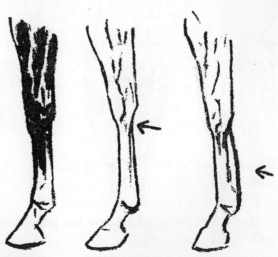

a. Good cannon   b. Tied-in tendons   c. Bowed tendon
and tendons

Fig. 23. Lower leg

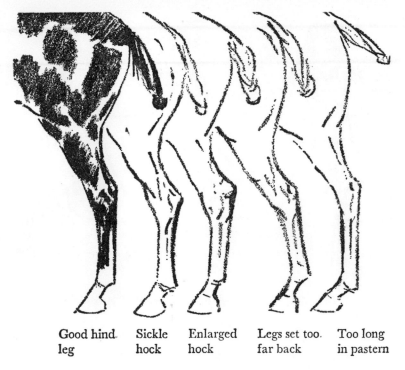

Good hind. leg   Sickle hock   Enlarged hock   Legs set too. far back   Too long in pastern

Fig. 24. Back legs seen from side

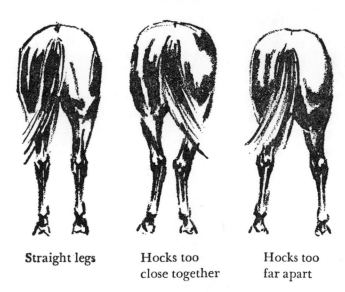

Straight legs   Hocks too close together   Hocks too far apart

Fig. 25. Horse's back legs seen from rear

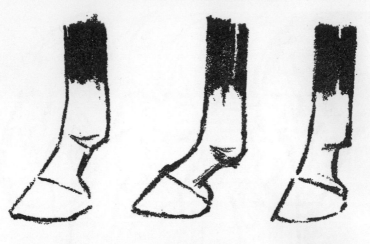

| a. Good foot | b. Pastern too long | c. Pastern too straight |
| and pastern | and sloping | and short |

Fig. 26. Foot and pastern seen from side

longer a straight line from the fetlock joint to the toe. The horse with a foot and pastern like the one shown in 26c will have hard, choppy gaits.

In Fig. 27a, we see a well-made fore foot and in *b* a hind foot with a wide heel and well-developed frog. The hind foot is generally rounder. In *c* we see a bad frog and contracted heels. The sole should be arched upward, away from the ground, and not be too flat. A flat sole is one indication of a condition known as "founder," which you will learn about in Chapter 8. Notice the ridges on the wall, as seen from the side, and how the wall itself sinks in halfway down. Never buy an animal with a foot like this even though he shows no signs of lameness.

Judging Soundness

What does the term "going sound" mean? It means that the horse travels squarely with no sign of weakness or injury. When you buy a horse, the seller, if he is honest, will guarantee him "sound in wind, limb, and eyes."

How can I tell whether the horse is sound? To find out whether he is sound in his legs, have someone ride him at the

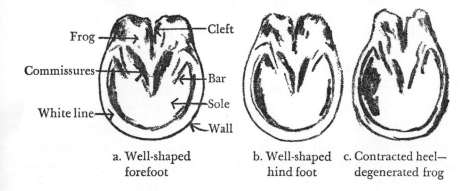

Frog
Cleft
Commissures
Bar
Sole
White line
Wall

a. Well-shaped
forefoot

b. Well-shaped
hind foot

c. Contracted heel—
degenerated frog

Fig. 27. Horse's foot

walk. Notice how he puts his feet down and listen to the rhythm
of the gait. The cadence should be regular and the feet planted
solidly, without hesitation.

Some horses move as though they were "walking on eggs."
This always indicates unsoundness. Look particularly at the
prints made by the horse's feet. At the walk, the print of the
hind foot should come well in front of that of the front foot.
This is called the horse's natural "overreach."

If the horse is only slightly lame, he won't show it at the walk
or the canter, but only at the trot. Have him trotted on a hard
surface so that you can hear the beat of the gait. It should be
perfectly even; one beat should not sound louder or heavier than
the other. While the horse is trotting, watch him carefully from
the front to be sure he "paddles," or throws his feet out as he
travels. Have him trotted in small circles in both directions as
well as up- and downhill, especially the latter. A horse with a
weak shoulder will go slightly lame moving downhill and on
sharp turns.

If the horse goes evenly through these tests, he is probably
sound as far as his legs are concerned.

Can I tell anything about a horse's sight just by looking at his eyes? You can tell whether or not he sees well, and whether or not he has "ophthalmia." The eyeball of a horse with this disease will have a bluish look and may be covered with what looks like a slight film. Sometimes, deep within the eye itself, there is a whitish or greenish spot. The eyes should not be inflamed, nor the lids puffy, and there shouldn't be any unusual discharge.

Some horses have bad eyesight from other causes that have no obvious symptoms. As a simple test, stand by the horse's shoulder and wave your hand gently near the eye, though not hard enough to cause a breeze and let him know that something is near his eye. Don't stand in such a position that he can see what you are doing with the other eye. The instant your hand moves toward the eye, the horse should blink, cock his ears, or pull away.

How can I test a horse's wind? There are two main ailments of the "wind," or respiratory system. One, called "broken wind," involves a thickening of the cartilage at the horse's throttle. Usually it is an after-effect of some such disease as "shipping fever," common in horses shipped in public conveyances. In broken wind, the horse breathes very loudly, in a "roaring" manner that is particularly noticeable when he is raced or run rapidly. The other ailment, "heaves," is a condition of the lungs themselves. There is a breakdown of the cells by means of which blood coming back from the veins loaded with carbon dioxide is exchanged for fresh blood loaded with oxygen. The main characteristic of this disease is difficulty in expelling the air. There is often a thickness in the breathing. If you watch the flanks of the horse just below the hipbone, you will notice that the flanks move once as the horse inhales and twice as he exhales. Other symptoms include a cough and an unusual development of muscle below the flanks, leading to a marked line called the "heave line." The test for both these ailments is the same. Gallop the horse for five minutes; then have him stand while you listen to his wind and watch his flanks as he breathes.

Tests for Manners and Way of Going

How else should I test a horse before buying him? You will want to ride him and see if he is the type of horse you can manage and enjoy. This, as explained earlier, will depend on what you intend to do with him, and on your own riding experience. You will also want to test his manners, both under the saddle and in the stable.

How can I test the horse under the saddle? First, find out whether you can mount him easily by having everyone stand away from him as you climb on his back without assistance. Does he stand perfectly still or does he fidget? Does he try to bolt before you are firmly seated? If you can mount alone, even though he may not stand to perfection, you will be able to correct his manners a little in this respect, later. If you can't mount alone, and yet you plan to take care of the horse yourself and ride alone, you'd better look further. Next, check his gaits to see if they are comfortable, and to find out how well he obeys your legs and hands.

Is there a special way to check obedience and gaits? Yes. Move out on a loose-rein long walk. Make several circles and halt several times to see if the horse responds willingly. Ride him both toward and away from the stable. If he walks freely and is willing to turn or go in either direction, put him into a slow trot and sit to it without posting. This will tell you whether the trot is comfortable. Then once again, ride in circles, stopping and starting near the barn area. Follow this with the posting trot. Try to get the horse to extend and take long strides. Is he willing to maintain his gaits without either slowing down or breaking into a faster gait without permission?

Finally, try his canter. Does he take both leads readily? Can you gallop fast toward the barn and pull up without difficulty? Will he gallop, come down to a halt, and then move on at a loose-rein walk?

These tests will tell you a great deal about the horse's training, gaits, and disposition, as far as going by himself is concerned. However, since you may be riding him in company at times, it is well to test him with a companion, too.

How should I test the horse's manners in company? Have another rider join you and ride beside him, close enough so that you can hold hands. Now, have the other horse go ahead, as you follow. Does your horse try to run into the horse in front? Does he continually fight to get past and be in the lead? Finally, ask your companion to ride behind you. Is your horse willing to move out in the lead? If he puts back his ears and switches his tail when the other horse comes up a little close, it is his way of warning the other animal to expect a kick.

How can I test a horse's stable manners? See whether he will let you walk into his stall after his feed has been put into his manger, without pinning his ears back and turning his haunches toward you. Put the saddle and bridle on the horse yourself. Does he snap at you when you try to adjust the girth? Does he put his head up very high and clinch his teeth together when you try to slip in the bit? These are not very serious faults and you will learn later how to correct them, but you want to be sure that you can manage your horse without help from the very beginning. Otherwise all these vices will become worse and worse. Next, run your hand over every part of the horse's body, and pick up his feet. This will tell you whether you will be able to groom him properly.

How do I test a horse's pasture manners? With the horse wearing only a halter to which a lead rope (halter shank) is attached, lead him in and out of the stable and around the barn area. Does he try to pull away? Does he stand still, brace his feet and neck, and refuse to budge? Tie him to a fence or to the corner of the barn and walk away. Does he stand quietly?

Next, turn him loose in a small paddock and see what he does. Probably he will lie down and roll, stand up and shake himself thoroughly, and then gallop around a few minutes. When he has settled down and begun to graze, try walking up to him, holding out a little grass or tidbit. Will he let you walk up to him and snap on the halter shank? Does he throw back his head and gallop away? Does he pin back his ears and charge at you? The latter is a serious vice. It can be cured, but a horse with such a habit is not suitable except for a very strong and experienced boy or girl.

Is there any other way to test a horse for soundness, manners, and suitability? Ask for a veterinary certificate of soundness, and also for permission to take the horse home for a few days and try him. Most reputable dealers will let you do this if you pay the costs of transportation and assume responsibility in case of accident.

Where should I look for a good horse or pony? You might visit a reputable dealer, since this is where you can often find what you want at a reasonable price. Remember, however, that any horse in the hands of a dealer is probably being sold because someone else doesn't want him. Be sure the dealer is honest and will guarantee the horse's physical fitness and manners. Another way to find a horse is through advertisements. You can put an ad in a horse magazine such as the *Middleburg Chronicle,* which is published in Virginia, and read by people interested in showing and hunting. You can also watch for ads in the sports sections of the *New York Times* and *New York Herald Tribune,* and in the classified sections of local papers.

The ideal way is to find a breeder who specializes in the kind of animal you want, go to his farm, and try out several horses. Although you will pay more, you will be getting a horse or pony that has not been spoiled and one trained especially for riders such as you.

The Cost of a Horse or Pony

How much should I pay for a good horse or pony? It is difficult to be very specific about this. The time of year and where you live make a difference. A few years ago, before ponies became so popular, a really good one could be bought for around three hundred dollars, and a serviceable one for as little as one hundred and twenty-five. Now the prices are much higher, and if you are looking for registered stock, you will be lucky to find one under a thousand dollars.

Horses are easier to find; nevertheless, a sound, young, good-looking, well-built, well-schooled horse cannot be bought cheaply. Once in a while a bargain comes up. A boy or girl with an ideal pony may have to sell it for a small amount because he has outgrown it, because the family is moving away, or because the owner is going away to school. The same applies to horses. However, in buying your horse, remember that, unlike a car, it will last many years, provided it is given good care.

Don't expect to find perfection. Horses are not machines, and don't come in standard sizes and colors. Each, like a person, has his good and bad points. Keep an ideal in mind. Make sure, above all, that the animal is sound in wind, eyes, and limbs; that you can manage him by yourself; and that he is suitable for the type of riding you want to do. Then choose the animal closest to your dream.

Hiring a Horse

Perhaps you are not in a position to own a horse or pony but have the opportunity of hiring one at a riding stable. Before doing so you should ask yourself the following questions: "Am I a good enough rider to ride a strange horse? Would I be able to manage him without help if he should shy or bolt? Would I know what to do if something went wrong with the saddle or the bridle?

If your answer is "yes," then you are capable and should find a stable of well-kept, sound animals. Be sure to try out any horse that is offered to you before taking him away from the stable. In this chapter there are tests for soundness and manners. Give your horse these tests before you leave. Especially important is the one in which you gallop the horse toward the stable, pull down to a walk, and walk in on a loose rein.

Is there anything special I should remember in riding a "hireling"? Treat your hireling, horse or pony as the case may be, with the same care and consideration that you would give him if he were your own. Walk the first ten minutes and the last. Don't gallop or trot fast on hard surfaces. Change gaits frequently and never gallop him until he is covered with lather and blowing badly. When you get him back to the stable, walk him until he is cool.

The good and bad features of particular types and breeds of horses and ponies are in Chapter 2. How to judge the animal's age is in Chapter 3.

6

Tack, Equipment, & Stable

Suppose you have found the perfect horse or pony. What equipment and supplies will you need? Where will you find these, and what about a place in which to keep your new companion? Is there an unused building which could be converted into a stable, or would you like to build one? In that case, you will want to know how large a space you need, what materials to use, and the most practical layout for a stable.

The Tack

What is meant by "tack"? Originally, the word was "tackle." Like fishing "tackle," it refers to the items you need in order to enjoy a certain sport—in this case, riding. It includes such items as the bridle, saddle, saddle-pad, stable blanket, and martingales, but not the grooming or stable tools. These come under the heading of "stable equipment."

The Bridle

Since the bridle is the first thing you put on your horse when you "tack him up" (put on his wearing apparel), let's start with that. The bridle holds the bit or the hackamore in place so that the rider can control his mount through the use of the reins.

Are all those straps shown in the picture of the bridle necessary? Yes, and although the bridle looks complicated, each strap has a purpose. (See Fig. 28) The cheek-straps are attached to the bit at one end and to the crownpiece at the other. The

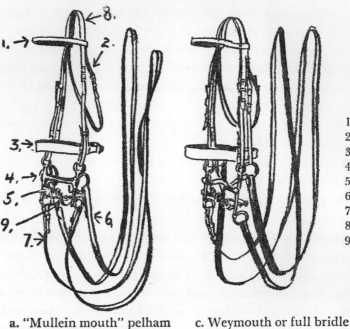

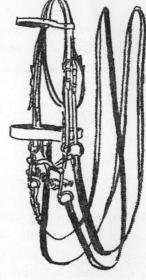

1. Brow-band
2. Throat-latch
3. Cavesson
4. Bit
5. Curb chain
6. Snaffle rein
7. Curb rein
8. Crownpiece
9. Lip strap

a. "Mullein mouth" pelham   c. Weymouth or full bridle

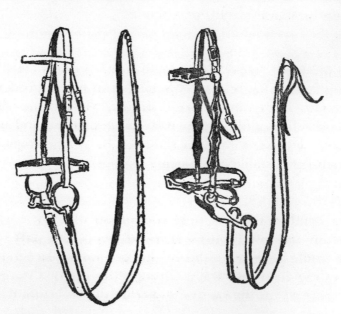

b. Simple snaffle   d. Hackamore

Fig. 28. Bridles

crownpiece, which goes over the top of the horse's head, keeps the bit from falling out of his mouth. By having the two cheek-straps buckle to it, instead of having cheek-straps and crownpiece all one, the bridle can easily be made longer or shorter to fit different horses. There is a type of bridle, not shown in the drawing, which, instead of having separate cheek-straps, has a buckle on top of the crownpiece for adjusting the size, but this is generally used only for racing.

Why does the bridle have a throat-latch? This keeps the horse from shaking the bridle off over his head.

What is the purpose of the brow-band? This keeps the bridle from sliding back on the horse's neck.

What does the curb chain do? As you will learn a little further on in this chapter, the curb chain acts against the horse's chin groove, making the curb and Pelham bits more severe.

What is the purpose of the lip-strap? To keep the curb chain in place, to keep the curb chain from getting lost when the bridle is not on the horse, and to keep the horse from taking the branch of the bit in his mouth.

What is the cavesson? The main part of the cavesson (KAve-sun) is the noseband. When fitted snugly, it prevents the horse from opening his mouth wide to avoid the action of the bit. In harness bridles, the horse wears a noseband which slips through loops in the cheek-straps; he does not wear a complete cavesson. Another type of cavesson, called a "dropped noseband" is so adjusted that it is below the bit and fits tightly around the lower nose of the horse. Like the ordinary cavesson, it keeps the horse from opening his mouth, and used with a snaffle bridle, gives a little more control. For ordinary use, the regular cavesson is fitted loosely and is really just to dress the horse up a bit.

Is there any way to tell the curb and snaffle reins apart? Yes, the curb reins are narrower. Also, the snaffle reins have a buckle which joins the right and left reins together, whereas the curb reins are stitched. This buckle makes it possible to put on a running martingale.

Are there many different kinds of bridles? Generally speaking, the bridle is known by the name of its bit. There are five main classifications of bridles, and one, the "Kimberwicke," whose bit is a sort of cross between two other types, the Pelham and the snaffle. The six types of bridles, as classified by bit, are the snaffle, the Pelham, the Kimberwicke, the Weymouth or full bridle, the Western bridle, and the hackamore.

What is a "snaffle" bit? There are two main types of snaffle bits, the bar snaffle and the jointed snaffle shown in Fig. 28. Then there are many variations of each of these types, and each has its special use. The bar snaffle, which is not as popular as the jointed type, is often used in driving. Some snaffles have two little "branches" extending downward. These prevent the inexpert rider on a stubborn animal from pulling the bit all the way through his mount's mouth, so that it lies along the cheek, instead of where it belongs. Some jointed snaffles have different sizes and types of rings than others. The larger ring gives a little more control and is popular for use in the hunt field. The "egg-butt" snaffle is a good design too. The rein does not slide around and the ring works easily. Wire snaffles, sometimes single, sometimes double, are a very severe type of bit. A horse that needs one of these would not be a suitable mount for the average rider.

How does the jointed snaffle bit work? The snaffle is the lightest and mildest type of bit. It is the one to which the young horse is first introduced. It acts on the corners of the horse's lips rather than on the bars. To work well in a snaffle, a horse must have a very light mouth and be obedient.

Is the snaffle the best bit for an inexperienced rider? There is much disagreement about this. Many people feel that the beginner should ride only on a snaffle because with this light bit the heavy hands of the beginner are less apt to hurt the horse than with the more severe Pelham. This is good advice as long as the horse is not the type that leans on the bit and pulls against the rider, or as long as the rider doesn't use his reins as lifelines to pull on in order to keep his balance. If either of these conditions exists, the rider and horse will go on pulling harder and harder, and the horse's mouth will become more and more insensitive, while the rider will never develop any true balance. On the other hand, if the heavy-mouthed horse is bitted in a Pelham, he

e. "Kimberwicke" bit   f. Western bit and bridle

Fig. 28. Bridles

will stop readily when the rider pulls; if he doesn't, he will be made very uncomfortable. Also, the rider will find that he cannot use his reins as a means of support; if he does, the horse will not go forward.

What is a Pelham bit? As you see in Fig 28, the Pelham is quite differently designed from the snaffle. It has two reins, the "snaffle rein," and the "curb," as well as a chain which rests against the horse's chin groove. This chain hangs loose except when the rider pulls on the rein. Then it presses against the chin groove. At the same time, the mouthpiece of the bit presses on the bars of the horse's mouth. Thus, the lower jaw at the bars is literally pinched between the chain and the mouthpiece. You can see how much stronger the action of the Pelham bit is than the action of the snaffle which merely pulls up on the lips.

Some horses are so sensitive that they do not go well in the Pelham bridle, and must be ridden in some other type. For the inexperienced rider, it is often wise, in riding with a Pelham bridle, to tie up the curb rein and let it hang on the horse's neck, where it can be used as an "emergency brake" if the need arises.

What is the difference between the many types of Pelhams? Pelhams vary a great deal in severity according to the length of the "shank," or type of bit. The longer the branch, the more severe the bit. Some Pelhams have a straight bar mouthpiece, and some have a mouthpiece with a sort of curved hump, called a "port." The purpose of this port is to allow room for the horse's tongue. In some countries and even in our own West, one sometimes sees bits with ports so high that they hit the roof of the horse's mouth when the reins are used. These are very cruel, but a shallow port, which is more common, is not severe. Notice Fig. 28, showing the "mullein mouth" Pelham. The term "mullein mouth" refers to the fact that the mouthpiece of the bit is slightly curved and more comfortable for the horse.

What is a Kimberwicke? A Kimberwicke bit is a Pelham with the lower branch and rein taken away. It is often a good compromise for the horse that won't obey the snaffle, but is too sensitive to wear the ordinary Pelham.

Is a full bridle, or Weymouth, more severe than a Pelham? No, it is less severe. The Weymouth, as you see, has two bits— a simple jointed snaffle, and a "curb" bit. The latter is just like the Pelham, but without the top rein. When riding with a Weymouth, the horseman may use either his snaffle or his curb separately. With the Pelham, he never really gets a true snaffle effect (the Pelham never works directly on the lips of the horse instead of on his bars) though he does have the choice of a severe action or a less severe action, depending upon whether he uses the top or the bottom rein.

What is the hackamore bridle? As shown in Fig. 28, the hackamore has no mouthpiece. The action is on the horse's nose and on his lower jaw at the chin groove. This type of bridle is very good on the average horse that is being ridden by a beginner. It is not good if the horse tends to try to avoid the rein by ducking his head, or by bucking. Nor is it successful if he leans against the noseband. Many horses work much better in hackamores, when ridden by beginners, because they are more comfortable. This is also a good choice of bridle to use when a rider is first learning to jump, for with this type, it is impossible to hurt the sensitive mouth of the horse. A kind of bridle called the Western hackamore has very long shanks and is severe. In buying a hackamore, be sure to get only the kind shown here.

Do cowboys use a curb bit? The Western type of curb bit, as we have said, is very severe. The cowboy uses it only in an emergency. His horse is trained to work on his own, and to stop the instant the rider touches the reins. This is the only practical way to train the stock horse, for the cowboy has to have his hands free to use his rope. The Western curb bit is not suitable for a person who rides "on contact," as described in this book, or for those who jump.

How much does a bridle cost? This depends on the quality of leather, and on the type of bit. A good, serviceable Pelham, snaffle, or hackamore bridle will cost from fifteen to twenty-three or twenty-four dollars. A full bridle (Weymouth) will cost more. A hand-stitched "hunting bridle" or a Saddle Horse "show bridle" can cost as much as fifty dollars, or even more.

What are martingales? These are pieces of equipment classed as "artificial" aids. They help the rider control the horse that is difficult to manage with the simple bridle. The "running," or "ring" martingale, gives more control in the snaffle bit. As you see in the picture, the reins of the snaffle run through the rings of the martingale. With this properly adjusted, the snaffle no longer works on the corners of the horse's mouth; it works downward on his bars. People who feel that their hands are not light enough to use a Pelham in the hunt field, often use a running martingale. Those who do not understand its correct use, or how to fit it properly, often have the two straps to which the rings are attached so long that the martingale has no effect whatever.

What is the standing martingale? Its purpose is to keep the horse from raising his head too high, from poking his nose out, and from "star gazing." Usually the result is that the horse forms the habit of leaning on it, so that it does not teach him anything. It is far better to train your horse to carry his head correctly through exercises.

What is the Irish martingale? This gives a little more control in a snaffle bridle, and also prevents the reins from getting out of position when the horse tosses his head, as some badly trained horses do.

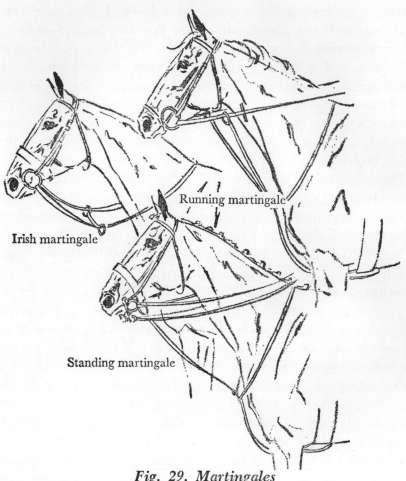

Irish martingale

Running martingale

Standing martingale

Fig. 29. Martingales

The Saddle

Fig. 30 shows four types of saddles. One of these is old-fashioned and not well-designed. The others are well-designed, and each has its special use.

Why is "the well-designed flat saddle," better than "the old-fashioned English hunting saddle"? As you will learn in the chapter on basic position, when the rider sits correctly, he is in the center of the saddle, over the center of his horse. By sitting this way, he makes it easier both for himself and for his mount. Notice that the well-designed saddle, in Fig. 30a, dips quite noticeably, with the deepest part of the dip at the center point.

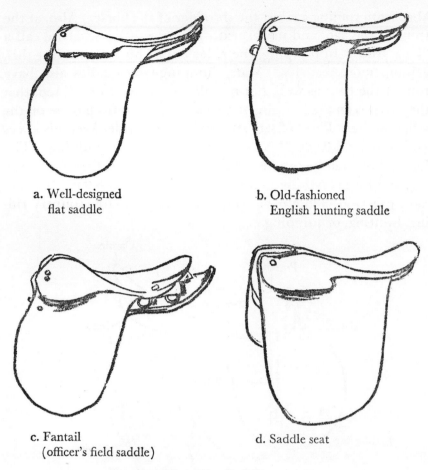

a. Well-designed
flat saddle

b. Old-fashioned
English hunting saddle

c. Fantail
(officer's field saddle)

d. Saddle seat

Fig. 30. Saddles

In Fig. 30*b*, on the other hand, the lowest point is farther toward the cantle or back end of the saddle. Also, in the latter, the pommel is flatter, which might cause trouble by rubbing the withers of the horse. The saddle shown in Fig. 30*a* can be used for all ordinary riding and for dressage. It is not as good for jumping, however, as the "forward-seat saddle" in Fig. 31.

Why is the saddle shown in Fig. 31 better for jumping? There are several reasons. In jumping, the rider uses a slightly shorter stirrup. His knee is bent more, extending in front of the pommel. Notice that the flap of the jumping saddle is slanted forward. With a short stirrup, this type of flap prevents the rider's knee from coming against the shoulder of the horse. Also, at the front of the flap, and underneath it, you will see what we call a "knee roll." In jumping, the rider braces his knee against this, gaining more security. Many jumping-type saddles also have rolls at the back as well, but not all do. You will find, too, that the stirrups on the jumping saddle are different from those on the other saddle. This "offset" stirrup helps the rider keep his knees against the saddle and his heels down when he is jumping. The forward-seat saddle can be used for all ordinary riding, for jumping, and for everything except very advanced dressage. It is the most practical saddle for anyone interested in cross-country riding, hunting, or jumping.

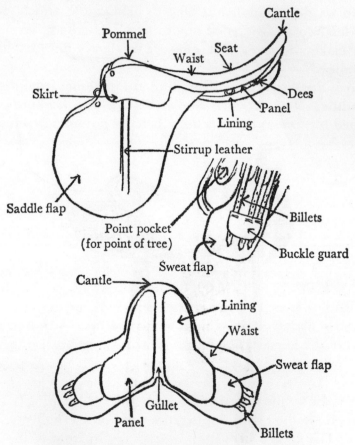

Fig. 31. Forward seat (jumping) saddle

What is the saddle marked "saddle-seat"? This saddle (Fig. 30d) is adapted only to the showing of Saddle Horses, and for riders who adopt the so-called "saddle seat," in which the rider sits back instead of in the center. This saddle is entirely unsuited for jumping, dressage, or ordinary riding.

What is the purpose of the "officer's field saddle"? Designed for ordinary riding, this saddle (Fig. 30c) is especially good for overnight rides, or for riding in climates where rain comes on very suddenly, since a raincoat or blanket roll can be fastened on behind. Though it does not have the knee rolls of the regular jumping saddle, the flaps are cut a little forward, and it can be used for ordinary jumping and hunting. If you cannot afford a good forward-seat saddle, the officer's field saddle, which sells for much less, would be a good one to buy. There are several different makes, however, and some are too heavy for a boy or girl to handle.

Why is the Western saddle so different in design from the English saddle? The Western saddle (Fig. 32) is a working saddle, designed for use on the ranches. It has a pommel to which the

Fig. 32. Western saddle

rider can attach his lariat. No doubt, on the screen you have watched cowboys rope a calf or steer, then jump off and let the horse hold the rope taut while the cowboy runs and ties the animal up. Without the pommel, this would be impossible. Since this puts a great strain on the saddle, the Western saddle has two girths instead of one; they do not buckle but are fastened by means of straps which can be pulled very tight. Because the Western rider often has to ride through sagebrush, his stirrups have flat wooden treads and leather protectors on the front.

Do saddles come in different sizes? Yes, they are measured from the pommel to the cantle, and the number of inches is the size. Children's saddles go up to size 16, and have shorter flaps than adult saddles. Most boys or girls of twelve years or more need adult saddles.

How can I tell if the saddle is the right size for me? When you sit in the saddle, be sure that there are at least four inches between the back of your buttocks and the end of the cantle. Place your feet in the stirrups. Do your legs come where they should on the flap? Do they stick out forward over the flap? Or are they too short to hit the knee rolls, if the saddle has these? Above all, is the saddle comfortable? Every make of saddle differs slightly from every other, and even those of the same make differ from each other. For this reason, you should never buy a saddle without first sitting on it. Stores that sell saddles have special wooden "horses" on which they put the saddle for you to try it.

How can I tell if the saddle fits the horse? Put the saddle on the horse and adjust the girth. Now examine it, both at the pommel and at the cantle. Does the saddle touch the horse at either of these points? If it does, then it will give the horse a sore back. Mount and check again. You should be able to run your fingers under the saddle at either of these points. However, the saddle can be too high off the horse's back also. Horses with lower withers need saddles with wider throats, and those with prominent withers need a narrower, higher pommel, with perhaps a "cut-back" throat as shown in the officer's field saddle.

Where should I go to buy a saddle? There are many manufacturers of saddles, and many harness stores which carry them.

If at all possible, go to such a store and try out a number until you find one that fits you. Then make arrangements to take it home and try it on your horse. If you can get a well-broken-in second-hand saddle, you will be doing well. Unfortunately, these are hard to find, except for the old-fashioned flat saddles, which are worthless. If you cannot go to a good saddler, write for a catalogue, study the pictures of the various types of saddles, write to the company, give your height, describe your horse, and ask them to pick one out for you. Be sure it is understood that you will be allowed to return it for another saddle if it should prove unsuitable.

How much does a good saddle cost? A new saddle for a boy or girl costs about eighty dollars, for a medium grade. There are cheaper ones, but they are usually poor in both workmanship and cut. For an adult saddle, one pays from one hundred and thirty to two or three hundred dollars. Don't make the mistake of buying a saddle just because it is cheap. A good saddle, if it is properly cared for, will still be in fine condition long after the original horse for which it was intended has died.

Other Tack

Why are saddle pads sometimes used? A properly fitted saddle, on the ordinary horse, does not require a saddle pad; but some horses have especially sensitive backs and do need this protection. Of course, if the saddle does not fit properly, a pad is a must. The saddle pad also keeps the lining of the saddle clean. If you do not have one, be sure to scrub the lining of your saddle thoroughly each time it is used. Otherwise it will become soaked with sweat and will soon rot.

What is the best kind of pad? Some people like the plain wool or felt ones. These are inexpensive, but are hard to keep clean. They are not easy to wash and quickly become stiff from sweat. The sheepskin pad is more easily kept in condition, provided you wash it in lukewarm water with a mild soap, and do not hang it to dry near heat. Many riders like the cotton quilted pad. This may be improvised from a bed pad. Get a large one which can be folded in half, and still be long and wide enough to protect the horse from the saddle at all points.

When does a horse need a stable blanket? A horse needs a stable blanket if he has been clipped (the hair shaved off close all over the body), if he is alone in a very cold stable, or if you want to keep him from growing a heavy coat. The pony or horse that is turned out most of the time, and has grown a heavy coat, does not need a blanket even in very cold weather.

Stable Equipment: Grooming Tools

What tools do I need to keep my horse clean and healthy? In Fig. 33 you will see the various articles you need in order to give your horse proper care. In the next chapter we will discuss in detail what these are for and how to use each one. Be sure to get all of them, as well as a suitable box or bag in which to keep

Sweat scraper

Mane and tail comb

Hoof pick

Dandy or mud brush

Body brush

Rubber currycomb

Fig. 33. Grooming tools

them. The little overnight zipper bags which the airplane companies often give away make excellent grooming-tool bags.

What stable tools will I need? You will need two pitchforks, one with three tines and one with four or five. The three-tined fork is to be used for hay, and the other for cleaning the stall. You will also need a shovel with a broad, flat front edge, an iron rake, a stiff push-broom, and a wheelbarrow.

The Stable

How big a building will I need for my horse? First of all, you will need space for your stall. The minimum requirement for a full-sized horse is an area ten feet by ten feet. An area twelve by twelve is better. A large pony needs a stall nine feet by nine feet. Smaller animals need less room, and a very miniature Shetland can get along comfortably in a stall 6 feet by 7, or 5 by 7. You will also need storage space. Enough covered area for grooming is desirable, too, though not absolutely necessary.

Hay catches on fire very easily, of course, so it is important to see that no one smokes or uses matches in or near a stable. Learn how to use a fire extinguisher, and keep one in the stable, ready for use, at all times.

What are the best materials for the floor of the stall? Clay, cinders, or sand are best for flooring. Wood absorbs odors, and rots easily. Cement and asphalt are too hard and dry. Horses stabled on these develop foot ailments.

What material should be used for the walls and partitions of the stall? The only material which will stand up under the wear and tear of the stable is 2-inch oak planking. Rough oak, directly from the sawmill, is excellent; but other types of wood are dangerous since a horse can kick them into splinters. If more than one horse is stabled, and the two are in adjoining stalls, the oak, beginning at the floor, should extend upward for 5 feet. Above that use a very heavy gauge woven wire. With this arrangement, the animals can keep each other company but cannot hurt each other.

What do I need to keep in the building besides my horse? Grain, bedding, hay, and tack. Grain and hay are best stored

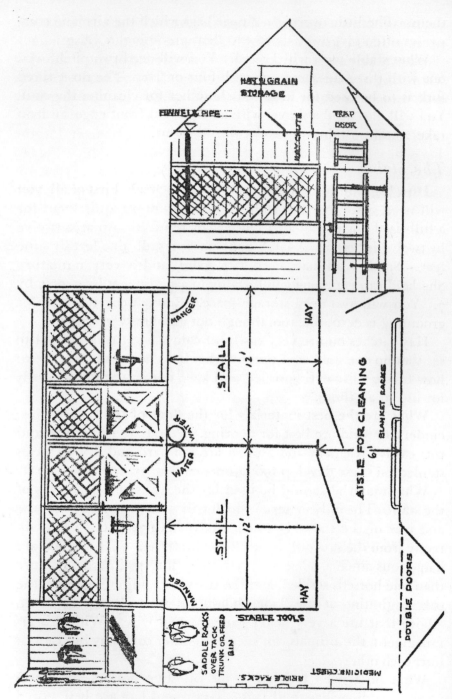

Fig. 34. Floor plan of two-stall stable

overhead. It is easier to feed from above, and there is no danger of an animal getting out of his stall and into the grain barrel. Tack can be hung on a wall, or on the outside of the stall, with a covering of some sort to protect it from dust and hayseed. You will also need an area where water is available for cleaning your tack.

What do I need in the stall? You need a manger for the horse's grain and something to hold his drinking water. Fig. 35 shows how a water bucket can be attached to the wall so that it is easily lifted out for refilling and cleaning. The manger, which

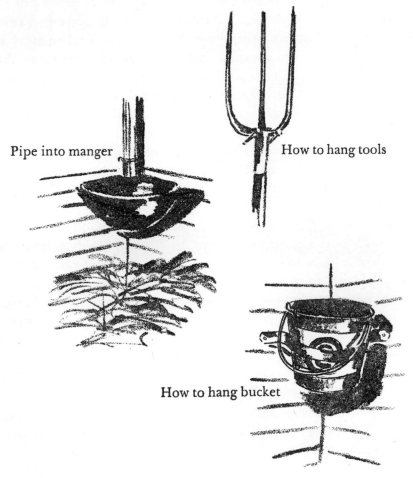

Pipe into manger

How to hang tools

How to hang bucket

Fig. 35.

is usually of iron, must be high enough from the floor so that the horse cannot get his foot into it, but not so high that he is unable to eat from it comfortably. In a large stable, automatic water fountains such as those used for cows, are by far the most practical. If your grain and hay are kept overhead, a large iron pipe can be fastened to the wall and the grain poured down through it into the manger from the loft above. A hole cut into the flooring will enable you to pitch the hay down. You also need a container attached to the wall to hold a brick of salt.

What is the best way to solve the manure problem? Many communities require that all manure be kept in fly-proof pits or rooms. In many rural areas, you can pile your manure in a suitable spot some distance from the stable and have it taken away at intervals. Mushroom growers and nurseries will often buy the manure from you, but they usually require that you do not use shavings for bedding. Occasionally, one finds a mushroom grower who will supply straw and take all the manure in exchange.

Is a paddock necessary? You should certainly have some area where you can turn your horse or pony out when you are not riding him. This can be a paddock adjoining the stable, or a field.

What kind of fencing will I need around the paddock? Since horses are herd animals, one kept by himself needs a stronger fence than a horse that has a companion. Post-and-rail fencing, 3 feet 6 inches to 4 feet in height, with a gate or draw bars, is usually adequate for the average horse or pony. Most horses and ponies will knock down or scramble over the average stone wall. Woven-wire fencing is not usually good because horses can get their feet caught between the meshes. Also, they often lean over the top to get the grass on the other side and so bend or break down the fence. Barbed wire is dangerous. Electric fencing, if the horse is trained to respect it, can often be successful, but it must be checked at regular intervals to make sure that the current is on.

7

Care & Handling

All the rules for correct feeding, watering, and general care are important. Keeping them or breaking them will mean the difference between success or failure in your career as a horsemaster. Remember that your horse or pony has nerves and feelings, just as you have. He is dependent on you for his health and happiness. Before thinking of yourself you must think of your horse. This has been the maxim of good horsemen for generations.

Do not spoil your horse or pony with too many tidbits or by overfeeding. Ponies, especially, should not receive sugar, carrots, or apples out of your hand except as a reward for some definite act, such as coming to be caught when called. If you want to give carrots or apples, put them into the feed manger. As we discuss the feeding schedules, suitable rations for different sizes and types of animals will be recommended. Try and stick closely to these, and only change if you notice that your pony or horse is losing weight rapidly, or is gaining too much.

Feeding

What should I feed my horse or pony? Horses and ponies should not be fed alike, so we'll discuss them separately. Let us start with the horse. If he is being used for either riding or driving for an hour or more a day, he will need grain and hay as well as salt. If he is kept turned out most of the time and the grass is good, he will need only grain and salt.

What kinds of grains are used for horses? In the United States, we use oats as a basic grain. In some parts of the West and South, corn on the cob is used. There are also several brands of mixed feed which contain a variety of grains, ground alfalfa, minerals, vitamins, and molasses. Bran is often used either by itself in the form of a mash or mixed with oats.

Are all oats alike? No, they vary in quality and also in type. We have whole oats and also crushed or "crimped" oats. The latter do not need to be chewed as thoroughly. Sometimes, however, a poorer quality of oats is used for crimped oats. In big stables, oat-crushers are used, the oats being crushed after delivery.

How can I tell good oats from poor oats? Good oats are plump and heavy and do not have any other seeds mixed with them.

What amount of oats should I feed a horse? This will depend on three factors: the type and size of the horse, his physical condition, and the work he is doing. Some horses, especially those with Quarter Horse, Morgan, or draft ancestry, are generally short-coupled and somewhat chunky. Because they require much less feed than the lankier Thoroughbred types, they are called "easy-keepers." Such a horse, doing ordinary work, rarely requires more than from 2 to 6 quarts of grain a day in two feedings, one in the morning and the other at night. A tall, lean, long-coupled, or high-strung horse will need from 8 to 12 quarts per day, preferably given in three feedings. The best course is to find out what ration the horse is accustomed to and what his previous work has been. If his condition is satisfactory, and he has been doing about the amount of work you expect from him, continue to give him his regular rations. If he is thin, or is going to be working harder than before, you can increase his rations. But they must be increased very gradually; give not more than one additional quart at a feeding every three or four days until the desired amount is being fed. There is one other very important point to remember. If your horse is going to be laid up for a day or so because of injury, bad weather, or any other reason, his regular ration of oats should be cut in half, though he should be fed at the same hours as before.

What is the purpose of feeding bran? Bran is a mild laxative, and also helps provide bulk. Although it is lower in proteins than oats and corn, it does contain a certain amount. Bran is somewhat heating to the blood, and horses fed too much of it in hot weather will often break out with pimples. A good ration is 1 quart of bran to 3 quarts of oats in cold weather, and 1 to 4 in hot weather. Bran is not a supplement, but takes the place of some of the oats. In other words, if you want your horse to have 8 quarts of grain a day, he would get 2 quarts of bran and 6 of oats given in two feedings.

Another way to give bran is in the form of a hot mash the night before a day of rest, in place of the evening grain ration. To make a bran mash, put three or four quarts of bran in a pail, add salt, and pour on boiling water until all the bran is thoroughly wet. Put a burlap bag over the mixture and allow it to steam until cool enough to eat, then feed. Any horse that is not being worked over a period of time, and is being kept in a stable, should receive a bran mash every three or four days.

How do I give "mixed feed"? Mixed feed is excellent for winter feeding, but many horses do not thrive on it in summer because of the high bran, corn, and alfalfa content. Since mixed feed is heavier than crushed oats, you can feed about one-fourth less by measure. In changing from one type of feed to another, however, always do so gradually.

Are there different kinds of hay? Yes, a number of different kinds. Some hay is very rich and must be fed sparingly. Hay grown on poor, unfertilized soil, has almost no value except as roughage. A person who feeds his horse poor hay because it is cheap practices poor economy. The better the hay, the less you will have to feed of either hay or grain. Furthermore, horses fed bad hay may develop many incurable ailments.

What are the most common types of hay? In the East, timothy hay is generally preferred for horses. It should be cut while green and then thoroughly cured. A mixture of timothy and clover is often satisfactory, but not for horses that have a tendency toward heaves. Straight clover is not good, as it is too laxative and soon becomes very dusty. A little alfalfa mixed with timothy is all right if the horse is used to the mixture, but horses not accustomed to it often get very loose bowels ("scours") from alfalfa.

Feeding procedures vary according to locality. In the West, horses are accustomed both to alfalfa hay and to oat hay.

How can I tell good hay from bad? Number One hay, which is the best, is a first cutting. This means that it is cut in June before the hot summer sun has dried it up. After it is cured, it should not be a lifeless brown color, but should retain some of its natural green. It should smell fragrant rather than musty. When you break it, it should be crisp and not dusty, limp, or rotten. The heads of the timothy should still be on it. There should be no black mold, or broken sticks, or strange-looking plants mixed with it. There are a number of wild plants which poison horses. Examine the hay you buy carefully to be sure it is all timothy or other edible grass.

How do I feed baled hay? Unless you have a great deal of storage place, you will probably be using baled hay. If it is baled with cord, you need only scissors or a sharp knife to cut the cord. If it is baled with wire, you need wire cutters. In an emergency, you can slip one tine of the pitchfork under one of the wires, then twist the wire around the pitchfork by walking around and around the bale, holding the pitchfork. When the tension gets too high, the wire will snap. You can break the other strands the same way. Once the bale is open, pull out one or two sections, according to your needs, and holding them with the fork, shake them out thoroughly. If you feed the tightly packed hay directly to the horse, he may not chew it thoroughly and so not digest it as he should. Also, in shaking it out, you can watch for weeds, sticks, or mold. When it is thoroughly loosened, push it down into the horse's stall. Always pick up the wire or cord as fast as you take it off the bales. Otherwise, they may be swept into the stall where the horse can get caught up in them.

How much hay should I feed? Just as with the grain ration, this depends on the type and condition of the horse. Most people feed too much hay and thus endanger their horse's health. In the morning, your horse should have about as much hay as he will finish in an hour. At night, he can have half as much again.

The Army ration of hay for an average-sized horse doing hard work is from twelve to sixteen pounds per day in three feedings. A medium-sized feeding is given in the morning, a very small feeding at noon, and a large feeding at night.

How should I give my horse salt? There are three ways of giving salt. Coarse salt can be mixed with the feed, a lump of "rock" salt can be kept in the manger at all times, or a brick of salt can be placed in a metal container, called a *lick,* fastened to the wall. Most people find the last method the easiest. The horse can get the salt as he needs it, and the owner can tell at a glance whether the salt ration needs replacement.

How much water does my horse need? An average horse drinks from three to five gallons of water a day in ordinary weather. In hot weather he will drink much more. A constant and sufficient supply of cool water is a must, if your horse is to be comfortable and in good condition.

How do I make sure that my horse always has enough water? Either keep a pail of water in his stall at all times, or provide him with an automatic drinking fountain, which he will soon learn to work for himself. The sketches in Figures 34 and 35 show where and how to hang a water bucket in the stall so the horse cannot upset it.

When should my horse not have water? He should not be allowed to drink a full pail of water and then stand still in his stall, if he has just been working hard and is hot. Of course, you should never put a hot horse away in his stall without first walking him slowly, until he is thoroughly cool and has stopped breathing hard. Better still, after he is cool, give him a good rubdown before putting him away. You need not deprive him entirely of water if he is thirsty. Fill a pail one-fourth full and let him drink it after you have walked him for five minutes. Then walk him for five more minutes and give him a little more water. Continue this until he is cool, and you will probably find that he has had all the water he wants. This method, by the way, is the one used at race tracks, and is called "watering out" a horse.

In what order should I feed hay, grain, and water? Before giving either hay or gain, fill the water pail in the horse's stall and let him have five minutes to drink. Next throw his ration of hay to him. Wait another few minutes and give him his grain.

What is the reason for following this order? When a horse drinks, the water goes directly through his stomach and into his kidney and bladder. If the stomach is full of oats, some may be washed into the intestines undigested and cause gas and colic. Also, if the water enters a full stomach, the grain in the stomach has a tendency to swell, and this, too, can cause colic. After the water, we give hay because some horses are very greedy. If they are given grain first, they gobble it down without chewing it properly. Since the digestive juices are not very strong, this may cause partially digested grain to be carried into the intestinal tract where it may start trouble. If the horse first eats some hay, he will not be quite so greedy. Those that insist on eating too fast should be fed crushed or crimped oats. There are also special types of mangers made with divided bowls which prevent the horse from taking too large mouthfuls.

How does the feeding of ponies differ from that of horses? Since the pony is much smaller than the horse, he will need much less feed. Also, ponies become bad tempered and nervous when fed much grain. If possible, omit the grain entirely from your pony's rations. If you feel you must give him some, perhaps because there are horses in the stable and he gets restless if they are grained and he is not, put only a handful of grain, mixed with a handful of bran, in his manger once or twice a day. It is generally far better, however, not to give him any. Above all, don't feed him out of your hand. If you do, he'll start biting you, and later charging you to get the desired morsel.

As for the amount of hay to give, this depends on how soon your pony finishes his ration and how fat he is. If he is kept turned out all the time, in summer he won't need anything other than grass. Watering procedure is the same for ponies as for horses.

Bedding

What should I use for bedding in the stall? There are several types of bedding considered suitable for use in stalls. The first is wheat straw. Never use oat or rye straw. Horses will eat oat straw, and rye is long and too hard to manage. Wheat straw is probably the most common type of bedding but it is by no means the most satisfactory. Straw is not very absorbent, it retains odors, and is exceedingly heavy to handle. Another material used for bedding is "peat moss." This is a dark-brown, very absorbent material, which decomposes readily. Many people will pay higher prices for manure mixed with peat moss than for manure from horses bedded on other materials. Peat moss has the disadvantage of being very expensive. Also, because of its color, it is not always easy to distinguish it from manure when the stall is being cleaned.

A finely shredded material made of sugar cane is still another type of bedding. Its commercial name is "Stays-Dri." It is very absorbent, very light, easy to handle, and much less expensive than peat moss. Unfortunately, since it is rather sweet, some horses tend to eat it and it also attracts flies. It decomposes less quickly than peat moss, but more quickly than shavings.

Shavings are the cheapest type of bedding. They are light to handle and absorbent. However, you must clean your horse's feet very carefully each day, for shavings tend to pack in the crevices and bring on a condition known as "thrush." Shavings can be purchased in bales or in bags. Of the two, bags are preferable, because the baled shavings are usually packed so tightly that it is hard to fluff them out again. If there is a woodworking mill in your locality, you may be able to get your shavings for nothing by going there with burlap bags and getting them yourself.

How often should the bedding be changed? If you take out droppings and dirty and wet spots once or twice a day when you feed the horse, and clean the whole stall out twice a week, putting in new bedding, your horse should be comfortable.

Why can't I use hay for bedding? It is not good to use hay for bedding because the horse will eat it. Very often he will eat it when it is wet and dirty. This is bad for him. Even if he eats only the clean hay, it is not good because, as we learned earlier, a horse should not have unlimited amounts of hay.

Handling and Leading the Horse in the Stable

In order to handle and lead your horse safely and successfully inside the stable, you must learn how to avoid hurting him and how to avoid being hurt yourself.

Why am I more apt to get hurt working in the stable than outside? A stable is a small space with solid walls. For this reason, if your horse should kick or bite, it is harder to avoid him, for you cannot jump out of the way. Many horses are more irritable when confined in a stable. It is not the way nature intended them to live. As we learned in an earlier chapter, horses often sleep standing up, with their eyes open. If awakened suddenly, they sometimes make sudden movements. When a horse is eating, he doesn't like to be disturbed any more than a dog does when he is munching on a delicious bone.

What is the most important rule for safety in the stable? The first safety rule is to *keep alert*. When working around your horse, be sensitive to the way he reacts, especially in regard to his ears. Nearly every horse puts his ears back when he is annoyed. Be ready to move out of the way of danger if you should see his ears go back suddenly.

What is the best way to enter a stall? If your horse is in a box stall, speak to him and try and get him to turn his head toward you. Try not to go into his stall while he is still eating his oats. Above all, don't go in carrying a saddle. He may think you are not going to let him finish his meal. If you are carrying a pitchfork or other stable tool, don't wave it around and frighten him. If your horse is in a standing stall with his head tied at the front, speak to him first, and put your hand gently on the left side of his rump, pushing him over a step to the right. By doing this you will know for certain that he is not asleep. When you go in, walk directly up to his head and pat him.

If I know that my horse kicks, how can I go behind him in a small space without being hurt? As a rule, it is best to go around a horse's head to get behind him, but sometimes, especially if the horse is in a standing stall, it may be necessary to go around his rear end. In such a case, put your hand on his rump, speak to him, and go around slowly and as *close* to him as you can get.

If he kicks when you are right up against him, you will receive only a little shove from his hocks, whereas if you are two or three feet away, you will get his iron shoes in your middle!

What else do I have to watch out for besides being kicked or bitten? Be careful not to let the horse step on your toes. Although no horse will deliberately step on you, this is not out of fear of hurting a human being. He is afraid of hurting his own feet. But at the walk, and while standing, horses are often inattentive. When you are leading a horse, keep in step and keep your own feet out of the way. If he moves toward you when he is in a box stall, be alert and move your feet aside. In putting him into his stall, walk ahead of him, right up to the front of the stall.

How can a horse get hurt in the stable? First, there is the danger of slipping. Many stable aisles are made of concrete. If oil is spilled on this, it becomes very slippery. Keep your aisles clean and don't use oils near an area where horses pass. A second danger is that of knocking their hipbones when going through doorways. Many stables have sliding doors, and some people are careless about making certain that the door is pushed all the way back before leading a horse out. Hinged doors sometimes tend to swing shut after being opened. It is important to see that hinged doors are hung correctly. If you ever have to lead a horse through a very narrow opening or over rough ground, turn and face him, with a rein in each hand as shown in Fig. 36a. Then, walking slowly backward yourself, guide him carefully through the narrow opening.

Is there any other way a horse can hurt himself in the stall? Yes, a horse can be "cast" in his stall. Many horses like to lie down and roll, especially when the bedding has just been changed. A horse having an attack of colic invariably rolls to ease the pain. If, in rolling over, his legs become jammed up against the wall or doubled under him, he is said to be "cast," for he can't get up again, and will sometimes struggle until he ruptures a blood vessel in his brain and dies.

How can I help a horse that is cast? If you find your horse or pony cast, speak to him and try to reassure him through your

a. Leading horse through narrow doorway

b. Correct way to lead a horse

Fig. 36

voice.   Then go and get help.   A man or a strong boy can take hold of the animal's tail, and usually will be able to pull him away from the wall so that there is room for him to get up. Sometimes, after he has been pulled away, it may be necessary to go to his head and straighten his front legs so that he can get up. Other times, once he is pulled away from the wall, he will roll back over by himself and then get up.   If he is jammed very tightly, and there is no way of pulling him by his tail, you will have to slip a soft rope around the pasterns of both of the feet that are under him and turn him over.   If the horse is very nervous and excitable, you will have to have a veterinary come and give him a tranquilizer before you can work with him.   To avoid getting hurt yourself, watch out for flying hooves and always keep behind the animal's spine.   Never go into the stall on the side toward his legs in attaching a rope.   Always work from the other side.

Leading and Tying

Is there any special way to lead a horse?   Yes.   Walk beside his left shoulder.   Hold his halter shank (rope) or reins in your right hand about three inches from his chin, and hold the end of the reins or shank in your left hand to keep it from dragging on the ground, where you or the horse might trip over it.   Do not look at the horse while leading him, but walk straight ahead. If the horse pulls back and refuses to go ahead, either have some-

Fig. 37. Pulling cast horse out of corner

one else speak to him from behind, or if you are alone, turn him suddenly to the right and then to the left to break up his opposition. Once started, he will probably follow unless there is something that frightens him.

How should a horse be tied for grooming? In tying the horse, either for grooming or any other purpose, we must think of the possible need of untying him quickly in an emergency. For grooming, we generally use two ropes fastened by rings on each side of an aisle or in the doorway of the stall. Attached to the ends of the rings are snaps which fasten to the rings on each side of the halter. This is called "cross-tying." (See Fig. 38.)

How should I tie my horse in the stall? When tying the horse in the stall, even though a shank with a snap is used, it is well to tie the other end to the ring by the knot shown in Fig. 39. If an emergency occurs, such as the horse getting his leg over the rope, and the snap jams from pressure, simply pull the end of the rope and the whole thing will then come untied. One good way to tie a horse in a stall without any danger of his leg getting caught is the one shown in Fig. 40. As you see, the rope, with a

Fig. 38. Cross-tying

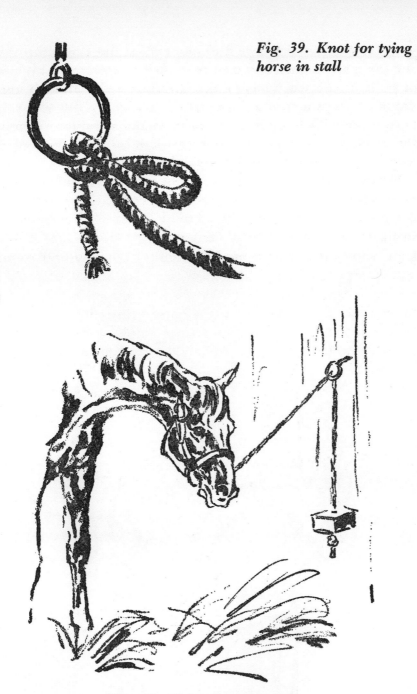

Fig. 39. Knot for tying horse in stall

Fig. 40. Tying horse in stall (block-of-wood method)

solid block of wood attached to one end, is slid through a ring and the snap fastened to the halter. As the horse raises his head or pulls it back when lying down, the rope pulls through until the block stops it from coming all the way out. But when the horse lowers his head or goes nearer to the wall, the weight of the block pulls the rope the other way and there is no slack or loop in which he can become entangled.

How should I tie a horse when I am out on the trail and want to stop for a while? Your horse should be wearing a halter under his bridle. To the halter should be attached a shank. A shank of any length can be carried on a horse if the "cavalry knot" shown in Fig. 41 is used. When you come to your resting

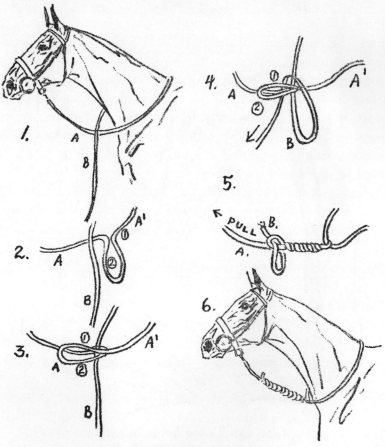

Fig. 41. Cavalry knot

spot, pick out a tree that has a long limb. Tie the shank to a point on the limb where a branch will prevent its sliding farther down. Don't have the rope so long that the horse can get his head to the ground. If you want your horse to eat grass, hold onto the rope yourself. Otherwise, he may turn and get his legs caught in it. There is a good reason for using a swinging limb instead of the trunk of a tree. If the horse pulls back suddenly, the limb will give a little and he will be less apt to snap his rope or halter. If there is no suitable limb, you will have to use a post or the trunk of a tree. Be sure that whatever you use is solid and will neither break nor pull away, and that the rope cannot slide below the level of the animal's shoulder.

Grooming

Brushing and cleaning the horse and picking out his feet are called grooming.

Is there any reason for grooming other than to make the horse or pony look nice? Yes. Thorough grooming stimulates the circulation of the blood, and the body gets more nourishment. A horse or pony in bad condition from neglect recovers faster if he is thoroughly groomed at least once a day, than if he is just allowed to stand and eat a great deal.

The second reason for grooming is that, in doing it, one can search for signs of injury or illness: unusual body heat, abrasions or cuts, and lumps under the skin. If a horse gets a bad cut high up under his belly, for example, it can go unnoticed for several days if he is not groomed. If neglected, it can easily become infected and then you are in for much trouble.

How do I groom a horse? On page 108 are sketches of all the grooming tools. The rubber currycomb is used to remove caked mud on the *body*, and to bring hidden dandruff to the surface of the coat where it can be brushed away. It is not used on the face or lower legs of the horse.

How is the currycomb used? Standing on the near, or left side of the horse, opposite his shoulder, take the currycomb in your right hand, and either the body brush or the dandy brush in your left. Begin just behind the ears on the side of the neck, and

Fig. 42a. Shortening a mane

Fig. 42b. Brushing tail

scrub the horse in circular motions. Keep your elbows stiff and press hard, unless the animal is very sensitive. Every twenty seconds or so, tap the currycomb against the heel of your shoe or against the wall, to knock off the dirt which will have collected in it.

What do I do with the brush? As soon as you have scrubbed the dandruff to the surface, holding the brush in your left hand, sweep the dirt away. Always sweep with the hair, never against it. Clean the brush with the currycomb, at every fourth or fifth stroke. Continue working with both currycomb and brush until you have gone over the horse's whole body. When you move around to his off (right) side, start again at the front, but hold the currycomb in your left hand and the brush in your right.

How do I clean the lower legs and face? If these are not very dirty, use the soft body brush. If they are really dirty, you will have to use the coarser dandy brush. With the coarser brush, don't scrub hard, because the bones are near the skin in these areas and the horse is particularly sensitive here. Be sure to get all the dirt and sweat from behind the ears and from the back of the pasterns.

How do I comb the mane and tail? Use the mane-and-tail comb and also the dandy brush. First brush the mane, then comb it. If the hair is very tangled, comb the ends first. Don't worry about hurting the horse, since there are no nerves in the neck or dock where the hair is rooted. Most people prefer a thin mane and tail because this indicates Thoroughbred blood. Thinning is not done with scissors. Instead, hairs are pulled out, a few at a time. In working on the tail, grasp the end and hold it out, as shown. Then brush and comb each little clump of hair, working from the end and from the side. If the hair is badly tangled, first separate it with your fingers.

Horses turned outdoors often get into burs, which become matted in the hair. Don't try to get these out by combing. With your fingers, pull each hair away from the bur, *not* the bur away from the hair. When the burs are out, brush and comb as directed. For a final finishing touch, dip the dandy brush in water and, standing on the side of the mane opposite to the one on which it falls, brush the mane along the neckline.

Fig. 43. Picking up forefeet

How do I clean the feet? Start with the near forefoot. Facing the horse's tail, put your left shoulder against the animal's left shoulder. Now slide your left hand down the tendons behind the cannon bone, pinching slightly as you do so. At the same time, lean hard against the horse's shoulder to throw his weight onto his opposite front foot. As you do this, give some voice command such as "lift." As soon as the horse lifts his foot, continue to slide the left hand down until the hoof is cradled in your hand. Bend the fetlock joint as much as possible. This turns the bottom of the foot upward, in a flat position, and makes it harder for the horse to pull away from you. Take the hoof pick and, very gently, pick out all the dirt, being especially careful to clean very thoroughly the crevices down the center of the frog and on each side of it. Be sure to start at the heel and work toward the toe. Then, if the horse should jerk away suddenly and the hoof pick slip, it can do no damage. Cleaning toward the heel is dangerous, for a sudden movement can cause the point of the pick to injure the sensitive heel.

Fig. 44. Picking up hind feet

After cleaning the near front foot, move forward, still facing the tail, and pick up the back foot the same way, leaning against the stifle to push the horse's weight over. Don't pull the back foot to the side. First pull it forward and then straight back. The picture shows just what your position should be. Horses and ponies whose feet have been neglected will often put up a fight the first few times you try to clean them. Before long, however, they will learn to lift each foot in turn on command, especially if you praise them highly and perhaps give them a tidbit when you have finished.

What do I do when I have finished the feet? Check the horse's eyes to be sure they are clean. Swab them with a little absorbent cotton dipped in water. If the eyes seem irritated, add a teaspoon of salt or boric acid to the water. Wipe each eye carefully, especially at the lower corner.

Now check under the tail and, if you have a gelding or stallion, check the sheath. If these parts are dirty, wash with a clean sponge and soap. Now that your horse is clean, take a soft piece of flannel or toweling and wipe him all over to give him a polish.

Is there anything else I should do? There is one more thing which is most important. With your bare hand go over the entire body and legs of your horse or pony. Any spot you have missed will feel rough. At the same time, feel for heat, hidden bumps, bruises, or broken skin. Put one hand on one front foot and one on the other. Is the temperature of both the same? What about the hind feet? Are they cooler than the front? Heat in the front feet can be a sign of the condition known as "founder," and should be checked further. Be sure to feel carefully along all the tendons of both front and back feet. Heat in this area is an indication of strain. In checking for cleanliness, pay particular attention to the girth and saddle areas, as well as to the area around the ears and the backs of the pasterns.

Does a horse ever need a bath? In hot weather, a warm or cool bath is very pleasant for the horse that is sweaty. Put a little soap powder or a mild detergent in a pail of water. Add 2 tablespoonfuls of some sort of light oil. Mineral oil is good and salad oil is all right. Starting behind the ears, slosh the horse off with a large sponge, using plenty of water. Then, take the sweat scraper shown in the sketch and scrape off the excess water. Bend the flexible scraper into a curve and use the edge, always

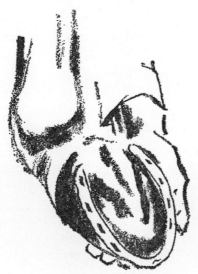

Fig. 45. Holding the foot

Fig. 46. Using the sweat scraper

working from the top down and following the way the hair lies. When the horse is as dry as possible throw a light cover over him, if you have one, and then walk him until he is completely dry. He will not look nice again until you have once more given him a thorough grooming, for the hair usually dries in mats.

When should a horse's legs be bandaged to rest them? After a day's hunting or polo, or an exceptionally hard day at the shows or on the trails, the horse will recover from fatigue and be less apt to be stiff and muscle-sore if you rub his legs with liniment and bandage them lightly but snugly. To put on the rolled bandage, follow the directions for putting on the shipping bandage on pages 150–151, but don't use cotton and do not go below the fetlock joint.

Clipping

Why are horses clipped in the winter when it is cold? We only clip horses in winter if they are stabled, and if their work is such that they get overheated. Horses sweat much more profusely then do human beings. If we take the heavy hair off the horse's body, he doesn't sweat as much, and any sweat that does form dries out immediately.

Is there more than one type of clipping? Yes, your horse may be clipped all over. He may have what is called a "hunting clip," shown in Fig. 47a, or an Irish "trace clip," as in Fig. 47b. Many people prefer the hunting clip, in which the hair is left on under the saddle and on the legs. For one thing, the stable blanket does not cover the legs, and if your barn is very cold, you will probably prefer this type of clip. Also, some horses have tender backs and get sore under the saddle area if they are clipped there.

In Ireland, where horses are used mainly for hunting, and

Fig. 47a. Hunting clip

where storms come up without warning, a trace clip is popular. This keeps the hair over the loins, where the kidneys are located, for protection, but takes it off the lower parts of the body where the horse gets the muddiest.

How do I use the clippers? Always clip against the hair. Do not press down too heavily. Dip the running clipper blades in kerosene every two or three minutes. The whole head of the clippers should be submerged in the kerosene, to wash away the hairs and dirt. After that, they should be wiped with a rag, and several drops of a good grade of light machine oil should be put on the blades and into the oil holes in the head. Clippers become overheated easily. When this happens, stop clipping until they have cooled. In clipping around the elbows, lift the front foot and pull it forward so that you can get into the folds of skin.

Fig. 47b. Trace clip

Try never to stand directly in front of the horse while clipping. If he lunges forward or brings his knee up quickly, you can be hurt.

How do I control a horse that is afraid of the clippers? Most horses will allow you to clip their bodies without giving too much trouble; and a few will allow you to clip their heads and legs. Some won't let you come near them, but begin plunging and fighting as soon as you start the motor of the clippers. The best way to control such horses is by means of a "twitch," shown in Fig. 48. A twitch is easily made from an old broom-handle and some soft cord. Don't use hard cord or very thin cord. The principle of the twitch is based on the fact that a horse cannot think of two things at the same time. It is attached to his upper lip, as shown (never to the ears or tongue).

To put on a twitch, slide your right hand through the loop. Grasp the horse's upper lip firmly and hold on tightly, while someone else quickly twists the handle of the twitch until the cord is tight around the lip above your hand. This pinches the lip just enough to distract the horse's attention. Perhaps it seems cruel to you, but actually it is the most humane way of handling a horse that will not allow you to work around him. Don't keep the twitch on too long, or the lip will become numb and the horse will get restless again. When you take it off, rub the horse's lip for him and give him a tidbit.

What do I do after clipping my horse? When you finish clipping, give him a good currying to remove all the dandruff and dirt that has come to the surface. Then, with the oily rag you used for wiping the clippers, go over him lightly. Most of the extra dandruff will stick to it and your horse will be shining. Don't make a regular practice of using kerosene on your horse's coat, however. If you do, all his hair will come off. When you have finished clipping, you may be surprised to find that your horse is quite a different color!

Braiding

As you learned in Chapter 2, horses of different breeds have different styles of hairdo. Several of these styles require that

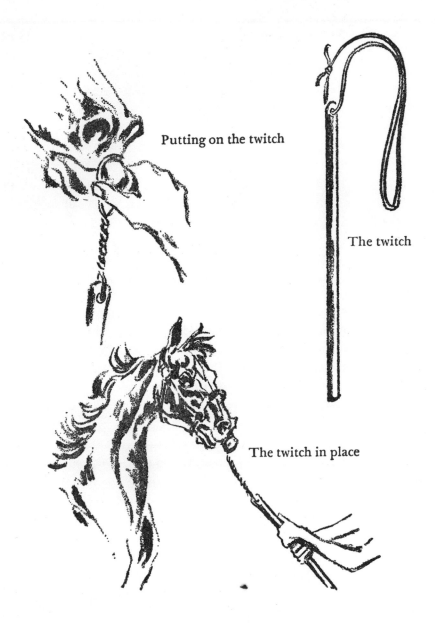

Putting on the twitch

The twitch

The twitch in place

Fig. 48. Putting on the twitch

Fig. 49. Hunter with braided mane and tail

the horse's mane and tail be braided. Fig. 49 shows you how a hunter's mane and tail look when he is ready for the show ring or the hunt field. As you see, the mane is braided in a series of little pigtails, which are turned under, and either sewn or held in place with small elastics. The mane must first be thinned and shortened by pulling. When it is about 4 inches long, it is divided into clumps, braided, folded under, and sewn or tied.

Braiding the tail is much harder. Starting at the top, take some of the hair from each side of the dock as high up as possible, and some from the middle. Then braid, at each crossing of an outside clump of hair adding a few more hairs (about an inch at a time). Work your way about 12 or 14 inches down the tail. Finish with a long, thin, pigtail of center hairs, then roll this back, and tuck it under, sewing it in place if possible.

Fig. 50 shows a "mud-tail." Here, after being braided past the dock, all the rest of the hair is picked up and made into a braid, which is then turned up. The purpose of the mud-tail is to keep the horse's tail out of the mud in the hunt field.

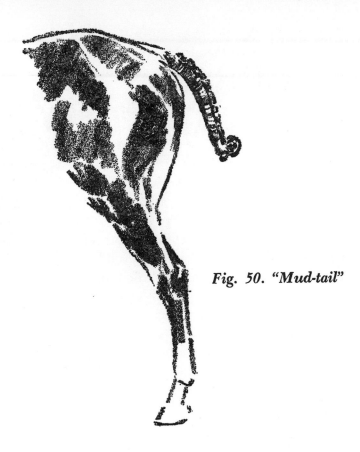

Fig. 50. "Mud-tail"

Shoeing

As we learned earlier, nature gave the horse a protective covering for the hoof which renews itself as needed, an insensitive but not rigid sole, and well-designed shock absorbers (the frogs). Nature intended the horse to run on moist, grassy pastures, however. In the beginning, no allowance was made for the fact that he would be required to carry weight on his back, and travel on hard or rocky roads, or that he would jump over high barriers when going fast. Nature also assumed that the horse would be on the move most of the time. Now that the horse is stabled for long hours, fenced in small pastures, and made to carry weight, the foot is no longer able to maintain itself without protection and care.

The Romans, feeling that hardness was the essential factor desirable for good hooves, used small rocks and stones for bedding instead of straw. Both the Romans and the Arabs shod their horses with metal shoes that covered the whole sole of the foot. Today we know that the sole and frog should be kept moist. We know that the horse turned out in a small pasture often needs no shoes, but must have his feet trimmed regularly, for he will not run enough to wear away the walls. Horses whose feet are not cared for in this way can develop hooves so overgrown and deformed that they can barely move at a slow walk.

Shoes protect the hoof from breaking off when the horse travels over rocky ground, or from wearing away so that the sensitive laminae (LAMinee) are exposed. By means of projections called "calks," or of heels, they also keep the horse from slipping when he works on icy, hard, or muddy surfaces. They correct a faulty way of walking, and enable the horse that toes in, toes out, or paddles (swings his feet out as he trots), to travel more normally. Horses of special breeds, such as the racing trotter, wear delicately balanced and fitted shoes which enable them to trot faster. Saddle horses wear very heavy shoes and their toes are allowed to grow very long. This makes them pick their feet up higher. Some horses are awkward and hit the front foot with the toe of the back foot. This is called "forging." Good shoeing can correct this also.

How does a blacksmith shoe a horse? After taking off the old shoes, the blacksmith carefully trims the feet, rasping away the lower edges of the wall and cutting off any ragged edges of the frog. He does this to shape the hoof so that the horse stands flat and even, with neither side of his foot higher or lower than the other. Many blacksmiths trim off more of the frog than is necessary, and cut away the bars entirely, to make a neater-looking foot. When you engage a new blacksmith, be sure and tell him that you do not want this done.

In the old days, the blacksmith would take a straight rod of iron, heat it until it was red-hot, and then shape it to fit the individual foot. This is still done on trotting tracks, where many of the shoes must be beveled off or accurately weighted, according to how the horse travels. Usually, however, the blacksmith starts with a factory-made iron shoe. Already shaped like a horseshoe, this has a U-shaped perforation in which the nails are set. Factory-made shoes come in sizes starting with #oo (double zero) for small ponies, and running to size 3, 4, or larger, for draft horses.

The blacksmith heats the shoe in the glowing coals of his forge until it is red-hot and then hammers it on his anvil. He must form some little liplike projections called "clips" (see Fig. 51), which turn up over the wall and help hold the shoe on. These can be either "toe clips" (one in the center of each shoe), or "quarter clips" (two on each shoe, placed as shown in the diagram). Usually he uses toe clips on the front feet and quarter clips on the back feet. The factory-made shoes are cut long enough so that if the blacksmith wishes, he can make heels by turning the ends back on themselves, or he can make wedges by pounding the hot metal.

At frequent intervals, the blacksmith stops pounding and holds the shoe against the bare foot of the horse to see whether he has it exactly the right shape. The hot metal makes a mark on the sole and wall. Thus, the blacksmith can easily tell what more he has to do to make the shoe fit properly. Although smoke

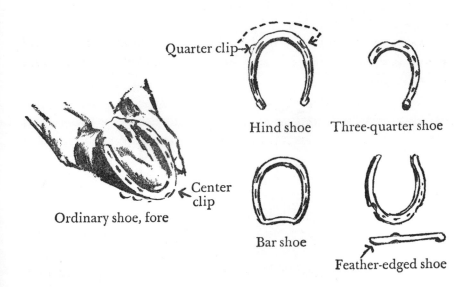

Quarter clip→

Hind shoe   Three-quarter shoe

←Center clip

Ordinary shoe, fore

Bar shoe

Feather-edged shoe

Fig. 51.

arises when the hot shoe touches the foot, the horse doesn't feel any pain.

When the blacksmith is certain that the shoe has been shaped to fit the foot exactly, he plunges it into cold water to cool it, then nails it on the foot. The finished job should look like Fig. 52a. Notice that the line from the coronet to the toe is straight. Fig. 52b shows the foot of a horse that has been improperly shod. The blacksmith tried to fit the hoof to the shoe instead of the shoe to the hoof.

Are there other kinds of shoes besides the ordinary ones? There are several types used for corrective purposes. Fig. 51 shows a "bar shoe," which is used in cases where the veterinary wants to be sure that there is pressure on all parts of the frog. The three-quarter shoe shown is often used on a horse that has suffered from a corn under the inside of the shoe; it takes the pressure off the sole at that point. If the horse forges, the blacksmith will put on a "feather-edged" shoe in front. In this, the bottom is beveled or rounded off slightly. (See Fig. 51.) With this type of shoe, the horse will turn his front feet over faster, and get them off the ground and out of the way faster. The blacksmith may also set the front shoes slightly back, and set the back shoes slightly forward.

When the blacksmith finishes shoeing my horse what should I do? Ride at the trot to make sure the shoe does not pinch and that the horse moves correctly.

Fig. 52.

a. Well-shod foot   b. Shoe too small—
foot made to fit shoe

At what age should we begin taking care of a colt's feet? The blacksmith should watch the foal moving around in the pasture before he is six months old, and, if necessary, trim the little feet. This will prevent bad habits such as paddling or toeing in or out from developing. The first shoes, which are often only tips, should be put on as soon as you find that the feet are breaking off or becoming too worn down. Tips protect only the toe and leave the heels free. Sometimes they are necessary only in front, since you need not put anything on the back feet until you begin regular work over hard or rocky ground.

How often should the shoes be checked? About every four weeks, the blacksmith will probably take them off, trim the feet, and if they are not worn, put the same shoes back on. This is called "resetting" the shoes.

Do ponies always need to be shod? No. Ponies do not carry as much weight as horses and are not required to jump as high. Their hooves are usually thick and strong, so many ponies do not need shoeing at all. If your horse's or pony's feet do not either break off or wear down too much, it is far better not to shoe him. The feet must be trimmed regularly, however. Sometimes only the front feet chip or wear down, for they support the most weight. In that case, you can have your pony shod only in front and leave his back feet bare.

Is there any other way to fit and put on shoes? When the blacksmith uses a forge and fits the shoe while it is hot, we call it "hot shoeing." Less experienced people sometimes put the shoes on cold, without doing the final and precise molding of the hot iron. This is not good and should be done only in an emergency.

Putting on the Saddle, Bridle, and Stable Blanket

There is a right and a wrong way to tack up your horse. Learn the right way in the beginning, and stick to it.

How do I put on a stable blanket? Before answering this, let us talk about taking it off so that it is correctly folded. First, unbuckle the surcingles (the body straps). Then undo the chest straps. Now fold the front half of the blanket back over the back half, as shown in Fig. 53. Next, take hold of the point marked "a" with your left hand, the place marked "b" with your right, and lift off the blanket. It is now folded neatly in a square and you can hang it up as it is. To put it back on, lay it across the hindquarters of the horse with the folded-back front half on top. It should be a little farther forward than the way he wears it. Unfold the front section, do up the chest straps, pull the blanket back into position, and do up the surcingles.

Should I put the bridle or the saddle on first? If you are going to ride as soon as your horse is tacked up, put on the bridle first. If he is going to stand around in the stall for several hours, put the saddle on and girth it up lightly, hanging the bridle outside the stall.

Fig. 53. Putting on and taking off blanket

How do I put on the bridle? Putting on the bridle takes a good deal of skill. How much skill depends on how tall you are and how cooperative the horse is. If you can reach the top of the horse's head easily, use the following procedure:

a. With the cavesson noseband and the curb chain undone, hold the bridle with your right hand, as shown in Fig. 54.
b. Stand beside the horse's near shoulder, facing front. Slide the rein over the horse's head and leave it just behind the ears as in Fig. 55.
c. With your right hand, pull the bridle up until the bit rests against the teeth. Be sure that the horse's nose is in the noseband of the cavesson.

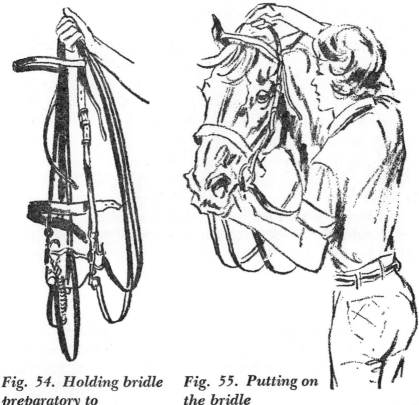

Fig. 54. Holding bridle preparatory to putting it on

Fig. 55. Putting on the bridle

Fig. 56. Putting bit into horse's mouth

d. Cup his lower lip in your left hand as shown. Keep your thumb on the center of the bottom of the bar of the bit.

e. If the horse does not open his mouth of his own accord, slide your fingers into the mouth at the bars on the right side. The taste of your fingers will cause him to open his mouth, at which you immediately *pull up the bridle with your right hand*. Don't try to force the bit into his mouth with your left hand.

f. Keeping the bit in the horse's mouth by pulling up with your right hand, use your left hand to pull his left ear through the head stall. Then go around to the other side and pull the right ear through. Buckle the cavesson and the curb chain, taking care that the latter is untwisted and lies flat.

g. Finally, slip the reins back to the withers.

How do I put on the bridle if my horse won't hold his head down and I'm not tall enough to reach up to his poll? Instead of holding the bridle by the top of the crownpiece, grasp the two cheek-pieces and the cavesson in the right hand just above the bit, as shown in Fig. 57. Slip your arm under the horse's head, and hold onto his nose just above the nostrils. A little molasses on the bit will often make the horse anxious to be bridled.

How do I put the saddle on? Put the pad on somewhat farther forward than you want it, then slide it back into place so that the hair will lie flat. Be sure that the stirrups are run up on the leathers and that the girth is over the seat, as shown in Fig. 58. Now lift the saddle and set it lightly down on the pad. It should fit snugly up on the withers. Rock it with your hand to be sure it is not too far back. Attach the girth on the near side. Then go around the horse, reach under the saddle, pull the girth up, and attach it.

If your saddle has three billet straps and your girth has only two buckles, use the two outside straps, letting the middle one hang free on top of the girth. If your girth has girth guards to protect the under part of the flap from being rubbed against the buckles, pull these down into place as shown in the picture. Be sure that your girth is buckled evenly. Don't have it on the

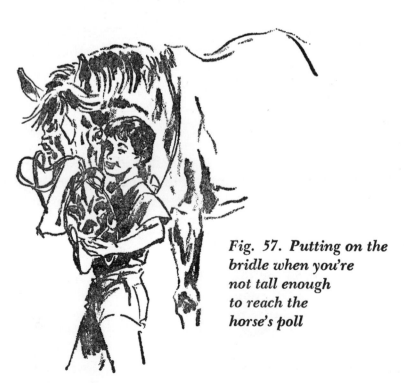

Fig. 57. Putting on the bridle when you're not tall enough to reach the horse's poll

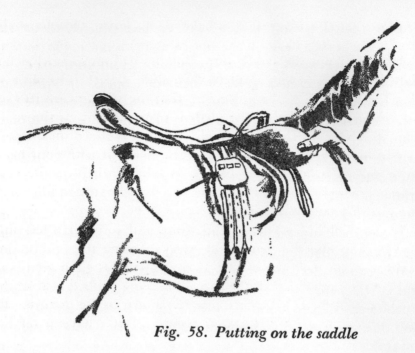

Fig. 58. Putting on the saddle

second hole on one side and the fifth or sixth on the other. Don't buckle the girth too tightly, especially on a cold day. When you are ready to mount, you may tighten it up a little more, but it should never feel tight on the sides of the horse, only at the bottom. Slip your hand in between the girth and the horse on each side and run it down to the bottom to make sure that it is not too tight and that the hair will lie flat.

If you are using a folded leather girth, put the fold to the front so that the sharp edge will not hurt the horse. If you are not using a saddle-pad, put the saddle on well ahead of the withers and slide it back into place. When the saddle is correctly placed and the horse is standing with his legs under him, there is usually a space of about four inches between his elbows and the front edge of the girth.

Catching the Horse in the Pasture

What is the best way to catch a horse in the pasture? This will depend on the type of horse. If he is the kind that likes to be caught and if he wears a halter when in the pasture, carry a tie-rope (halter shank) with a snap on one end. Quietly approach the horse's head on the side away from the stable, so that the horse is between you and the stable. Hold your hand out and offer him a tuft of grass or a carrot. Speak or whistle to your horse, and walk up to him. Give him the tidbit, slide one arm over his neck and, with the other, snap the halter shank onto the halter.

If he wears no halter, carry a bridle out with you. Slip the reins over his head and leave them just behind the ears. Then bridle, as explained in a previous paragraph. Gentle horses can often be led into the barn with nothing but a halter shank or your own belt slipped around the neck behind the ears. Hold the two ends together just under the throttle.

What about the horse that doesn't like to be caught? A horse that is really wild and either runs away or charges you presents a problem. If you don't need him immediately, spend a few days training him. Fix a box or bucket to the gatepost nearest the stable. Two or three times a day go to the box, whistle or call to the horse, and put a little grain in the box. The first time you do it, move well away, and let the horse come up and eat it without attempting to approach him. The second time, if he seems less shy, walk a little nearer to him.

Continue this for several days or a week, moving closer each time. When the horse lets you come close while he is eating, stand and stroke his neck. Keep talking to him, but don't try to take hold of the halter or slip a rope around his neck until he is willing to have you move around him freely. Of course, this takes patience, but one day the horse will come up to the box and let you walk quietly over to him and attach the shank.

With a horse that is only a little wary, go into the field carrying a pail of grain. Get the horse's attention by shaking the pail and moving the grain around in the pail with your hand. As soon as he comes toward you, turn around and start walking back toward the stable. Many horses will willingly follow someone right into the barn so long as the person doesn't try to catch them in the field. There are also many that will come up to you if you kneel on the ground, take a wisp of grass, and rub it briskly between the palms of your hands. It goes without saying that every movement you make must be very slow and quiet.

In an emergency, when you must catch a horse that refuses to be caught, the following method can be used. Have two people take hold of each end of a thirty-foot rope and stand along the fence, near a corner. A third person should drive the horse up into the corner as slowly as possible. Take plenty of time. When he is in the corner, one of the two people holding the rope moves across into position, as shown in Fig. 59. Gradually the two shorten the rope and move in toward the horse until they have him pinned in the corner, when the third person walks up to him. Although this method is not very effective with a frightened horse, it does work with the horse that simply doesn't feel like being caught.

Vanning

How do I protect my horse's legs from injury during vanning? Use *shipping bandages*. These are rolled bandages put on over *sheet cotton*. If you cannot get sheet cotton, use ordinary cotton batting; but sheet cotton is cheaper and can be used over and over again. Most harness and saddle stores that sell the bandages also carry the sheet cotton.

How do I put on the shipping bandage? First, roll up each bandage with the tape end in the center. Starting with the near

Fig. 59. Catching the horse in the corner of the pasture

front leg, kneel beside the horse and wrap a layer of sheet cotton around his leg. It should run from just below the knee, over the fetlock joint and pastern, and entirely cover the coronet. Holding this in place with your left hand, and with the bandage still rolled up in your right hand, begin to wrap the horse's leg, starting about halfway down the pastern. Work upward first, leaving the top inch of the cotton uncovered, then work downward until you have completely covered the coronet. Now work up again to where you started. When you come to the end of the bandage, tie it in place with the tape, making sure that the knot is on the outside. This will keep him from catching the heel of his other foot in the knot if he should be restless and start pawing. Use the same type of knot that you use to tie your shoestrings, but cross one end over the other and bring it up from underneath *twice* instead of the usual once; also, after forming the second loop, bring it around and through the knot a second time (see Fig. 60) before pulling it tight. This knot is much more secure than the ordinary bowknot. To untie it, pull both ends at the same time.

Is there any special way of getting the bandage to go on smoothly and snugly? Yes. Because the horse's leg is not exactly the same size all the way down, and also because you have to go over the fetlock joint, you will find it impossible to roll the bandage on neatly unless you take a *half-turn* every so often, as shown in Fig. 60. Each time you do this, the bandage will tighten itself and conform to the shape of the leg. Around the fetlock and pastern, you will have to make a half-turn each time you go around the leg with the bandage. Further up the leg this will not be necessary. If you should end with the bandage wrong side out, make another half-turn to put the tapes on top.

Are all four legs bandaged when the horse or pony is shipped? Yes. Horses and ponies often injure their legs while getting in and out of vans and trailers, if they get excited and plunge or shy into the tailgate or the sides.

Should any other part of the horse be bandaged when he is shipped? Bandage the upper part of the tail (the dock) with the ordinary rolled bandage and no cotton. Start 2 or 3 inches

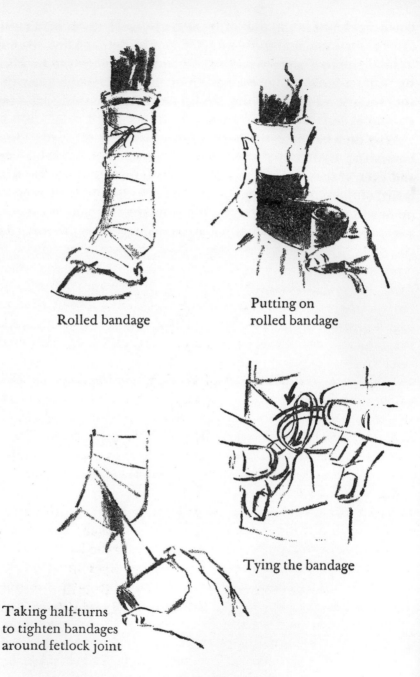

Rolled bandage

Putting on
rolled bandage

Taking half-turns
to tighten bandages
around fetlock joint

Tying the bandage

Fig. 60.

down from where the tail joins the body, work up as high as you can go, then down about 12 inches, and back up again. Be sure to hold the hair tightly and keep it smooth under the bandage. By using a half-turn at each wrap of the bandage, you can fit it very snugly. Tie as you did the leg bandages, wrapping the tape around at least twice with the knot on top.

Why do I bandage the horse's tail when he is shipped? Some horses rub their tails from nervousness when they are in vans, and even if they don't, the tail is often pushed against the backboard of the van or trailer. In any case, the hair is easily roughed up or even rubbed off, and the skin injured. If your horse takes a few very high steps when he wears bandages for the first time,

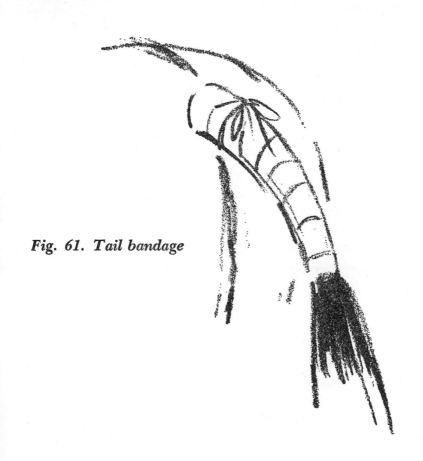

Fig. 61. Tail bandage

this is his way of telling you that they feel strange. Many horses and ponies do this.

How do I teach a horse to go willingly into a van or trailer? First, put a bridle on the horse. Don't try to control him with just a halter and shank. Most horses are afraid of stepping onto the ramp or of falling off, once they are on it. Sprinkle sand or bedding on the ramp and, if necessary, construct temporary sides for it. Ladders make good ramp sides. You may be able to back the trailer or van up to an alleyway between two buildings and lean rails against the vehicle, as shown in Fig. 62a. Sometimes it is necessary to extend the rails so that they form an alleyway up to the ramp. This can be done with jump standards. Lead the horse up to the ramp between the rails. Let him stop when he reaches the ramp, where he will put his nose down and sniff. The person who is leading should go up the ramp and coax him from the top with oats. If he still refuses to go up, lift each of his front feet in turn and put them on the ramp. Often, when a horse finds that he can stand on the ramp, he doesn't mind walking on it.

A timid horse that refuses to come anywhere near the ramp can sometimes be led into the van on the heels of another that is not afraid.

Otherwise, you will need two people with two long ropes. Attach one end of each rope to the van or trailer, as shown. Each person then holds a rope about three feet off the ground, forming an alley. As soon as the horse is between the ropes, the two people change places quickly. This crosses the ropes just above the horse's hocks. They both then walk toward the van, pulling in on the ropes. The horse will probably try to sit back on the ropes, but the people must hold fast and keep on pulling him into the trailer. The sketch makes this clear.

For the third method, the ramp must have sides. One person walks briskly toward the ramp, while two others, each holding the end of a jump rail or two-by-four, follow immediately behind the horse. Should he stop on reaching the ramp, it is their job to bring the rail in against his hind legs just above the hocks, and push him in.

a. Making temporary sides for ramp of trailer

b. The "rope" method

c. The "bar" method

Fig. 62. Vanning the horse

8

First Aid for Ailments & Injuries

When a horse shows symptoms of being ill, or suffers an injury in which the skin is broken or in which his movement or his eyes are affected, you must call the veterinary. There are things, however, which you can do either before the veterinary comes or as follow-up treatment. Learn the danger signs so that you will know when your horse is sick. Be able to tell the veterinary about the symptoms, and always have certain necessary supplies on hand.

How can I tell if my horse feels sick? Loss of appetite is usually the first sign of illness. If your horse does not finish his ration of grain, or leaves the major part of his hay, you may be sure there is something wrong. Horses run fevers just as human beings do. The normal temperature of the horse, taken with a rectal thermometer, is about 100 degrees. If your horse feels hot and has not eaten, take his temperature by putting petroleum jelly on the thermometer and inserting it under his tail. Leave it there for three minutes and then read it. You can also take the horse's pulse by feeling under each side of the jaw where the large artery runs. The normal pulse rate is thirty-six to forty beats per minute. Besides refusing food, a horse with a bad sore throat will not drink, so this can be another general indication of illness.

What types of ailment are most common? "Colic," "parasites," and contagious diseases.

What is the most common contagious disease? "Shipping fever," which is similar to distemper in other animals. The symptoms are loss of appetite, a cough, a discharge from the nostrils. In advanced cases, there is a swelling of a little gland under the jaw and the disease is called "strangles."

How do horses and ponies get shipping fever? They catch it directly from an infected animal or from using the same water-bucket or manger. We call it shipping fever because so many animals that are shipped in public conveyances contract it.

What should I do if my horse or pony shows symptoms of shipping fever? Call the veterinary at once! He will probably give the animal an injection of penicillin or of some other drug which will fight the virus. Meanwhile, keep the animal warm and quiet.

Is shipping fever a serious disease? It can be, for it sometimes leads to pneumonia. If it develops into a severe case of strangles, the gland will have to be opened and drained; sometimes the horse's respiratory system may be permanently affected. Heaves have been known to develop after a bad case of strangles. The horse may also become "broken-winded" if the cartilage in the throttle thickens, causing the horse to wheeze as he breathes.

Is there any way of preventing a horse from getting shipping fever? Preventive injections for shipping fever can be given to the animal several days before he begins his journey. When effective, they either ward off the disease entirely or lighten the attack. So, if you plan to ship your horse from one part of the country to another, it is a good idea to have him inoculated first.

If a horse with shipping fever comes into the stable, how can I keep the other horses from catching it? Isolate the newcomer, if at all possible, and be sure that he does not use the common water-pail. When any new horse first arrives in a stable, it is well to take these precautions for the first week, even though you do not see any symptoms of the disease, since he might develop it.

Are there any other common horse diseases which are contagious? "Horse encephalitis" (sleeping sickness) is carried by insects which first bite an infected animal and then transmit the disease to a healthy animal by biting it in turn. This is a fatal brain disease. Horses that develop it must be destroyed. There is a preventive serum, and if you live in a part of the country where there have been any known cases, you should have your horse inoculated once a year.

"Glanders" is another fatal disease and one that can be transmitted to man, but it is very rare today. Horses about to be shipped to districts where glanders has been known to exist can be inoculated. In fact, some states insist that horses and ponies which travel by rail be inoculated against the disease.

Sore throat, laryngitis, pneumonia, influenza, etc., are all as common in horses as in human beings. The veterinary must be called and will prescribe treatment and diet.

Colic

Is there more than one kind of colic? Yes, there are three types. In "flatulent colic," the horse develops a great deal of gas in his stomach and appears badly bloated. If this gas presses against the heart, the horse may die. In "spasmodic colic," the horse is obviously in great pain, but is not as bloated. "Impaction," a severe constipation in which the bowels are momentarily paralyzed, is also a serious condition with colic symptoms.

Is colic dangerous? Colic is an exceedingly dangerous ailment which can come on very suddenly; if not treated at once, it can lead to complications which cause death. One such complication is "twisted gut." The horse tries to relieve the agonizing stomach pain by rolling violently. In doing so, he may displace and knot his intestines and die. After calling the veterinary in this kind of emergency, we must try to relieve the pain and keep the horse walking slowly so that he does not lie down and roll.

What are the first symptoms of colic? The horse refuses to eat, bites at his flanks, and seems very restless, lying down and standing up repeatedly. If you notice your horse behaving like this, call your veterinary.

What kind of medicine do I give? The first-aid kit of every stable should have a bottle of colic remedy and an instrument to get the medicine into the horse. Since colic medicine is very bitter and strong, it is usually given in large capsules which are shot into the back of the horse's throat with a "balling gun." Having done this, hold his muzzle high and pinched tightly closed until you see the horse swallow. Otherwise, he will spit the capsule out again. If you have no balling gun, you will have to push the capsule by hand as far back in his mouth as you can, holding his muzzle as described. Then keep the horse walking in slow circles.

Parasites

What are parasites? A parasite is a living organism which spends at least part of its life cycle on another living creature (or plant) using it for a home and for food. In other words, the larger being acts as host to the parasite that robs him of nourishment and is often an uncomfortable guest. There are three main classes of parasites in horses: those that live within the body, either in the stomach, colon, or blood stream; those that live outside the body; and those just under the skin.

What kinds of parasites live inside the horse's body? Long, white "stomach worms" are often extruded by the horse. They eat the food which should be nourishing him. His coat becomes dull, his skin seems tight; he often gets very thin; no matter how much you give him to eat, he does not gain weight.

The larvae of "botflies" that are sometimes found in the stomach also take nourishment that the horse needs himself. Perhaps you have noticed these flies that look like small bees buzzing around the horse's legs. They do not sting, but lay tiny eggs that look like little seeds on the legs. They stick very tightly and must be clipped off with clippers or scraped away with a razor blade. Otherwise the horse may get them into his stomach by biting or licking them, and then the trouble begins.

"Blood worms" are the most serious of the worm parasites. Nearly invisible, they work their way through the walls of the intestines into the blood stream, where they multiply and take nourishment needed by the horse.

Do many horses and ponies have worms? If you have a young animal, and he is turned out to pasture with other animals, you can be pretty certain that he will become infected. When asking the veterinary for the proper medicine, take a specimen of the manure to him. He will put it under his microscope, and will know just what kind of parasites he must deal with. He will give you instructions about the diet to use before and after worming. Be sure to follow them exactly.

What kinds of parasites live on the outside of the horse? Lice are the most common. To get rid of them, clip the animal, then give him a warm bath with a solution of Lysol. Wipe him off with a kerosene rag, and put more kerosene in his mane and tail. One treatment is usually enough, but you may have to repeat it in a week.

What kinds of parasites live under the skin? The "warble fly" lays its eggs under the skin of a horse, especially in the saddle area. You notice nothing until the egg hatches and a grub emerges and grows into a lump shaped somewhat like a pecan nut. The horse doesn't feel anything, unless this lump happens to be where weight presses on it. In that case, the veterinary will have to come and cut it out.

Skin Ailments and Infections

Since several types of virus attack both horses and human beings, always disinfect your hands after treating a horse. These viruses spread easily from one animal to another, so the grooming tools used on infected animals should be kept separate and dipped in a Lysol solution after each use.

What are the most common types of skin viruses which attack the horse? Horses and ponies often get "ringworm." This is not a worm but a virus. Ringworm can be identified by the round, bare spots about the size of a quarter that develop on various parts of the horse's body. Later, raised scabs will form. An ointment named Iodex is good for these, but your veterinary may suggest something better.

There are also various types of "mange." Some are easily cured, while others are serious and difficult to treat. Large, itching bare spots will appear, which the veterinary will have to clear up.

What other skin ailments are there? There are many kinds of eruptions and pimples which are caused by a sudden change in feed. Ask your veterinary.

Other Ailments

Perhaps the most common ailment in horses, and this too is usually a virus, is the foot condition known as "thrush." There is a strong-smelling discharge in the frog area, and the horse may be very lame. If powdered copper sulphate (sometimes called blue stone) is used when the symptoms first appear, the ailment can be cured in a few days, but if the case is advanced, something stronger will be needed.

How do I apply the copper sulphate? Clean the foot thoroughly, especially in the cleft and the *commissures*. (Have the blacksmith do this if possible.) When the foot is completely dry, pack as much of the copper sulphate as you can into the commissures and cleft, and wad it in place with dry cotton, using the back of an ordinary table knife. Every twenty-four hours, remove the cotton and repeat the treatment. If the horse continues lame for more than three days, call the veterinary.

"Navicular disease" is an affliction which attacks the navicular bone and the coffin bone which are inside the foot of the horse. The various causes include overwork on hard roads, improper shoeing, and heredity. It is incurable, but can be relieved in certain cases either by special shoeing or by removal of the nerves in the heels of the horse.

What is "Navicular bursitis"? This is an irritation of the covering of the navicular bone. The veterinary will prescribe treatment. Often ice packs, used with a water boot, are recommended.

What is "founder"? This is a foot condition and is sometimes called "laminitis." It can be brought on if the horse is allowed to stand, hot and sweating, after drinking too much water, by overeating, bad feed or bad hay, or too much work on hard ground.

Founder is one of the most painful diseases. The horse is hardly able to put his feet to the ground, and both front feet are very hot to the touch. The blacksmith must pull the shoes as

quickly and as gently as possible. The horse must then be per-
suaded to stand in a tub or stream of cold water for several hours.
In a bad case the animal will have to be destroyed. If he recovers
enough to do light work, he will have to wear rubber pads under
his shoes and his hooves will be deformed.

Wounds

How many types of wounds are there? There are four, but
the "puncture wound" caused by a nail that is driven into the
foot or other part of the horse is most dangerous. If you know
that your horse has stepped on a nail, even though he may not
be lame, have the veterinary come and give him a preventive shot
against tetanus. While waiting for him, wash out the wound
with hydrogen of peroxide, but do not bandage it.

An "abrasive wound" is one in which the outer skin is rubbed
off. Unless the abrasion covers a very wide area, simply paint it
with gentian violet or any other good disinfectant recommended
by your veterinary. Abrasions of the knees and of the back of
the pastern take the treatment recommended for *mud fever*.

An "incised wound" is the type made with a sharp knife and
is not very common. Bleeding is the primary danger in deep
incised wounds. Cover the wound with a gauze pad, and press
hard on it until the bleeding stops. The veterinary will prescribe treatment, but may forget to tell you to put veterinary
petroleum jelly on the hair below the wound. This will prevent
the discharge from sticking to the hair if the wound should become infected.

A "lacerated wound" is one in which the flesh is torn and the
edges are rough. A veterinary must be called, and every effort
made to avoid infection. Do not try to treat the wound yourself. If the veterinary cannot come at once, however, bathe the
wound gently with either a mild Lysol solution or peroxide.
Then apply either sulfathiazole ointment or B.F.I. powder.

What is "mud fever"? *Mud fever,* or "cracked heels," is a condition which affects the back of the pasterns. Since it occurs only
in some parts of the country, we think it may be caused by a
virus which lives in certain soils. The horse's skin becomes in-

flamed and cracks open. There is a discharge, and scabby sores develop. If not checked, this condition can spread and cripple the horse completely. The treatment is as follows: Gently soak and wash the animal's foot with warm water. When the scabs are softened, pick them off and apply one of the following remedies: cod-liver oil, sulfathiazole, or Resinol ointment. Keep the stall very clean and dry, and do not turn the horse out. The condition should heal from underneath without forming new scabs. If new scabs do form, you will have to soak them off again and apply your ointment more heavily.

Other Injuries

A very stubborn type of injury is a boil called a "fistula" (FIStula). This is the result of a blow or heavy pressure, and usually occurs on the withers or on the poll. Unless treated at once, it may spread and become very serious. Hot applications, followed by either sulfathiazole or a healing powder are the usual early treatment. If the wound remains open for more than a day or so, a veterinary may have to operate. Of course, if the fistula is on the withers, the horse must not wear a saddle until it is entirely healed.

Strains, sprains, and bruises are to be expected with horses that hunt or jump a great deal. Even the horse that never jumps may go lame from twisting his foot, from too much fast work on hard ground, or from some weakness. In any case, the veterinary should be called, and he will advise treatment.

"Bowed tendon." This is a sprain. The tendons swell, there is heat in the leg, and the horse is very lame. If the sprain is not too severe and is taken care of, the horse may recover completely. In other cases, the tendon may never go back to its original shape. Cold wet compresses are usually advised.

"Capped elbow" or "shoe boil." This is an enlargement on the point of the elbow caused by the horse bruising it with the heel of the other foot when lying down. Treat with hot Epsom salts solution. Unless it subsides or opens of its own accord, the veterinary will have to lance it. Continue to treat with hot applications, and cover the hair below it with petroleum

jelly, as there will be a heavy discharge of pus for some days. A shoe-boil boot must be worn until the horse has entirely recovered.

"Capped hock." Although the horse may not be lamed, this is unsightly and sometimes never goes away entirely. It is usually caused by a blow or by the horse's constant kicking in the stall.

"Curb." This is a strain of the tendon which runs down the back of the hind legs. The horse is usually quite lame. Liniment, or a mild blistering agent such as Churchill's Iodine painted on every day for three days, then left off for three days, and repeated until a scruff forms is sometimes enough, but the veterinary should be called.

"Ringbone." This is an enlargement which goes all the way around the pastern. It is serious and does not always yield to treatment.

"Side bone." This is an enlargement on the coronet. The horse often goes lame, and when rested, seems to go sound. But he goes lame again as soon as he is put back to work. Blistering by the veterinary sometimes helps, as does the wearing of rubber pads under the shoes.

"Sit fasts." These are hard, callous-covered lumps which form in the saddle area. Sometimes they are painful, sometimes not. There is usually no successful cure.

"Spavins." "Bog" spavins are a soft, puffy swelling on the inside and front of the hock. They are a form of sprain, though often the horse is not lame. Hot or cold wet compresses usually help. When the horse is put back to work, he should be reconditioned very carefully. "Bone" spavins, sometimes called "jacks," are more serious. They are bony growths located on the hock joint.

"Splints." Common to most young horses, these are injuries to the splint bone which runs along the cannon and is joined to it at the top. While splints are forming, the horse will be very lame. After they have become hard, the horse will usually go sound. As the horse grows older, they often disappear entirely. Churchill's Iodine sometimes hastens the healing.

"Stifle." The stifle is one of the points on the horse most prone to injury. A dislocation of the stifle is very common. A perfectly sound horse may suddenly be unable to bend his hind leg. Often, after a minute, he goes sound again. If this occurs more than once, the veterinary will probably advise blistering him and then turning him out for several months.

"Stringhalt." Some horses lift their back legs very high when first brought out of the stable or when backed. It is considered by many to be a nervous affliction, and there is no cure.

Swollen leg or "stocking up." The hind legs of some horses swell at night, usually because of too much hard work without proper conditioning. When the horse is worked, the swelling subsides. After work, the horse's hind legs should be thoroughly massaged with a good liniment and wrapped in loosely rolled bandages. When first brought out, he should always be walked at least fifteen minutes before he is trotted, and again fifteen minutes before he is put away after work.

"Thoroughpins." Puffy enlargements on both sides of the hocks, seldom serious enough to cause lameness.

"Wind puffs." These are similar to thoroughpins, but occur in the ankle area.

Bandaging

Don't wait until your horse is injured, or until you want to ship him somewhere before learning how to bandage him properly. Study the pictures that show bandaging, and practice until you can do it quickly. To see if you have put the bandages on firmly enough and tied them well, leave them on until the next day. A bandage that falls off after an hour is of no use.

Bandages are used to protect and support other dressings in case of injuries, to keep wet compresses or poultices in place, to support and rest tired legs, and to protect the horse's legs from being injured in vanning or shipping by rail. For shipping bandages and for bandages to rest tired legs, see Chapter 7.

What kinds of bandages are used in cases of injury? In injuries in which the skin is broken it is best to leave the wound open to sun and air. Sometimes, however, after treating the wound, the veterinary may recommend that you keep the part bandaged with rolls of three-inch gauze, gauze squares, and rolls of two-inch adhesive tape. How these are attached will depend on where the horse is injured. Since any injury serious enough to need bandaging will require the help of a veterinary, it is best to have him show you exactly how he wants the wound cared for, including the application of bandages.

In cases of injury where the skin is not broken, the bandage is used to keep wet compresses or poultices in place.

What kinds of bandages are used to hold compresses in place? Cotton batting and "rolled" bandages are used. The rolled bandage is a long strip of a jersey material with one square end and one pointed end, to which is attached a piece of tape.

How do we bandage to keep medications in place? Sprains and strains, especially of the leg tendons, can be relieved by cold compresses. Prepare a half-pail of clear cold water with a cup of Epsom salts dissolved in it. Wrap dry cotton batting in layers as thick as possible around the affected part, and over it wrap a rolled bandage. While holding back the bandage at the top, pour the Epsom salts solution all around the leg until the cotton will hold no more.

In cases of infections, and in some types of sprains, the veterinary may want you to use either a hot Epsom salts solution, or a poultice. Make the Epsom salts solution the same way as before, but with water as hot as you can bear on your hand. Dip an ordinary bath towel in the hot water, wrap it around the leg, and hold it there until it stops steaming. Take it off, re-dip in the water, and repeat. Continue this for at least twenty minutes. If your horse or pony is calm, the injury not too high up the leg, and you have a suitable tub, you may induce him to put the injured leg right into the tub of hot water. Have him hold it there for fifteen or twenty minutes while you talk to him and give him tidbits.

After the injury has been thoroughly bathed in the way described above, put on the dry cotton with the rolled bandage over it, and soak the cotton with the hot Epsom salts solution.

If a hot poultice, of a substance such as Antiphlogistine, has been recommended, first, bathe the injured part. While you are doing this, have the unopened tube or can of Antiphlogistine heating in a pan of water on the stove. Next, open the can or tube and test the Antiphlogistine by putting a little on the blade of a knife and holding it against the back of your hand. If it feels very hot but does not burn you, it is the right temperature. Smear it all over the injured or infected area at least a quarter of an inch thick and cover with dry cotton. Over this place some sheets of newspaper, or a plastic sheeting which clings, and cover these with your rolled bandage, wrapped in the usual way. A poultice applied in this way will keep hot for many hours, and should be left on undisturbed for at least forty-eight hours.

Basic Equipment For the First-Aid Kit

(Except for minor ailments or injuries, always call your veterinary instead of trying to treat the horse or pony yourself.)

Six rolled bandages

Four rolls of 2-inch gauze bandage

One package of 3-inch gauze squares

One roll of antiseptic absorbent cotton

Several rolls of sheet cotton

Several rolls of 2-inch adhesive tape

Five-pound package of Epsom salts (For compresses and for internal use in cases of constipation)

Scissors

Balling gun
     or medicine syringe

Thermometer

Twitch

A clean pail

Antiphlogistine

Boric acid crystals (For bathing the eyes)
Blue Gall Remedy (For surface wounds)
Sulfathiazole ointment (For most wounds and infections)
B.F.I. powder; or other good disinfectant and fly-repellent powder recommended by your veterinary
Lysol (A general disinfectant for the stable and for large wounds)
Glauber's Salt (For constipation; a handful in the feed once a day)

Copper sulphate (Sometimes called blue stone. Be sure it is ground fine and is fresh. Use for "thrush")

A liniment or leg brace (Ask your veterinary to recommend one.)

White rock (A kind of clay that must be soaked twenty-four hours in cold water before it can be applied to reduce inflammation of the legs, or to pack the hoof when the sole gets very hard)

Colic remedy (Ask your veterinary.)

9

Basic Principles of Correct Riding

In a famous treatise on horsemanship written by Xenophon, before the time of Christ, the frontispiece shows a centaur (SEN-taur). This mythological creature had the head, torso, and arms of a man, and the body and legs of a horse. In other words, he was a horse with a man's brain, or, if you prefer, a man with the speed and strength of a horse. Xenophon wanted his pupils to be like centaurs. He wanted them to have so much knowledge of the horse, so much sympathy and understanding of him, that the rider and his horse would function as one being.

The really experienced horseman actually does become so much a part of his mount that the two appear to act as one. Such a rider can cause his horse to move in any direction, at any gait, to start and to stop, to execute many intricate steps and movements, all without the bystander's seeing how he communicates his wishes to the horse. It is as though the rider thought, and the horse obeyed. Nor is this very far wrong; horses often seem to read the minds of their masters.

Usually the rider does give the horse very exact commands. We have all seen the beginner who hauls his horse around a corner as though he were tugging on a rope, and who flogs him with his legs. Commands like these are easy enough to see, but the horse responds sluggishly to them. This does not necessarily mean that the horse is not well-trained; but it does show that the rider cannot speak "horse language" fluently. With another rider, the same animal might do everything willingly on almost imperceptible signals.

Try to become a rider who gets the most possible out of every horse or pony, with the least amount of effort on your part and his.

How can I become a good rider? It is best to have an instructor, but if you cannot get good instruction, read the principles of good horsemanship as given here and try to follow them as closely as you can. Perhaps you have a friend who is also learning. If so, you might study together, watch each other ride, and by comparing yourselves with the pictures, help each other to improve. Your horse is an excellent teacher also. You will be able to judge your improvement by the willingness with which your horse obeys you.

What is the first thing I should learn about riding? Learn to feel what the horse is doing under you. In order to do this, you have to sit correctly. In addition, you have to *interpret* what you are feeling. This comes with experience. Third, and this is the most difficult, you have to *influence* the horse to do what you want him to by learning the "language of the aids" or, as we call it, "horse language."

What is the right way to sit on a horse? You must sit in such a way at all times that you are in balance with your horse, and can maintain your position without having to hold onto the saddle or the horse's neck with your hands, or squeeze your legs against his sides. The exact position will change as the horse changes gait. This will be explained as we take up each gait.

Mounting and Dismounting

Is there more than one way to mount a horse? Yes, but the one most in favor for general use is shown in Fig. 63.

Horses are always mounted from the left, or *near* side. Face the horse's tail, with your left shoulder against the left shoulder of the animal. Take the buckle joining the two reins in your right hand, and slide your left hand down over the reins until it reaches the horse's neck in front of the withers (Fig. 67). Grasp a lock of mane, or the neck itself if the horse has no mane, in your left hand, together with the reins, which are now so short that

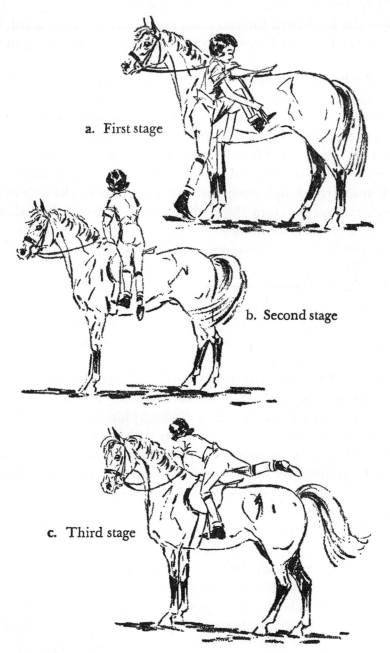

a. First stage

b. Second stage

c. Third stage

Fig. 63. Mounting

you can easily control the horse. Next, with the right hand, take hold of the stirrup and insert the toe of your left foot. Now comes the hard part, for you must push your toe downward, but not so far through the stirrup that it digs into the belly of the horse.

If the horse is tall and you are short, you won't be able to get your toe low enough. In such a case, face the shoulder of the horse instead of the tail, and when your toe is in the stirrup, turn the foot forward, as shown in the picture, so that the inside of the foot runs along the side of the horse. When your foot is firmly planted in the stirrup, take hold of the pommel of the saddle with your right hand, push your left knee against the side of the horse, and spring from the ball of the right foot. You should now find yourself standing in the left stirrup. Next, swing your right foot high over the croup of the horse and settle lightly in the saddle.

Try not to dig your horse with your left toe in mounting, or touch him on the croup with the toe or leg of your right foot as you swing it over his back; and try not to hit the saddle with a thump. Any of these things may cause him to start forward suddenly or even buck.

Why do I face the tail or the shoulder of the horse in mounting? Some horses kick when a rider mounts. If you mount from the rear, a kick will catch you in the back; but if you mount from the front, the horse cannot reach you with his hind foot. Some horses, Western-trained ones especially, tend to move forward when mounted. By standing near the forward end of the horse, you will be able to control him as he moves ahead.

Is it ever permissible to mount from the rear? Yes, under some circumstances. In cavalry maneuvers, for example, mounting from the rear makes it possible for each soldier to keep his eye on his officer at all times. Also, a very short person with a tall horse finds it easier to mount from the rear. If your horse tends to back away when you mount, it is best to mount from the rear. But, be sure your horse does not have the habit of kicking at the rider as he mounts. The reins are held in the right instead of the left hand, with the rider grasping them and the pommel of the saddle together. With his left hand he grasps the

Position of rider's left foot in mounting

Fig. 64. Mounting facing shoulder

mane. The second and third steps are the same for both methods of mounting.

How do I dismount? Take your right foot out of the stirrup. Hold the reins short in your left hand, and grasp a part of the mane with that hand as you did in mounting. Your right hand, as before, should be on the pommel. Swing your right foot high over the croup and bring it down to your left foot, which is still in the stirrup. Putting your weight on both hands, and keeping both knees straight, take your left foot out of the stirrup. Next, drop to the ground with knees and ankles relaxed. As you drop, push your body slightly away from the saddle, and turn so that you land facing in the same direction as the horse. If you do not push away like this, you may lose the buttons off your jacket. If you do not have both feet out of the stirrups, and your horse should step forward as you reach the ground, you will fall on the back of your head. By turning to land so that you are facing the way the horse is facing, you can get quickly to his head should he try to move on.

The Position of the Rider with the Horse Standing

How should my legs and feet be held when sitting on a horse? Notice in Fig. 66a that the rider's toe is directly under the point

Fig. 65. Dismounting facing front

b. Rider with legs too far forward—rider leaning back

Fig. 66.

of his knee. If he were to look down, he would not be able to see his own toe without bending forward. Compare this leg position with that shown in Fig. 66b. Here, the rider's foot is pushed much too far forward, and he is sitting as though in a chair instead of on a horse. The position of the lower leg is the first and most important thing to master.

Why do I have to keep my toe directly below my knee? Only in this position will you be balanced in your saddle. With any other, you will either have to hold onto the saddle with your hands, or grip tightly with your legs to keep from falling off, if your horse goes fast or does something unexpected.

What is meant by "balancing in the stirrups"? When you try this exercise, you will find that it is impossible unless your lower legs are in the correct position. To take the balance position, rest the tips of your fingers on the horse's neck, just in front of the withers. Look up and arch your back slightly, then bend forward until your belt buckle touches, or almost touches, the pommel of the saddle. Now put your weight on your stirrups, and raise your buttocks one or two inches out of the saddle. Then, when you are comfortably balanced (and you will probably have to make several attempts the first time you try this), take your hands off the horse's neck and put them on your waist.

Why is the rider in Fig. 66a bending his feet inward? This position of the foot helps keep the knee, thigh, and lower leg close to the horse.

What is the right position for my upper body when the horse is standing? Your upper body must be erect, chest up, back slightly arched, and shoulders neither forced unnaturally back nor allowed to slump. To attain this position, raise your hands

Fig. 67. Rider taking up reins

above your head as high as possible, stretching upward as you do so. Then lower them to your sides with palms out. The rider in Fig. 66a, you notice, is sitting in the very center of the saddle. There should be at least the width of the palm of your hand between the end of your buttocks and the cantle of the saddle.

How do I pick up and hold the reins? The reins are held in two hands except when the right hand is needed for something else, in playing polo, for example, or in roping cattle. To pick up the reins, first do as shown in Fig. 68, in which the rider has

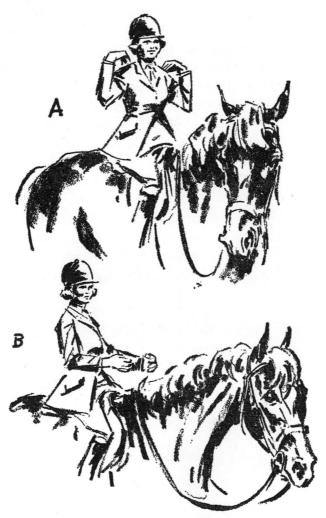

Fig. 68. Picking up reins

raised his hands over his head as he did in getting a good upper-body position. Fig. 68a shows him with the tips of his fingers resting on his shoulders. From this position, he brings his hands and arms forward and down (Fig. 68b). Notice that the wrists are slightly curved, as are the fingers. The rider looks almost as though he were going to put his arms around something. This position of the hands, neither completely flat nor completely vertical, is extremely important and should always be kept in mind.

Single reins are held as shown in Fig. 69. Double reins, used on Pelham and Weymouth bridles, are held as shown in the same picture. Notice that in both cases the extra end of the rein, called the "bight" (bite), which comes out at the back of the hand, is thrown forward and hangs to the right, with the thumbs of the rider on top. This keeps it from slipping.

Look again at Fig. 66a, showing a profile of the rider seated on a standing horse. Notice that you could draw a straight line from the rider's elbow along his forearm and the reins, ending at the bit. If the rider holds his hands correctly—not too close together or too far apart—this line would also appear straight if seen from above. It is most important always to maintain this straight line.

Why is the way I sit on a horse so important? When a rider sits correctly, as shown, his legs and seat are in contact with his

Snaffle→
Curb→

Bight

Fig. 69. Holding double reins   *Holding single reins*

mount. He himself is alert and prepared to change position suddenly if necessary. If he sits as if in a chair (Fig. 66b), and his horse suddenly plunges, it is as though someone had pulled the chair out from under him. With the correct seat, it is as if he were standing on the ground with his feet apart and knees bent and the horse were then brought up between them. With his legs, thighs, and seat close to the horse, he can feel every movement, and can also use them to indicate what he wants the horse to do. With the reins stretched and in a straight line, as shown, the rider will not have to shorten them, or raise or lower his hands when he wants to direct his horse. The lower back of the rider is very important, for he can use it to influence the horse in demanding many movements.

The rider's voice, his legs, hands, back, and the way he places his weight, are his "natural aids."

Using the Natural Aids

What is the most important natural aid? The legs are most important because they act on the hindquarters, where all progressive movements of the horse originate. Think of a tricycle. If you turn the handle bars, the front wheel will turn, but unless you work the pedals, which activate the back wheels, you won't get anywhere. Riding a horse is similar, in a way. The impulse of movement comes from the hindquarters. Merely pulling on the reins won't cause the horse to go.

Do I use both legs at once? Not always. Used together, your legs tell the horse to go faster or to stop, depending on what the hands do. Used singly, they tell the horse to move his hindquarters to one side or the other. Basically, the horse is taught to move away from the pressure of the leg. If you press with your right leg, your horse should move his hindquarters to the left; if you press with your left leg, he should move his hindquarters to the right.

Should I kick my legs hard? How hard you use your legs will depend on how sensitive your horse is, and on how good a rider you are. The good horseman starts with a slight pressure of the leg, and makes the pressure stronger and stronger until the horse obeys. If the horse is moving, the rider presses and then slackens the pressure with each step of the horse. This is called "using the legs in cadence with the movement." If the horse is standing and the rider wants him to move only his hindquarters without going forward, he gives a slight push with one leg, relaxing it the instant the horse takes a step with his hind legs in the desired direction. Then the rider gives another little push until the horse takes the next step, and so on.

How do I use my hands? We speak of the "passive hand," the "active hand," and the "fixed hand." A fourth, the "pulley hand," which is used in emergencies, should not be confused with the "pulling hand" (the hand of the beginner who tugs on his reins).

What is the passive hand? As the horse walks, his head bobs very noticeably. When he trots it bobs less, but at the canter there is again a great deal of head movement. If the rider holds his hands stiffly and rigidly, each time the horse moves his head he gets a jolt on the tender bars of his mouth, as the movement of his head brings him against the bit. To prevent this, the rider keeps his hands, wrists, and elbows relaxed, and follows the movement of the horse's head with his hands and arms. This is the passive hand and it is used when the horse is doing exactly what the rider wants him to do. There is still a slight tension on the reins, for without this, the rider would not be in communication with his horse. If the rider is using the passive hand, this slight tension should never vary.

The passive hand is very difficult to learn. The movements of the horse's body and head, as well as the shifting position of the rider's own body, make it hard to keep the same tension, never allowing the reins to get tight or to go completely slack.

What is the active hand? It is one way of using the hands to influence the horse. For the average rider on an average horse, it is the best method. With the active hand, the rider does not pull hard or steadily on the reins to influence the horse and cause him to turn, slow down, or stop. Instead, he gives little squeezes, relaxing slightly between each. The squeezes must be given in cadence with the stride, just as the leg signals are given.

What is the fixed hand? This is for more advanced riders and for horses in a higher stage of training. The rider "fixes" his hand in one position and then, by using his legs, causes the horse to push into the bit. As he pushes against the bit, the inflexibility of the fixed rein stops or turns him. Beginners or even intermediate riders cannot expect to master the fixed hand, for they must first learn to "coördinate" (work together) their hands and legs.

What is the pulley hand? Fig. 70 shows you the pulley hand. Used only in an emergency, to stop a runaway horse, it is very effective if used exactly as shown. The rider shortens up on both reins. He then grasps the horse's neck with his left hand, still holding onto the left rein. Throwing his own weight slightly back and down in the saddle, he lifts the right hand high and out to the side. In this way, he turns the horse's head to the right and also changes its angle so that the muzzle is pulled sideways and upward.

Fig. 70. Pulley hand

How is the back used? Do you like to swing? Do you know how to "pump," in order to make the swing go higher? This is exactly the way to use your back in riding. The French call it "stretching the loin." It enables the rider to sit tight to the saddle at the sitting trot and at the canter. It is used with the legs, or in place of them, to stop the horse, to get him to go faster, and with some of the more difficult special movements of the horse in advanced training.

How is the rider's weight used? Before starting, stopping, or turning, the rider indicates by a shift of his weight what he wants to do. If the horse is really well-trained, no other signal will be needed. In any event, the correct placing of the weight helps to balance the horse and makes it easier for him to do what you ask him. The general rule is that your weight is shifted in the direction of the movement you wish your horse to take. If you wish him to move to the right, press on your right stirrup, for example. If you wish him to slow down or stop, shift your weight slightly backward.

Walking

How do I get my horse to move forward? Get his attention by gathering your reins and holding them as shown, in a stretched position with a little tension on the bit. Now, squeeze your thighs and lower legs. If the horse is sensitive, he will move out at once. If he is sluggish, you may have to give a slight kick. As he moves out, let your hands become passive, following the movement of his head, as described earlier.

How do I stop my horse? First let your weight come back slightly and sit "deep in the saddle," as though you planned to sit right through it. Next, close your legs slightly on your horse and start using an active hand in cadence with the stride, as described. You may also "pump" slightly with your lower back. The use of the legs and back make the horse bring his hind legs under him, so that when he stops he will be standing properly and not all sprawled out.

Fig. 71a shows a horse that is halting as he should. The horse in Fig. 71b has not. Continue using the active hand, increasing

Fig. 71b. Horse stopping on forehand—all sprawled out

the pressure if the horse does not obey at once, until the horse has stopped. Then relax your aids and reward the horse with a pat on the neck.

Practice starting and stopping your horse again and again, allowing him to walk only a half-dozen steps, until he does it smoothly and quickly. Be sure not to lean forward, and be sure not to go on using your hands after he has come to a complete halt.

Sometimes a horse will swing his hind legs off the track in stopping, or turn his head and try to come into the center of the ring. If he swings his quarters, put a slightly harder pressure on both the rein and the leg on the side toward which he wants to move. For example, if you are travelling with the center of the ring on your left, and the horse keeps stopping with his hindquarters swung off the track to the left, use your left leg and hand more strongly. If he tries to turn in to the center, use your left leg and right hand more strongly.

How do I turn my horse? In turning, as in stopping, use three of the natural aids. As you approach the spot where you are planning to turn, step on the stirrup on that side and look in the direction in which you want to go. Then start using an active hand on the rein on that side. Use your legs, too. Otherwise, the horse will stop. Which leg to use more strongly depends on how sharp a turn you want to make. For a very sharp turn, carry the leg on the inside of the turn (the side toward which you are going) slightly back behind the girth and apply it strongly. Keep the opposite leg on the girth and use that, too, but not quite so strongly. If you want to make a half-circle, such as the one shown in the movement called the "half-turn" in Fig. 89 in Chapter 10, keep your inside leg on the girth, bring your outside leg slightly back, and use it strongly. If your horse does not respond to a light use of the hand, and changes direction, raise your hand slightly and carry it forward and to the side. Never drop your hand and try to pull the horse around by main force. The horse will brace his neck against this pull and, since he is stronger than the rider, will win the battle. By raising the hand and pulling slightly outward and up, the rider changes the position of the horse's head and breaks up his resistance.

Fig. 72. Turning the horse

How do I sit when my horse is walking? Sit erect, as you did when the horse was standing, but with the weight just a little more forward. To make the horse walk with longer steps, use your back with each step and keep your hands passive. To make him walk more slowly, use your back as before, but let your hands become slightly active. Give a tiny squeeze at each step with a quick release in between. Be sure to keep your legs under you and your head and eyes up. Test your lower leg position every so often by balancing in the stirrups, as you did when the horse was standing. Keep the ends of your fingers resting lightly on the horse's neck at first. Then, when you feel that your balance is good, put them on your waist, making your reins long enough so that you do not pull more strongly on the bit and cause him to stop.

Fig. 73. Correct position at walk

The Trot

How do I put my horse into a trot? When a horse trots, he holds his head higher than he does when he walks, so the first thing to do in demanding a trot is to shorten your reins. Hold the bight with one hand as you slide the other hand a few inches forward. Then shorten the other rein the same way. Next, apply your legs and back as you did to put the horse into motion. Be sure not to stiffen your wrists and elbows, but keep your hand passive. When the horse breaks into the trot, stop using the legs and back.

What do I do when the horse trots? There are two ways of riding at the trot. One is to sit the trot; the other is to do what we call *post* to the trot. The trot is a much rougher gait than the walk. At the walk, the horse plants one foot on the ground at a time, and there is little movement of the back. At the trot, he springs from one pair of diagonal legs to the other. First his left hind foot and his right forefoot strike the ground at the same

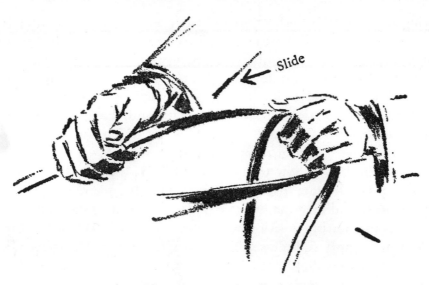

Slide

Fig. 74. Shortening reins before trotting

time; then his right hind foot and left forefoot. If he is trotting very fast, there is one point at which all four feet are off the ground. This movement causes the horse's back to bob up and down. Unless the rider has learned to relax his own back, and adjust his body to the bouncing of the horse, he will bump uncomfortably and make the horse uncomfortable, too. Yet the beginner can't help bouncing. This is one reason why a horse for boys or girls just learning to ride must not be too sensitive.

How do I keep from bouncing at the trot? You must use your back as you did to make the horse walk faster, although the cadence or rhythm will be much faster. Keeping your body erect, and your legs and hands steady, give little pushes as though you were pumping a swing. If you do this correctly, you will be able to keep close contact with the seat of the saddle. Be sure not to have your weight on the fleshy part of your buttocks. As you sit in the saddle, put your hand under you, and see whether you feel the two sharp points of your "sitting bones." If so, you are sitting correctly, for it is these which you must keep on the saddle. Your shoulders can be back slightly, but not so far that you have the feeling of leaning backward.

How do I learn to post? Posting, or rising up and down as the horse trots, is easy to learn and much more comfortable than sitting at the trot for both horse and rider, especially if the latter is just starting his riding career. There are three stages in learning to post. Start by putting a broomstick on the ground and standing on it. Your feet should be apart and bent inward; your knees should be bent. This is exactly how you sit on a horse. Next, straighten and then bend your knees in a quick rhythm to match the beat of the horse's feet which you hear when he is trotting: Up—down; up—down; up—down. If you have a friend who knows how to post, have him ride around you in a circle as you imitate his movement on the ground. Now mount your horse and take the balance position described on page 176. This is the posting position when you are "up." When you are "down," simply sink down in the saddle without changing the position of your shoulders or legs. Fig. 76 shows several mistakes often made by people learning to post.

What do I do with my hands when I post at the trot? Learn to relax your elbows and keep your hands steady. Extend the little finger of each hand and lightly touch the end of it to the horse's neck, just in front of the saddle. Now, as you rise up and down, try not to let your little fingers bounce off the horse's neck. You will find that you will have to straighten your elbows and push your fingers down slightly each time you rise out of the saddle.

Fig. 75. Posting to the trot—the "up" position

Rider too far forward
Legs too far back
Too "crouched"

Rider sitting up too straight
Rising too high
Weight behind the "balance"

Fig. 76. Common mistakes in posting

Even at the sitting trot, it is hard to keep the hands steady, so also practice the same exercise when you are learning to sit the trot without bouncing.

When I am posting and I want my horse to walk, what do I do? Take up the sitting-trot position, described earlier. Then use your aids as you would to make your horse halt from a walk.

Is it better to be going up when the horse's right shoulder moves forward, or when his left moves forward? This is a good question, and one which many riders, even quite experienced ones, ignore. When your horse moves his left foreleg and his right hind leg forward, he is said to be moving on his "left diagonal." His next step will be on his "right diagonal." When the rider rises as the horse is planting his left foreleg, he is said to be "posting on the left diagonal." When you rise out of your saddle, you take the weight off the horse's back momentarily. When you sit, you make it harder for the horse. If you always post on the same diagonal, the muscles which the horse uses when you are sitting down in the saddle will become more developed than the rest. Your horse will find it hard to trot evenly when you change diagonals, and will not be as well-balanced on both diagonals when he moves in circles. In short, he will become "one-sided." Even if most of your riding is done on roads and trails without sharp turns, don't post too long on the same diagonal. Keep changing from one to the other.

A second reason for learning to post on both diagonals is to help the horse balance on turns. In going around a corner, the inside hind leg acts as a "post of support" under the horse, and bears the major part of the weight of the animal. To make it easier, the rider should be going up when the inside hind leg and the outside (the one next to the wall of a ring) foreleg are planted. In other words, the rider posts on the "outside diagonal" when riding in a circle or in a rectangular area. When the center of the arena or field is on his left, he posts on the right diagonal. If he changes direction, he posts on the left diagonal.

How can I tell when I am posting on the left or on the right diagonal? Practice first at the walk, when your horse is moving slowly. Watch the action of his shoulder blades. As his left

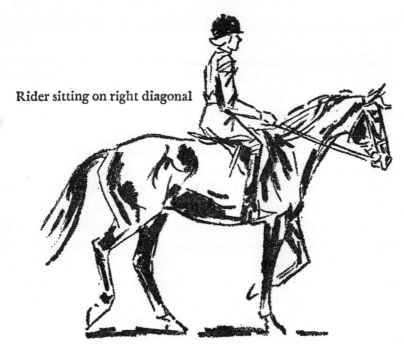

Rider sitting on right diagonal

Fig. 77. Posting to trot

shoulder blade moves forward, rise to the balance position and hold it until you see his right shoulder blade begin to move forward. Then sink back in the saddle. Repeat this until you can tell immediately when the left is moving forward, and learn to rise with it. You are now posting on the left diagonal.

Put the horse into a trot and do the same thing, watching the right shoulder blade rise as it goes forward, and sink when it comes back. Be careful to lower only your eyes and not your head as you practice this. As soon as you are sure you can tell the difference by watching the shoulders, try not looking, and see if you can tell the difference by feel. Pick up a trot, start to post, and without looking down, decide which diagonal you are on. Then check by looking. Fig. 75 shows rider posting on right diagonal.

The Canter and Gallop

What is the difference between the canter and the gallop? "Canter" is a fairly recent term which has come to mean a slow gallop. The movement of the horse's legs are the same in both gaits. The gallop is a three-beat gait, with one beat sounding louder than the other two: PLUckety—PLUckety—PLUckety. In galloping and cantering, the horse is said to "lead" with one or the other pair of legs. In Fig. 78, he is leading with his left front and left hind legs. He is on the "left lead." In Fig. 79 one horse is leading with the right hind and right fore and is on the right lead. The other horse is what we call "disunited." He is "cross-cantering," leading with his left fore- and his right hind legs. His left hind leg is sprawled out behind him, and he has no post of support under his left haunch. If he is turned sharply to the left he will fall. You can tell whether your horse is disunited at the canter, because his gait will be very rough. Stop him and start over again.

How do I put my horse into the canter or gallop? In an arena, hall, or field where the horse will be travelling in a circle or rectangle, be sure that he takes up the canter on the "inside" lead. This will be the right lead if the horse is moving to the right, with the center of the arena on the right, and the left lead if he is moving to the left. Sitting erectly at the walk, gather up your reins and press lightly with your legs. This will "collect" your horse, and tell him that you want him to do something dif-

Fig. 78.

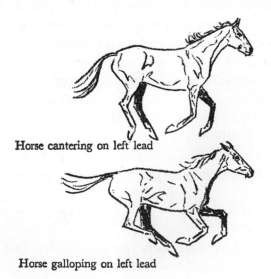

Horse cantering on left lead

Horse galloping on left lead

ferent. He will hold his head higher and shorten his back by bringing his hind legs farther under him.

Suppose you are moving to the left. Carry your right leg slightly back so that it is a little behind the girth. At the same time, increase the pressure on the right hand, raising it a bit. Now, when you feel that your horse is animated and ready to start, give a strong push with your back and with your right leg or heel. Don't let your shoulders come forward, but put them back for an instant. You should feel as if you are pushing the horse out from under you and lifting his "forehand." He shouldn't "fall into" the canter or gallop with his head down, but should reach up and out with his forelegs, and bring his back legs well under. As soon as he takes the canter, straighten the horse on the track by stopping, pushing with your outside leg, and by bending his head on the corners in the direction in which he is going.

This method of taking up the canter is called "the gallop depart on the lateral aids." We say "lateral" (side) aids because you have used the leg and hand on the same side. It is the method used by most beginning riders, and the one used in training the young horse. A more advanced and better way of doing this, on the diagonal aids, is in the next chapter.

Fig. 79.

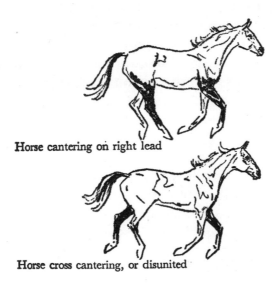

Horse cantering on right lead

Horse cross cantering, or disunited

How do I sit when I canter? Sit exactly as you do at the walk, but use your back very, very strongly, to keep from bouncing off the saddle. You must really feel as though you are pumping your swing very high. At first, in order to do this, you will have to let your shoulders rock backward and forward, but later you will be able to use your lower back and keep your shoulders erect and still. Learning to canter is like learning to ride a bicycle. It is a question of balance.

Don't try to learn the canter until you are perfectly at ease at the walk and trot, either with or without reins and stirrups. Practice both posting and sitting at the trot without your stirrups. Then learn to do the same with your hands on your waist. If you have a friend riding with you, try this: knot your reins so that they do not hang down too long, fall in behind your friend, and let your horse follow at the different gaits while you ride without stirrups and reins.

Other Exercises

What are suppling exercises? These are gymnastic movements (Fig. 80) to help make you strong, agile, and able to regain your balance when you feel you are losing it and may fall off. Practice them while the horse is standing, at the walk, and later at the trot. Finally, when you feel secure at the canter without stirrups and reins, do them at the canter.

Is there anything else to practice while I am still in the basic stage of riding? Practice dismounting, or vaulting off the horse when he is moving. Do this as you would with the horse standing, but first, take both feet out of your stirrups. Then, holding onto the mane and the pommel of the saddle, throw yourself off the horse. Be careful not to touch his haunches with your legs, and to land on your feet, facing in the direction in which he is moving. Practice this first while the horse is standing, then at the walk, later at the trot, and finally at the canter. Learn to come off quickly at any time, and land on your feet, still holding onto your reins, without having to think about it. Of course you will not attempt these things until you have mastered the basic principles.

Fig. 80. *Suppling exercises*

IO

Advanced Riding

Now let us talk about techniques that will carry you far beyond being satisfied with getting your horse to go in the direction of your choice at the gait you wish. This includes training your horse as well as improving your own riding technique.

Security of the Rider

What is the easiest and quickest way to acquire a really secure seat? Ride at all gaits without reins and without stirrups, until you are independent of them.

Is it easier to ride in a saddle without reins and stirrups, to ride bareback, or on a saddle-pad? It is easiest on a saddle-pad with attachments for a surcingle—a long strap with a buckle. The surcingle goes all the way around the horse, and buckles at the girth line. (See Fig. 81.) In putting the pad on, be sure to throw the buckle end over the horse and bring it up under him to fasten it.

Riding bareback is the next easiest way. Riding in a saddle without stirrups and reins is hardest, for the saddle is slippery and the rider does not sit so close to his horse.

How should I sit when I ride without stirrups and reins? Sit exactly as you do normally, on your sitting bones, your upper body erect, head and eyes up. There are two good ways to carry your legs. With the relaxed leg shown in Fig. 82, you will learn to ride entirely on balance. You should ride for many hours this way; it is comfortable and not tiring. With the fixed leg, shown

Fig 81. *Horse fitted with pad and surcingle*

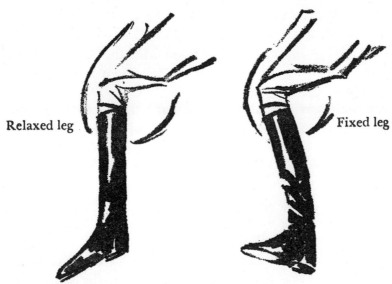

Relaxed leg   Fixed leg

Fig. 82.

in the same picture, the position is the same as if you were riding with stirrups. Although this is a good exercise for developing strong muscles, it is very tiring and should not be overdone.

Refining the Aids

What is meant by "refining the aids"? This horseman's term means that with practice you can learn to use your aids—hands, legs, body, and weight—so lightly and exactly that your horse obeys smoothly and willingly. Coördination of the aids, knowing just when to use each one in relation to the other, and when to stop using them is necessary, too.

How does coördination of the aids make the horse go better? Remember the principle of reward and punishment used in training the horse. Reward does not necessarily mean praise or a bit of carrot. Punishment does not always mean a blow with the whip or a sharp dig with the spurs. In training the horse, use of the aids can serve as a slight punishment, and relaxation of the aids as a reward.

How do I know how strongly to use my aids and when to stop using them? This depends on how quickly the horse obeys. If you want your horse to go forward, to turn or stop, use the active hand, the back, and the legs, very lightly. If the horse does not obey, use the aids more strongly. The instant the horse *begins* to obey, relax the aids. This gives him the reward that he is seeking and makes him willing to obey even more quickly the next time.

Are there any special exercises that help me to coördinate my aids? There are several. The first, and easiest, is learning to make your horse move backward. This is called "backing up" or, more correctly, "reining back." Start with your horse standing parallel to a fence or wall of the arena. Gather your reins and apply your legs slightly, as though you wanted him to move forward. Keep the light pressure on the legs, but increase the pressure on the reins until he takes one step backward. The instant you feel him *begin* to move backward, relax your aids completely. Then demand another step in the same way. If your horse does not move straight backward, but swings his quarters off the track toward the center, correct this, just as you did in teaching him to halt on a straight line, by using the inside hand and leg (the ones toward the center of the ring) more strongly than the others. When a horse moves backward at the walk, he does not lift and plant one foot at a time, he lifts and plants the diagonal feet, just as though he were at a trot.

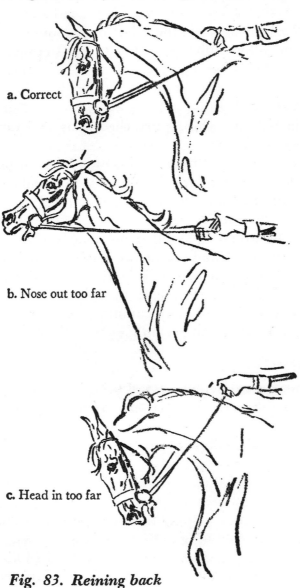

a. Correct

b. Nose out too far

c. Head in too far

Fig. 83. Reining back

When you are teaching a young horse to rein back and learning to coördinate your aids, ask for four to six steps, with a complete stop between each. After the last, move forward again. Next, ask for several steps without the complete halt, *but still relax the aids completely between steps.* The instant you feel the horse obeying and coming to a halt, use them again so that he merely hesitates, and then moves backward another step. As he takes the final step, use the legs a little more strongly. Use the back, and follow with the hands so that he steps forward again without completely halting.

Artificial Aids

These include the whip, spurs, checkreins, and various types of martingales.

Is it cruel to use a whip and spurs on a horse or pony? It is not cruel if the whip and spurs are used as aids, and not as severe punishments. In fact, a rider wearing blunt spurs punishes a sluggish or phlegmatic horse far less by the light pressure of his spurs, than he would by flogging his mount with his legs and heels. A beginner should never wear spurs, but it is all right for him to carry a whip or switch in his hand and use it lightly, if his horse refuses to move out on the leg pressure. Whips can and should be used for punishment in curing horses of vices such as biting and kicking, but are no substitute for proper training.

Rein Effects

Rein effects are different ways of using the reins to cause the horse to move in various directions. Don't confuse them with the various ways of using the hands.

How many rein effects are there? There are three fundamental ones: the "leading rein," the "indirect rein," and the "direct rein of opposition." Two others are combinations of these—the "indirect rein of opposition in front of the withers," and the "indirect rein of opposition behind the withers." These terms mays sound confusing until you look at Fig. 84.

What is the leading rein? The rider has carried his left hand a little forward, and to the side, and the horse has turned his head in that direction and is about to change direction to the left. This is the rein effect you have already learned to use in going around a corner, or in turning your horse into the center of the arena, before dismounting. If your aids are refined enough and your horse sufficiently well-trained, you will not actually have to carry your hand forward and to the side. By using an active left hand, a shift of weight to the left, and strong legs, you can get your horse to look to the left and turn in that direction.

What is the indirect rein? With the indirect rein, the horse turns his head one way, and moves his body the opposite way. Some people confuse this with the neck-reining used with the Western-trained horse, but there is a difference. In neck-reining, the rider holds the reins in one hand. If he wants to go to the right, he carries his hand to the right. When the horse feels the touch of the left rein on his neck, he simply turns to the right, just as he would if he had been turned to the right on a leading right rein. The indirect rein accomplishes a different

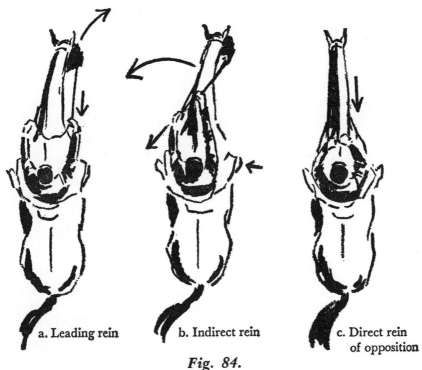

a. Leading rein   b. Indirect rein   c. Direct rein
of opposition

Fig. 84.

purpose. (Study Fig. 85.) The rider has brought his left hand a little forward, and has carried it to the right until it is above the mane of the horse. In so doing, he has bent the horse's head slightly to the left, but, since the rein is exerting a pressure toward the *right*, the horse does not turn in the direction in which he is looking, nor does he *turn* to the right. Instead, he *steps* toward the right. With the left indirect rein, the rider has shifted his weight to the right (for this is the direction in which he wants the horse to move), and is applying his left leg strongly at the girth.

When is the indirect rein used? It is used a great deal in advanced movements. For every-day riding, especially in an enclosed field or arena, it is used to cause the horse to move out

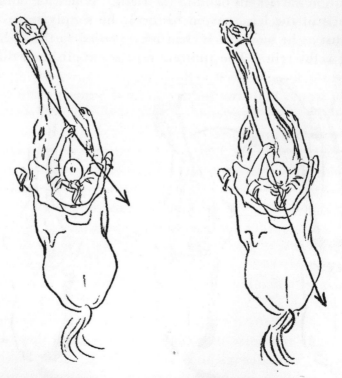

a. Left indirect rein of opposition in front of the withers   b. Left indirect rein of opposition behind the withers

Fig. 85.

into the corners of the arena, and still keep his head bent in the direction in which he is going.

What is the direct rein of opposition? In the different reins of opposition, what the rider is opposing is the forward movement of the horse. In the ordinary, or direct rein of opposition, sometimes called just the "direct rein," the rider pulls straight back. This is used to change from a faster gait to a slower one, or to halt the horse completely. You can also use opposition with one leading-rein effect, and make your horse both turn and slow down.

What is the difference between the indirect rein of opposition in front of the withers, and the indirect rein behind the withers? (See Fig. 85.) In the indirect rein of opposition in front of the withers, the movement of the rein is toward the rider's hip. It is a less severe use than when the direction of the rein is behind the withers and toward the horse's hip. This last rein effect is used in only a few movements, and in cases where the horse does not obey the less severe rein effect.

When would I use the indirect rein of opposition in front of the withers? The most common use of this rein effect is when the rider wants his horse both to move over and bend into a corner and, at the same time, to slow down. When two people riding side by side are rounding a corner, the inside rider, having a shorter turn to make, uses the inside rein of opposition in front of the withers. This slows his horse down just enough so that the outside rider does not have to hurry to keep abreast.

Schooling Movements

What are "schooling movements"? These are exercises to refine your own aids and to make the horse willing, strong, and flexible. They can be simple movements, such as reining back and bending the horse into the corners, or more difficult ones, such as the "shoulder-in" and the "two-track," described later in this chapter. Some people call these schooling movements "dressage," which is a French term for "training." The word dressage, to many people, however, implies only very advanced movements.

The first group of schooling movements, or "basic dressage," consists of "rating the horse"; "flank movements"; "change of hands" (sometimes called "change of rein"); "simple transitions" (from one movement to another, including the "simple change of lead"; "the pivots," "half-turns," "half-turns in reverse"; "circles"; "volts," "serpentine," and "figure eights.")

Rating the Horse

What is meant by "rating" the horse? There are three forms, or *phases,* of each of the three natural gaits—the walk, the trot, and the gallop. The first phase is the ordinary gait, the speed at which the horse moves naturally with light contact of the bit. The second is the "extended" or "strong" gait, in which the horse takes longer steps (though without changing the cadence or rhythm). The third is the "collected" gait. To "rate" a horse means to have him take up some phase of the gaits and maintain it until we ask him to change to another.

How do I make a horse move at the strong phases of the gaits? The horse must be induced to shift his weight forward, and take very long strides with both his front and back legs. To do this, he has to drop his head slightly and lean a little on the bit. The longer his strides, the more he will lean on the bit. Some horses can be trained to take up the extended phases of the various gaits easily. Others, because of lack of muscle in the haunches and loins, find it very hard. To get a strong walk, use a strongly active hand with each step, and push hard with the back. For a strong trot and a strong gallop, drop the hands lower than usual and fix them on the shoulders of the horse. Now, pushing with your legs and back, try to get the horse to lower his head and push against the bit.

How can I tell when my horse is taking up a strong phase of a gait, and when he is just going faster? Notice the cadence or rhythm. At the ordinary trot, for example, the beat of the gait is one—two; one—two. At the strong trot the beat should still be one—two; one—two; but, though the horse is obviously moving faster than he was, the beat should remain the same. You shouldn't have to count faster.

Fig. 86. Strong phase of trot

Watch the horse's legs. They will be flung forward with an instant of hesitation before each is planted. Without leaning over, you will see the front feet of the horse as he extends and plants them. At the ordinary trot, you will not see them.

Trot once around the ring or field at the ordinary trot, counting the number of strides the horse takes in completing the circle, and then counting the strides again as you go around on a strong trot. There should be many *fewer* strides at the strong trot, for the horse will be taking longer steps and won't have to take so many to cover the same distance.

At the walk, have someone on the ground examine the track and see if, in stepping, the horse plants his back foot well in front of his front foot on the same side. As we learned before, this is called the *"natural overreach."* Both at the walk and at the trot, this length of the overreach should increase when the horse takes up the strong phase of the gait. At the strong phase of the canter, the length of the whole stride should increase. A stride is the distance from the point at which one front foot of the horse touches the ground to the point where it touches again.

What is the collected form of the gaits? At full collection, the horse's length from nose-tip to buttock-point has been perceptibly shortened. Think of a coil or spring. The tighter you compress it, the more force it has when released. This is what happens when you "collect" a horse. You confine his forces in a shorter area. The strength which he used at the strong or extended form of the gait went into long steps and much forward movement. Now that same impulsion or strength is used to carry his body lightly, so that he moves along the ground like a feather. For light collection, the rider must use the aids more strongly and have them coördinated.

Why do we practice rating the horse? Practice at rating the horse develops his "longitudinal flexion." We ask him to go from full extension, with his silhouette as long as possible, to collection, in which his silhouette is at its shortest. This also improves the ability of the rider to feel what his horse is doing, to interpret what he feels, and to influence his horse. The rider must also, in feeling, learn to anticipate. If he pushes the horse on too much at the extended trot, the horse will break into a gallop. If he holds him in too much at the collected trot, the horse will break the cadence and walk.

What are "flank movements"? In the flank movement, the horse turns sharply on his center. The rider uses the leading rein effect, putting his weight on the inside stirrup, and using the inside leg just behind the girth.

It is fun to practice flank movements when riding in a group. Take the track with about four feet of space between the nose of one horse and the tail of the horse in front of him. Choose a leader and have him call, "By the left (or right) flank—now!" The "now" must be given when all the riders are in line along the long wall of the arena or field. At the command, each rider turns his horse as described, and then rates him so that, in crossing, the line of horses stays exactly abreast of the leader. As they approach the opposite wall, the leader again gives the command for a flank movement and the riders find themselves once more riding in a column (one behind the other).

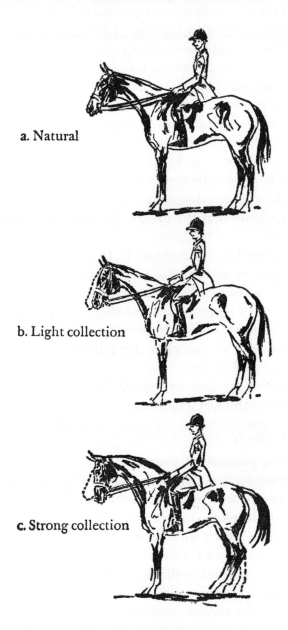

a. Natural

b. Light collection

c. Strong collection

Fig. 87. Collection

What is meant by a change of hands? It is not a good idea, of course, to ride always in the same direction when going around and around in an enclosed space. Change your direction often so that your horse will be equally developed on both hands. One way of doing this is to "change hands," or "change rein." Each rider, after he has ridden along a short wall of the arena, and turned the corner and gone one or two horse lengths beside the long wall, turns and rides on a long diagonal across the arena. When he reaches the opposite long wall, he should be the same distance from the corner as when he left the wall to start the change. If he is at a trot, as he passes the center of the arena marked X, he changes diagonal by sitting down or balancing in his stirrups. If he is at the canter, he changes from one lead to the other.

What is meant by a "transition"? In riding, it means a change from one form, or phase, of a gait to another form or phase of the same gait, or from one gait to a different gait. Sometimes it means a change of direction of movement, such as a change from posting on the left diagonal to posting on the right diagonal, or from the left lead to the right lead in executing a change of hands, as described above.

How should transitions be made? They should be as smooth, prompt, and rhythmical as possible.

Curving Figures

What is the purpose of practicing curving movements? All the movements, such as circles and half-turns, in which the horse must bend his spine in a curve, teach him to balance himself on curves and to develop "lateral flexion." Think of the horse's spine as a switch which we can bend in a curve. If the horse is to become well-balanced on turns, and able to travel in a circle correctly, he must develop this lateral flexion, or ability to bend his spine in a curve.

In executing all these schooling figures at the trot, the rider sits the trot so that he can use his back as an aid, and so that he can feel what the horse is doing.

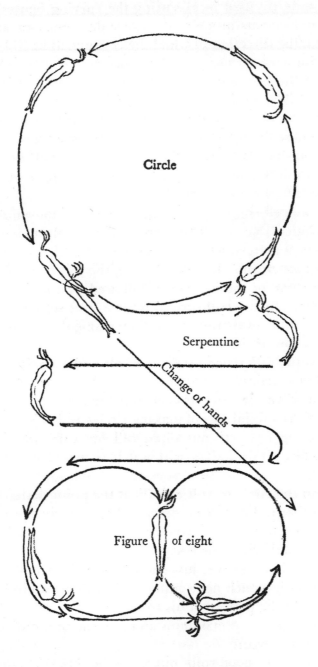

Circle

Serpentine

Change of hands

Figure of eight

Fig. 88. Schooling movements

What aids are used in executing the curving figures? In all curving movements in which the horse does not look and move away from the direction in which he is going, as he did in bending out into the corner, use the leading rein and put a little weight on the inside stirrup. If the horse tends to go around the circle stiffly, with his haunches pushed off the track and his spine straight use the inside leg (the one toward the center of the curve) against the girth, with the outside leg used strongly and well behind the girth. If he tries to make the circle smaller, use just the inside leg until you have him back where he belongs, then return to the use of both legs.

Study the patterns of these different curving movements carefully. Notice that the half-turn and the half-turn-in-reverse both follow a pattern which looks something like part of a cone filled with ice cream. In the half-turn, the feet of the horse first draw the curve of the ice cream, followed by the diagonal line of the cone. In the half-turn-in-reverse, you start with the tip of the cone, pull away from the wall on a long diagonal, and then curve back toward it.

What is the difference between a volt and a circle? A circle usually has a diameter of about sixty feet. A volt is a smaller circle, not more than twenty feet in diameter.

Is there any special way of making circles and volts? Dressage and schooling competitions often call for volts and circles at various gaits. The judges will watch to see that you do the following:

Take up the circle or volt exactly at the point designated and return to that point, having described an exactly round figure. The figure must be evenly balanced so that the two halves of the circle are exactly the same size.

Bend your horse's spine just enough so that the horse looks in the direction in which he is going, and so that his hind feet follow exactly in the pattern of his front feet.

See that your horse maintains an even, smooth, cadenced gait throughout the figure.

Many people do good volts, but when they are asked to execute a circle which uses exactly half the arena, they ride it as though it were a square.

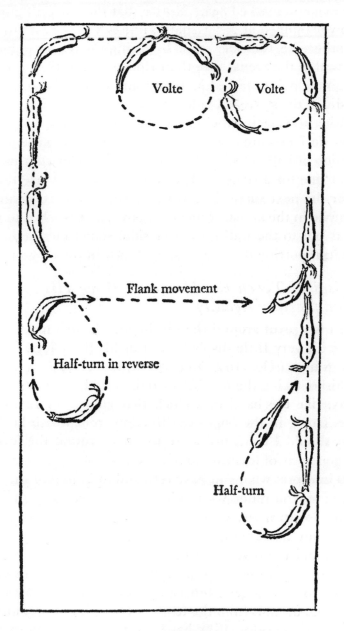

Fig. 89. Schooling movements

Is there a right and wrong way to execute a figure eight? Look at the diagram marked 89a. Notice that the correct figure eight is two volts joined at X. Usually, unless a judge asks to have it done otherwise, the rider starts by facing the center point of the short wall of the arena. He then rides a volt to the right, comes through the point marked X, being sure that he is facing exactly as he did at the start, and rides another volt to the left. He ends by halting at X, facing the center of the short wall.

How do I execute a serpentine? Think of a serpentine as a succession of half-volts. Between each, the rider continues on a straight line for a stride or two, then bends his horse the other way for the next succeeding volt. Serpentines are always done lengthwise in the arena. Sometimes the rider is asked to ride all the way out to the wall on either side; sometimes he uses only the central portion of the arena, as shown in the diagram.

Exercises to Teach the Horse to Move His Hindquarters Readily

What is a pivot around the forehand? In this movement the horse, with very little displacement of his front legs, moves his hind legs in a circle. In a full pivot, he moves all the way around and finishes facing the way he started. In a half-pivot, he moves halfway, like the hand of a clock that goes from 12 to 6, and finishes facing in the opposite direction from which he started.

Why should I teach my horse to pivot around the forehand? It is a good way of learning to feel what the horse is doing under you, to interpret what you have felt, and to influence your horse. In doing so, you refine your aids. Unless you use your aids exactly: not too strongly, or too lightly; nor for too long or too short a time, your horse will not pivot. Also, it makes your horse obedient and improves your control over him. The third reason is a practical one. Suppose you are riding across country and want to close a gate, but cannot quite reach it because the horse comes up to it from the front. There is not room to bring him in from the side. If he has been taught to pivot, it will be easy for you to cause him to move his hindquarters toward the gate so that he is standing close beside it.

How do I teach my horse to pivot? Begin by standing two feet

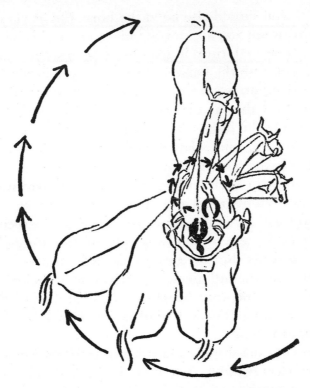

Fig. 90. Pivot around the forehand

in from the wall of the arena, or beside a fence. Collect your horse with your reins and legs. Now, put slightly more pressure on your right rein, and at the same time, apply your right leg slightly behind the girth. The *instant* you feel your horse begin to move his hindquarters to the left, stop using the aids strongly, but do not relax the legs and reins entirely. When he is again standing still, having taken one step with his hind feet and having turned his right front foot more or less in place, demand another step the same way. When you have completed the half-pivot in this way, let the horse rest a moment, then pivot with his hindquarters moving to the right. You should finish facing the same way you started, and in the same place.

Do most horses learn to pivot easily? Horses usually learn to pivot very readily, once they get the idea. With slow ones, it may be necessary to take a small stick and tap lightly on the flank above your heel, at the same time that you apply the heel, as described. You should also bend the horse's head very strongly to the right (when you are causing him to move his haunches to the left). The first time it may even be necessary to have a helper on foot push the horse's haunches as you apply your aids. Some sensitive horses get excited and try to whirl around. Be ready to correct this by quickly applying the opposite aids (if you are moving the horse's haunches to the left, using the right rein and right leg, immediately apply the left leg and bend the horse's head to the left with the left leading rein).

Some horses, in their excitement, try to go backward. To correct this, close both legs and push with your back.

The pivot will teach you how necessary it is in executing any movement with a given use of the aids, to have the opposite or assisting aids ready, in case they are needed.

Don't attempt the full pivot, which is done in the center of the arena, until you and your horse can do a half-pivot really well, stepping smoothly in the desired direction with only a brief hesitation between steps.

Are there any other movements which train the horse to move his hindquarters readily? Yes, there is the "leg-yield," in which the horse in motion, gives way, or yields his haunches to the rider's spur or leg. Look at Fig. 91. Here, the horse's hind feet do not follow in the track of his front feet, as he moves along the wall of the arena. Instead, the haunches are pushed a little off the track toward the center of the arena, and follow a track of their own. If the leg-yield is correctly done, when the horse is moving on the left hand as shown, each foot travels a path of its own instead of the hind foot stepping in the track of the front.

How do I make my horse leg-yield? Do not attempt the leg-yield until your horse can pivot on his hindquarters. To introduce the movement, ride along the short wall of the arena or field until you reach the corner. Take one step in the new direction on the long wall, and then check the horse with your hands to keep him from continuing on the same path. At the same time, apply your outside leg (the one toward the wall) strongly, to make him move his haunches to the side. Unless you coördinate your hands and legs exactly, you will find that your horse keeps running into the wall or proceeds in fits and starts instead

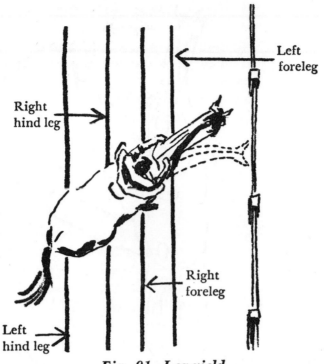

Right
hind leg

Left
foreleg

Right
foreleg

Left
hind leg

Fig. 91. Leg yield

of stepping smoothly. Just keep trying, a few steps at a time, stopping to reward your horse with a pat on the neck and a few encouraging words each time he does well. In all movements of this kind, be sure to practice going in both directions, not just in one.

Exercises to Mobilize the Forehand

What is the next exercise I should learn? You must next teach your horse to step to one side or the other with his front legs, just as in the previous exercises you taught him to step to the side with his hind feet. The first of these is the pivot on the hind-quarters, shown in Fig. 92.

How do I teach my horse to pivot around his hindquarters? Again, start beside the wall. The aim is to have your horse turn so that his inside hind foot, although it may be picked up and put down again, should not move from its original spot. Mean-while, the horse, crossing one leg in front of the other, makes a

Fig. 92. Pivot around hindquarters

half circle around this inside hind foot. On a pivot around the
hindquarters, to the left, the rider uses his right leg strongly,
behind the girth, to prevent the horse from swinging his haunches
to the right, and so turning on his center. He keeps his left foot
on the girth to assist. Both reins are used, but the right one pre-
dominates, and is used as an indirect rein of opposition in front
of the withers. The left assists as a leading rein. The diagram
shows clearly what to do with the reins. Your weight should be
on your own left hip. Only one step at a time is asked for, with a
full halt between each. Later the horse will learn to step
smoothly around without stopping. The worst fault, in the
eyes of the judges, is for a horse to step backward, so be prepared

for this and use both legs and back strongly in time to prevent it.

Are there any other movements which teach the horse to move his forehand independently? "Broken lines," shown in Fig. 93, is another such movement. The pattern is somewhat like a series of V's or W's. At each turn, the rider swings the forehand of his horse on a curve while holding the hindquarters to a smaller curve. The aids used are the same as those described already, but the horse continues moving and does not halt be-

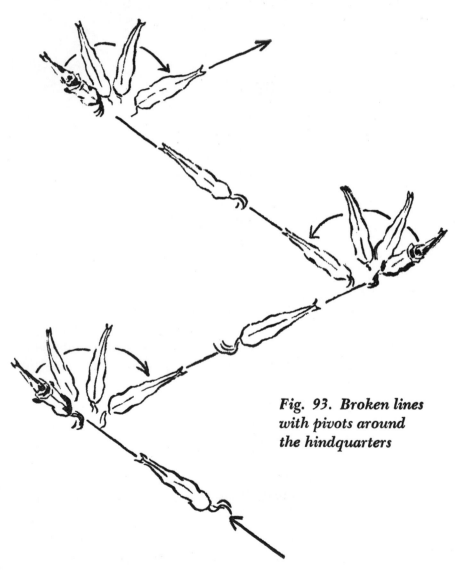

Fig. 93. Broken lines with pivots around the hindquarters

tween each step. You will know when you are doing the figure correctly by the sensation of swinging with your horse as though he were a gate. Broken lines may be practiced at the walk and the sitting trot.

Another exercise for "mobilizing" (causing to move) the forehand is to practice circles with the haunches "ranged in."

More Difficult Schooling Figures

What is the "shoulder-in"? This is a very difficult movement for the horse. Its purpose is to increase the lateral flexion.

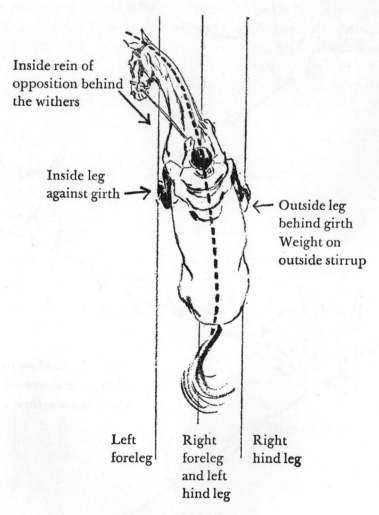

Inside rein of opposition behind the withers

Inside leg against girth →

← Outside leg behind girth Weight on outside stirrup

Left foreleg

Right foreleg and left hind leg

Right hind leg

Fig. 93a. Shoulder-in

To do the "shoulder-in," cross the short wall of the arena and turn the corner onto the long wall. After completing the turn, take one step toward the center as though you were going to do a volt, check your horse with your reins, and then cause him to travel along the wall in a curved position. To do this, use the inside rein of opposition behind the withers, the inside leg against the girth, the outside leg behind the girth, and the weight on the outside stirrup. Think of your inside leg as being the point around which the horse is bent, and be sure that his head and neck are bent no more than the rest of his spine.

Are there any other movements which horses and riders who compete in Intermediate Dressage Events and Schooling Rides must know? There are the "two-track" and the "counter-gallop." Fig. 94a shows the two-track, done correctly. In this movement, the horse moves to the side and forward at the same time. His spine remains parallel to the long wall of the arena.

Fig. 94a. Half pass (two track) or traversal correctly executed

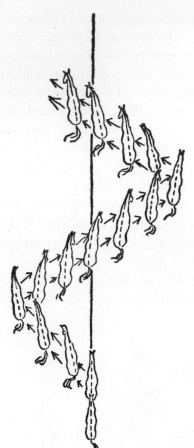

*Fig. 94b. Counter change
of hands on the
half pass or traversal*

His head, if bent at all, should bend in the direction of the movement and only very slightly. To two-track, the rider must have very finely coördinated aids, for what he does is to alternate those used in demanding the two kinds of pivots. First he moves the forehand, then the hindquarters, then the forehand, etc., so that the horse crosses both his hind and his front feet, yet continues to move forward. The worst and most common fault is to bend the horse's head the wrong way, as shown in Fig. 95.

The "counter-change of hands on the two-track" is a series of changes of direction made while executing the two-track. Although it is difficult, many horses that have learned the two-track, learn the counter-change very easily.

What is the counter-gallop? The horse canters or gallops a circle to the right on the outside or left lead instead of on the inside lead, and vice versa. Horses in advanced stages of training are taught the counter-gallop to give them balance, before they are taught the flying change of lead (when the horse goes from one lead to the opposite lead without coming down to a trot).

(Horse's head turned *away* from direction of movement)

Fig. 95. Half pass incorrectly executed

Fig. 96. Counter gallop

11

Jumping

Why Learn to Jump?

Many people think of jumping as something dangerous, and see no reason for it unless the rider plans to hunt or to enter jumping or hunting classes in competition at shows. Actually, jumping over obstacles of three feet or less is not so dangerous as many other forms of riding. The rider is forced to be more attentive and careful, and, in jumping low obstacles, he increases the security of his own seat. He learns to adjust his balance to sudden movements of the horse. When you are first

Take-off   Flight   Descen

learning to ride, even the ordinary gaits seem difficult and require effort and attention. Later you reach a stage at which you feel at home at the ordinary walk, trot, and canter. Then comes a day when, as you are riding on the trail, there is a sudden gust of wind and dead leaves rustle. The horse jumps sideways. This is called "shying." Unless you have accustomed yourself to such sudden movements, you are apt to lose your balance and either fall off or cling with your hands and heels to keep yourself on.

How the Horse Jumps

Fig. 98 shows the horse "approaching" the jump with head up, and ears pricked forward. On the "take off," he gathers himself and, with his head stretched out, pushes off the ground with his hindquarters. In the "flight," his back is arched. Then, as his hindquarters pass over the jump, in order to balance himself and keep from turning a somersault, the horse raises his head, only to drop it again as he lands. Notice that in landing, his front feet touch the ground and leave it again in what we call the "departure," before the back feet reach the ground.

Fig. 97. Movements of horse in jumping

Landing

Departure

Fig. 98. The approach

The Rider's Seat over Jumps

If the rider comes back on the horse, landing on the sensitive loins and jerking him in the mouth, the horse will soon refuse to jump any longer. The beginning rider, therefore, should balance in his stirrups from the beginning of the approach until the

Fig. 99. Point of departure

horse has completed the departure. The horse should be so well-trained that he will take a low jump calmly, and without having to be controlled by the rider. This permits the rider to hold on to a neckstrap, as shown in Fig. 100. Only in this way can he be sure not to hurt his horse as he learns to maintain his own balance.

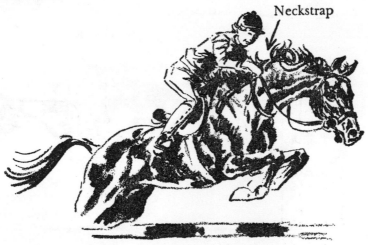

Neckstrap

Fig. 100. Neckstrap used in jumping

How soon should I start jumping? As soon as you can ride at the walk, trot, and canter without using your reins or stirrups, you are ready to begin jumping.

What equipment will I need? For the first few lessons, you will need two jumping standards and four long jump rails. The jumping standards, constructed as shown in Fig. 101, must be so designed that the height of the jump can be raised 3 inches at a time. Make a series of slots in the post and then have the blacksmith make you several pairs of "buckets," like those shown. These slide over the post and fit into the slots. The post should be a 4 x 4-inch timber. The jump rails are also made of 4 x 4's, the edges of which have been planed off. They should be 14 feet long. Both standards and rails should be painted. Divide

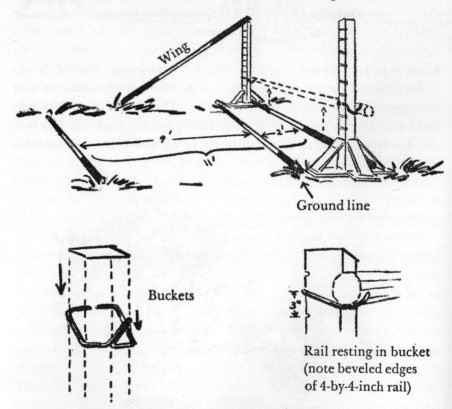

Wing

Ground line

Buckets

Rail resting in bucket
(note beveled edges
of 4-by-4-inch rail)

*Fig. 101. Jumping standards with four rails
in position to begin jumping*

the rails into three sections and paint each section a different color. Then, in jumping, you can tell at once which is the center of the jump.

The First Stage in Learning to Jump

How do I start learning to jump? First practice riding in the balance position at the canter. Take a stirrup leather and buckle it around the horse's neck about halfway between the withers and the poll. Put your horse into a slow canter, holding your reins in the normal way in the ordinary cantering position. When he is cantering smoothly and quietly, without shortening your reins, take up the balance position which you learned earlier, and hold onto the balance strap, as shown in the pictures. Notice that you don't grasp it at the top, but halfway down on the side of the neck, so that you keep the straight line from your forearm to the horse's bit. Your reins will be loose, and this will allow the horse to stretch out his neck without your hurting him.

Some horses get a little excited when first introduced to this exercise. When the rider balances and holds on as described, taking away all contact with the horse's mouth through the bit, the horse speeds up. If this happens, sink back into your saddle, quiet your horse, and practice the exercise first at the walk and then at the trot. Don't try it again at the canter until the horse is reassured, and will continue at the slower gaits when you assume the balance position.

When can I try my first obstacle? When you can maintain the balance position and your horse understands that this doesn't mean he is to go faster, you are ready. Set the jump standards as shown in the diagram. One rail should be on the ground just under the buckets of the standards. A second rail should be on the ground, two feet on the take-off side. This is called a take-off rail, or "ground line." Now, on the track of the approach, measure eleven feet from the center of the rail, which is later to be raised, and lay another rail on the ground. Finally balance one rail, as shown, running from the top of the standard that is farthest from the fence to the ground. This is called a "wing."

227

If your horse has never jumped, walk him up to the jump and let him smell it. Let him step across the rails, including both the take-off rail and the one which is eleven feet on the approach side. When he seems perfectly quiet, take up a trot on the track at least thirty feet from this first rail. As you approach it, balance in the saddle and grasp the neck strap. Your horse will canter across the first rail without any change of stride. When he reaches the double rails, you will probably notice that he extends himself just a little more. It will feel simply like an especially big stride. If he shows no excitement, and you have not felt off-balance, repeat this several times. If he does show excitement, let him walk over the rails again, and then, walking until you are only one stride away from the approach jump, put him into a trot at this point. He will trot over this bar and may even trot over the next two as well. Be sure to have a firm grip on your neck strap. Jumping from the trot is harder than jumping from the canter.

Should the jump always be approached from the same direction? No, and if you do always approach from the same direction, your horse will soon become bored. Move your equipment after a few minutes and practice coming from the other direction. Be very sure, even at this stage of your jumping, that you always look up, never at the jump, as you approach it.

How soon do I raise the bar off the ground? As soon as you and your horse are comfortable when negotiating the bars on the ground, you can raise it. But don't put the bar across the buckets on both standards at first. Instead, put the end up on the standard which is away from the wall, and let the other end remain on the ground. Your horse will now take a much more active spring. You must learn to prepare for this. As you cross the approach bar, start counting the horse's strides aloud, "One, two, three. . . ." When you think he has reached the point where he will take off, say "off." Remember that all this time you are looking up, balancing, and holding on to the neck strap. To teach yourself to feel the horse gather himself as he jumps, close your eyes as you start counting.

When you can jump the partially raised rail from both directions without losing your balance, raise the other end so that both are on the standards. The jump will now be from 14 to 18 inches high, depending on the construction of the standards. Don't be in a hurry to jump any higher, but give your horse variety by changing the jump from one side of the enclosure to the other, or by putting it up in different spots in the open area. You may have to use a second bar, as a wing on the other standard in the open area, so that your horse does not try to avoid the jump.

The Second Stage in Learning to Jump

When I can jump the low bar without losing my position, and my horse goes quietly over it, what do I do next? Raise the take-off bar, which has been lying on the ground, by using two more standards. This makes what we call a "spread jump," which is no higher than the original vertical jump of a single bar, but is 2 feet wide. Now you will find that your horse jumps both higher and farther. Practice over the low spread jump again and again, first having it set up alongside the fence or wall of the arena, and later away from the wall in different places.

Working over Cavaletti

What are "cavaletti"? These are a series of bars, so placed that the horse jumps one after the other. They can be spaced so that the horse lands and takes off again with no intervening stride, or so that he takes one, or even two strides in between each. Or they can be arranged so that he is forced to vary his stride.

Cavaletti bars can also be used flat on the ground and the horse trained to trot over them. This is excellent practice in teaching the horse to extend himself at the trot. It is also a good way for the rider to improve his seat.

Fig. 102 shows three sets of cavaletti. In the first, the bars are set 1 inch off the ground and 4 feet apart. These are properly spaced for trotting.

The second row shows a series of cavaletti set 9 feet apart and 18 inches off the ground. Here the horse springs, lands, springs, and lands without an intervening step.

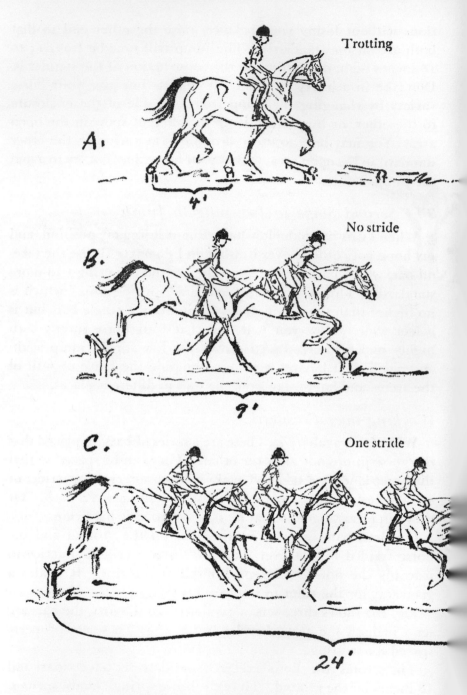

Trotting

A.

4'

No stride

B.

9'

C.

One stride

24'

Fig. 102. Jumping caveletti

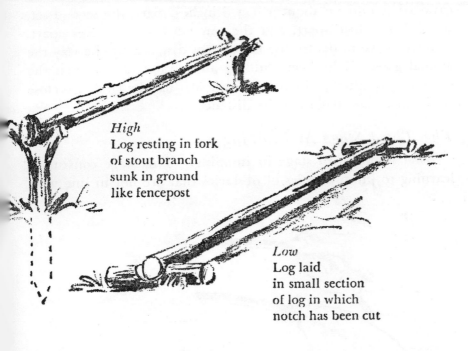

High
Log resting in fork
of stout branch
sunk in ground
like fencepost

Low
Log laid
in small section
of log in which
notch has been cut

In *a*, we have a row of spread cavaletti 24 feet apart. The horse will land, take a full stride, and spring again.

If you are riding a pony, shorten these distances. The trotting cavaletti should be about 3 feet 6 inches apart, the second set, marked *b*, 8 feet apart, and the row marked *c*, 21 feet apart. You will have to determine the proper distance by the way the animal goes. If he keeps adding an extra stride, shorten the distance. If, after springing over the first bar, he lands too close to the next one, lengthen the distance.

The Third Stage in Jumping

What is the third stage in jumping? This stage consists of learning to jump a series of obstacles that are not in line with

a. Jumping with contact
(note direct line from elbow to mouth)

b. Jumping without contact (note loose rein)

Fig. 103. Hand holding reins by driving method

one another, and to jump higher obstacles as well as strange-looking ones. Before you can do this, you must learn how to "jump on contact." This means that instead of holding on to your neck strap while jumping, you must learn to maintain a balance position and, at the same time, with your hands off the horse's neck, maintain a light contact with his mouth.

Start by practicing at the trot and canter. Hold the rein as shown in Fig. 103. This is called the "driving position." Now ride circles, turns, and half-turns at the trot and canter in the balance position, keeping a light feel on your horse's mouth. The rein should never get either tighter or looser, no matter how the horse moves.

When you have learned to guide and control him, go back to your original little jump that was flat on the ground with the take-off bar and the approach bar. Ride him at the canter over these, count your strides, as you say "Off," extend your hands with the movement of his neck, bringing them back as he resumes his original head position. Now you see why it was important to study how the horse moves in jumping.

Work up by steps, with the bar balanced only on one end of the standard, then on both, with the spread jump, and with the cavaletti. When you can take all these without being thrown off balance, without jerking your horse, coming back too soon into the saddle, or losing contact with the bit, you are ready for a series of jumps set in various positions around the arena. This is called "stadium jumping."

What equipment do I need for stadium jumping? There is no limit to the kinds of obstacles used in stadium jumping. Each year someone thinks up a new one. Since you have jumped only spread jumps at eighteen inches, you must have all your obstacles so designed that they can be lowered to this height. However, some of these obstacles are easily constructed. Fig. 104 shows some of the more common types of stadium jumps with their correct names.

What is the hardest problem in taking a course of jumps? *Setting* your horse, or riding him in such a way that when he approaches each obstacle, it is easier for him to jump it than to

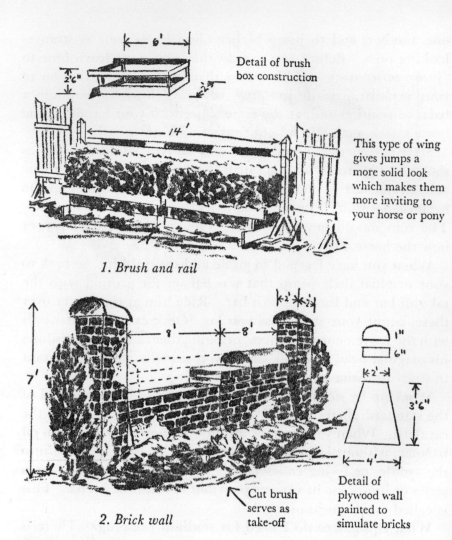

Detail of brush box construction

This type of wing gives jumps a more solid look which makes them more inviting to your horse or pony

1. Brush and rail

Cut brush serves as take-off

Detail of plywood wall painted to simulate bricks

2. Brick wall

Fig. 104. Stadium jumps

avoid it. As you go over each jump, look at the next one you plan to take, and turn your horse on his course in time, neither too soon nor too late.

When should I start jumping higher than 18 inches? You can begin to raise the jumps 3 inches at a time when your horse takes the lower height willingly, and when you can maintain your balance over it without holding on to the neck strap.

234

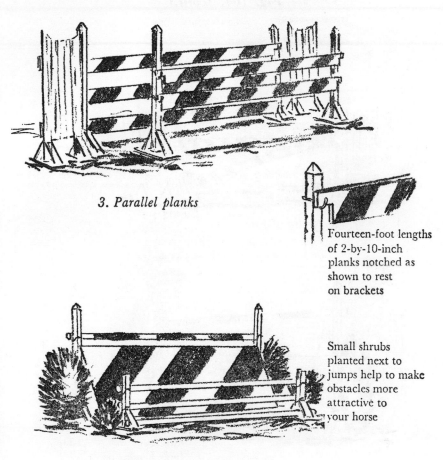

3. Parallel planks

Fourteen-foot lengths of 2-by-10-inch planks notched as shown to rest on brackets

Small shrubs planted next to jumps help to make obstacles more attractive to your horse

4. Panel and poles (spread)
Plywood panel 12 feet long by 4 inches wide

How many jumps should I take in one practice period? When the bar reaches 2 feet, limit the number of jumps. Perhaps twenty or thirty an afternoon at 2 feet, three times a week. When the jumps reach 3 feet, limit the number to twenty per session, and jump only twice a week. As you learn to jump higher, again cut down on the number of high obstacles you take at one session. Horses and ponies that are given too much

235

Fig. 104. (cont.)

5. *Railroad gate*
Flower boxes planted with geraniums
or other suitable foliage as ground line

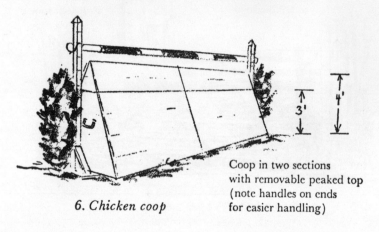

6. *Chicken coop*

Coop in two sections
with removable peaked top
(note handles on ends
for easier handling)

jumping, and that are made to jump too high, go lame or "sour."
When this happens, they stop jumping willingly and start balk-
ing and refusing.

**Must I always balance in the stirrups from the approach
through the departure when I am jumping?** No. As the jumps
get higher, you will have to learn to come back in the saddle
and use your back to control your horse as you approach the
obstacle. As the horse takes off, rise with him and keep bal-

7. *Oxer (with straw bales)*

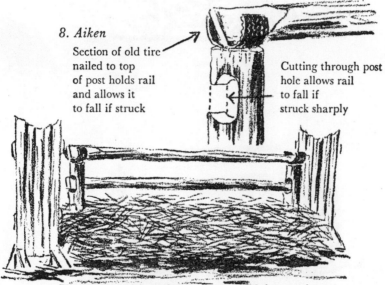

8. *Aiken*

Section of old tire
nailed to top
of post holds rail
and allows it
to fall if struck

Cutting through post
hole allows rail
to fall if
struck sharply

Pile brush and branches at base of 10-foot section
of split cedar three-rail post and rail

anced until after he has cleared the jump and has landed again.

Is it a good idea to practice jumping bareback? Bareback jumping over very low obstacles is excellent practice. Use a neck strap and lean forward slightly, but don't try to balance on your knees. If you can learn to keep your legs in a fixed position over the jump, you will feel much steadier. Dropping the reins and holding your hands out, or going over the low cavaletti with arms folded is also good practice.

Fig. 104 (cont.)

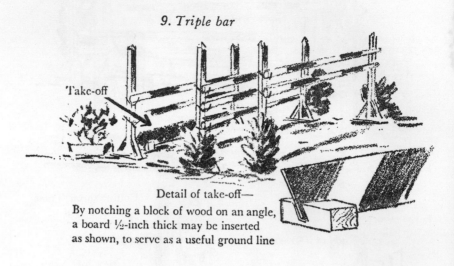

9. Triple bar

Detail of take-off—
By notching a block of wood on an angle,
a board ½-inch thick may be inserted
as shown, to serve as a useful ground line

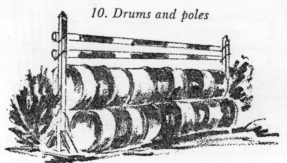

10. Drums and poles

Empty oil drums may be placed on top
of one another, used in a single row,
or placed on end in a row

Jumping on the Trail

When can I try jumping out on the trail? As soon as you have learned to jump 18 inches. You will probably find the horse much more willing to jump little logs along the trail than to jump stadium jumps. If you have no neck strap, hold on to the horse's mane. Count your strides and be prepared for a slightly bigger jump than when your horse or pony jumps obstacles to

11. Gate *(made of birch logs)*

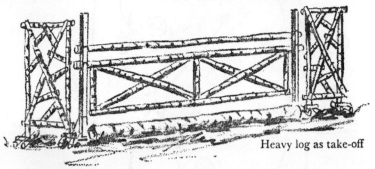

Heavy log as take-off

12. Stone wall

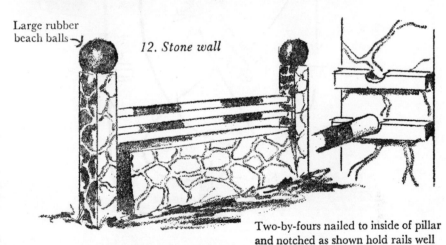

Large rubber beach balls

Two-by-fours nailed to inside of pillar and notched as shown hold rails well

which he is accustomed. When you are jumping three feet in the arena, it is time to start cross-country riding and jumping, especially if you live in an area where the fields are bounded by low stone walls. Just be sure to check the landing side, and see that there are no big rocks, wires, or holes in your path before putting your horse at the wall.

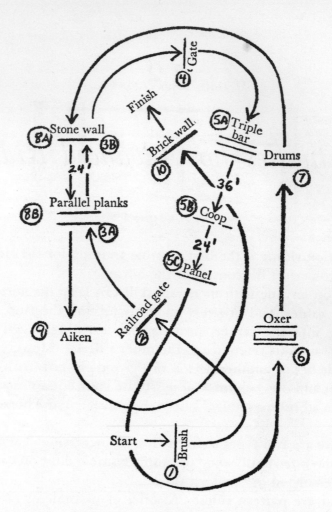

Fig. 105. Stadium jumps arranged in a course

A fairly difficult course requiring several changes of direction.
Note two different types of combinations: 3a and 3b and 8a and
8b require your horse to jump, take one full stride and jump
again; 5a, 5b and 5c require him to jump, take two strides, jump,
take one full stride and jump again.

12

Activities for Advanced Riders

Formation riding is the best possible training for the rider who wants to perfect his control of the horse.

Almost anyone with moderate skill can keep his horse at the trot or canter, and progress smoothly around the ring without cutting into the center, provided he is riding at will (as he pleases, without reference to the other riders). However, when you ride beside another person in a group of fours, with a group in front and one behind, you must rate your horse exactly, making him adjust his natural gait to the gaits of all the horses in the group.

There are two types of formation riding: "close-" and "open-order mounted drill" and "schooling figures" done on command, and memorized or "pattern rides."

What are pattern rides? A series of movements (a pattern) is first worked out, then the group practices them over and over, until they can be done from memory. Pattern rides, such as "Musical Rides" and "Dressage Quadrilles," are often used for exhibitions at horse shows, fairs, etc.

What is the purpose of mounted drill? The basic purpose is to move a group of riders from one place to another. The figures and movements are simple. They consist of riding in twos, fours, and single file, in changing direction one way or another, and in one or two other simple figures, all of which are done on command. The riders must be organized into "squads," and the squads into a "platoon" and there must be a "leader."

How the Mounted Drill Team Is Formed

What is a squad? Eight riders, one of whom is the "squad leader." It is his job to make corrections in the squad, to repeat the commands given by the leader, and to see that they are properly executed. In military units, he usually holds the rank of corporal. Where there are fewer than twenty-four riders in the group, it is a good idea to drill in "half-squads" of four riders each, one of whom acts as a squad leader. Thus, with twelve riders, plus a leader, you can form a platoon of three squads (half-squads), and do all the formations shown in this chapter. If you tried to ride in regular squad formation with this number, you would not even have two complete squads and so could not learn many of the movements shown.

Each platoon has a leader, who usually holds the rank of lieutenant. Generally, two sergeants, called "file closers," ride at the end of the platoon. Their job is to watch the whole unit from behind and make corrections. They also act as "road guards" when the unit is riding on public roads and comes to a dangerous intersection. Fig. 106 shows how the file closers can be of use here.

Two or more platoons make up a "troop." The leader of a troop holds the rank of captain. Several mounted troops compose a "squadron." The leader of a squadron is a major. Several squadrons form a "regiment," commanded by a colonel.

On the following pages are diagrams showing all the open- and close-order drills with explanations of how they are executed. The leader of the unit must learn how to give the commands. The following rules on giving commands also apply to those given by the instructor for schooling figures in formation.

Commands

Military commands are always given in two parts. The "command of preparation" tells the riders what they are going to do and gives them a minute to prepare. The "command of execution" tells them to carry it out. The command of preparation is given by the leader, then repeated by the squad leaders. In this way all the riders are sure to hear it. The squad leaders do

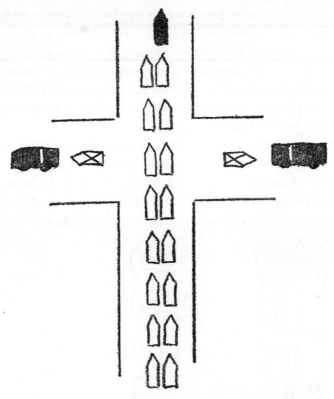

*Fig. 106. Crossing a dangerous intersection
with road guards in position*

not repeat the command of execution as they do the other.

Is there any special tone of voice for the commands? Yes, the command of preparation is given in a sustained (held) tone. If the gait is to be increased, the command is given in a high voice or in two-syllable words; the last syllable may be in a higher tone than the first: "Gal-*lo-o-o-op*—," "For-*wa-a-ar-d*—," or "Tro-*o-o-t*—," for example. If, on the other hand, the troop is at a trot and the leader wants them to walk, he will drop his voice slightly in giving the word, "Walk." The command of execution is the word "HO," or "NOW." For movements in which the gait remains the same or is increased, it is given in a clear, ringing, rather high voice. If the gait is to be decreased or the troop brought to a halt, the command of execution is given in a low tone.

How does the leader know when to give the commands? The leader must know clearly what he wants his troop to do, where he wants them to go, in what formation, and at what gait.

He must give his command of preparation in time for the squad leaders to repeat it. He gives the command of execution in time for the riders to understand it, then execute the movement at the gait he has indicated.

In increasing the gait, always go from the walk to the trot, from the trot to the canter, or the canter to the gallop. Never go directly from the walk to the canter, as you do in schooling movements. In decreasing the gait, come down gradually in the same way, with a different command for each gait.

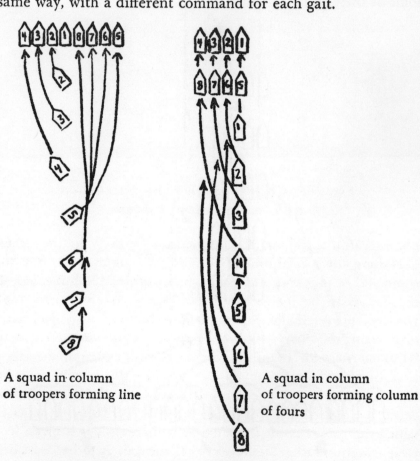

A squad in column of troopers forming line

A squad in column of troopers forming column of fours

Fig. 107a.

If your troop is not very experienced, it is a good idea to *decrease* the gait when you form twos or fours from "troopers." (Riders in single file are said to be riding in a "column of troopers.")

In decreasing the "front," you should increase your gait.

Except for this rule about a gradual increase or decrease of gaits, you can make your troop execute each of the formations shown from any other formation. The riders can go directly from a column of troopers to a "column of fours," for example, and the formation known as "line" can be executed from a column of troopers, twos, or fours. Now let us see just what some of these puzzling words mean.

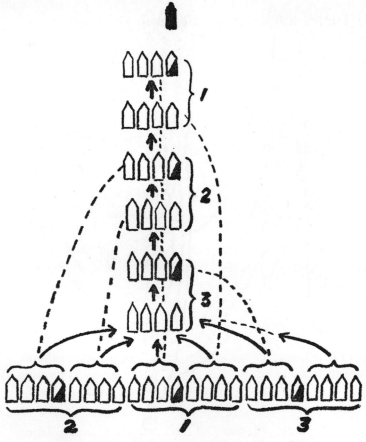

Fig. 107b. Column of fours from line

Forward. On this word, followed by the command of execution, the riders move out at a walk.

Trot. The riders take up a trot, either from a walk or from a canter.

Canter. The riders take up a canter (slow gallop), either from the trot or from the gallop.

Gallop. Generally used only in open-order drill where the troop is working in a large field. The riders must first be at the canter.

Column. Any movement in which the riders are following each other. It is used in combination with another command such as:

Column of twos. The riders who have been in either a column of troopers or fours move into a column of twos.

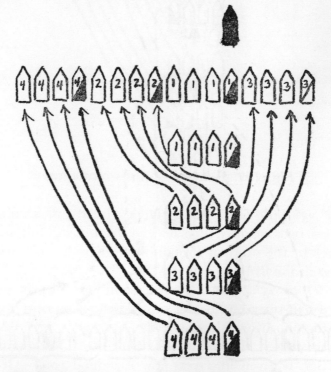

Fig. 108. *Platoon of half-squads forming line from column of fours*

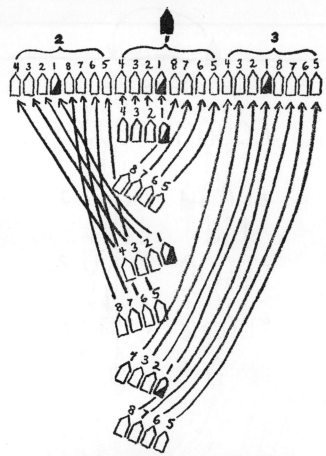

Fig. 109. Column of fours into a line

or:

Column right (or left). The riders, already in a column of
troopers, twos or fours, turn at a given point, still following one
another in the original formation. They do not turn all at
once as in the flank movements.

Column left or right about. As you see in Fig. 109a the unit exe-
cutes a half-turn, ending by riding in the opposite direction
from the one in which it started.

Troop (squadron, platoon, squad) Ho-o-o-. This command of
execution is given in a very low sustained voice. It means
halt, and every rider knows, by the tone of voice (whether he
understands the words or not) that he is to stop.

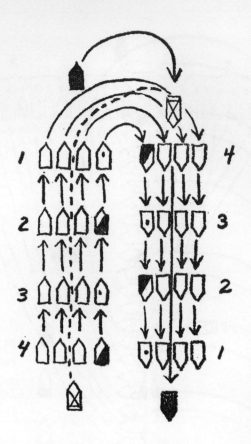

Fig. 109a. Column left (or right about)

Line. This movement is shown in Fig. 109.

Fours right (or left). This movement is shown in Fig. 110a.

Right (left) oblique (pronounced oblīque, to rhyme with *alike,* not with *week*). This movement is shown in Fig. 111.

Column half-right (or left). Don't confuse this movement (Fig. 111a) with right and left oblique.

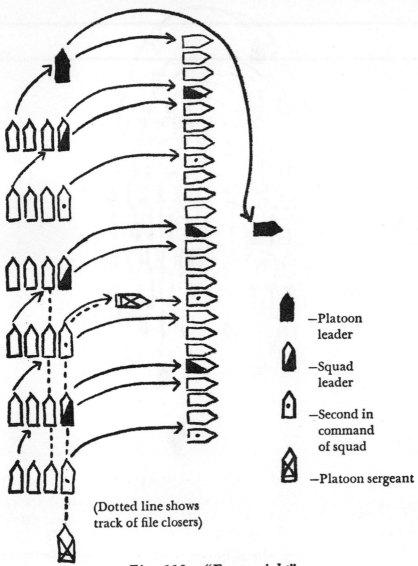

-Platoon
leader

-Squad
leader

-Second in
command
of squad

-Platoon sergeant

(Dotted line shows
track of file closers)

Fig. 110a. "Fours right"

Squads column left (or right) about. (Fig. 112b) The squad
leaders, instead of repeating the leader's command of preparation, say, "Column of Troopers (twos) follow me!" On the
command of execution, each squad leader makes a simple half-
turn, and is followed by the members of his squad. The
platoon ends up riding in the opposite direction.

249

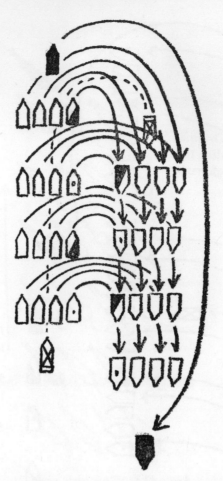

Fig. 110b. Fours right or left about

Remember that every one of the commands of preparation given above must be followed by the word NOW, or HO.

Must each command be given separately? Commands which give changes of gait, formation, or direction, all of which are to be executed at the same time, can be given as combined commands with only one command of execution. Where more than two such combinations are used, however, it is well to give the first two, wait until they are repeated, then give the third, and finally, the command of execution. Let us suppose that the platoon is riding in a column of twos at a walk. The leader

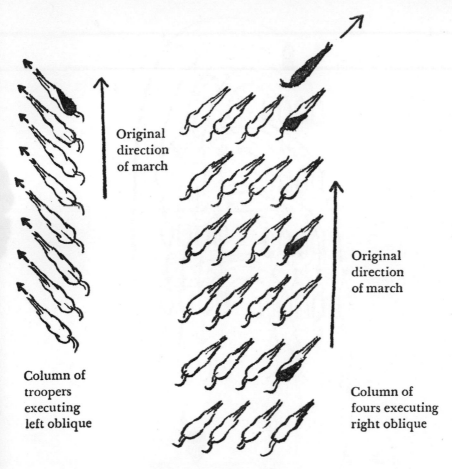

Original
direction
of march

Original
direction
of march

Column of
troopers
executing
left oblique

Column of
fours executing
right oblique

Fig. 111. The obliques

wants to bring them into a column of troopers, to put them at the trot, and, at the same time, to turn them to the right. The commands would sound like this:

Leader: "Column of Troopers, column right—"
Squad leaders: "Column of Troopers, column right—"
Leader: "Trot—"
Squad leaders: "Trot—"
Leader: "HO—"

On the command HO, the leader and the right-hand man of the first pair would break into a trot and turn to the right. The

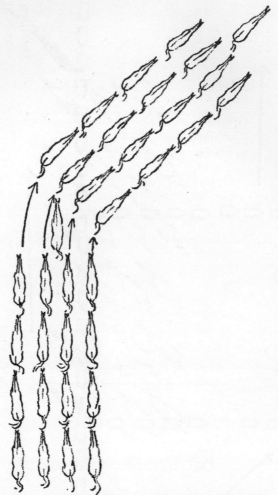

Fig. 111a. Column half right (or left)

other riders would follow in a column of troopers, one behind the other, taking up the trot as they moved into position. Each individual rider would turn right at the exact point where the leader turned.

What is the difference between close-order drill and open-order drill? In close-order drill, the riders are always at the specified distance (four feet from nose-tip to tail-tip). The word "distance" always means the space between riders, as measured from the front of the column to the back. They are also always at a specified "interval," meaning the distance between riders as

252

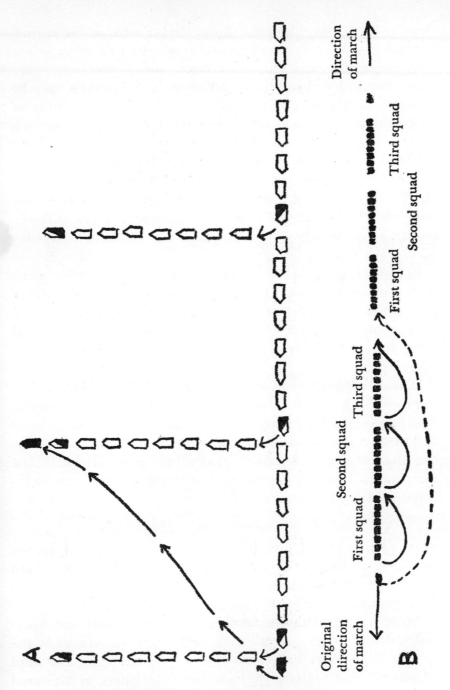

Direction of march

Third squad

Second squad

First squad

Third squad

Second squad

First squad

Original direction of march

B

A

Fig. 112a. Squads column right
Fig. 112b. Squads column left about

measured from one side of the "front" to the other. The normal interval is 3 inches from the toe of one rider to the toe of the rider beside him, and 6 inches between their knees.

In open-order drill, these distances and intervals can be changed. For example, the command, "Column of fours at 12-foot distance," would mean that the riders were to ride in a column, four abreast, and that each four should be 12 feet behind the four in front. In some of the open-order drill movements shown there are large intervals between the riders. For example, in the movement called "line of squad columns at 20-foot intervals" (Fig. 113b), the riders end in three columns of troopers, the squad leaders abreast of each other, but with 20 feet between each column.

In learning mounted drill, practice the changes of front (going from troopers to twos to fours and back again) and the changes of gait, again and again. Then practice the harder movements, such as fours right and left, and line. Twenty minutes of drill every time you ride will do wonders for the improvement of your control.

What is the purpose of schooling figures in formation? They improve the flexibility of the horse and the control of the rider. The figures which you have already learned—flank movements, half-turns, volts, transitions from one gait to another, and from one phase of a gait to another—are the ones generally used. For more advanced riders, figures such as the shoulder-in can be incorporated in the practice.

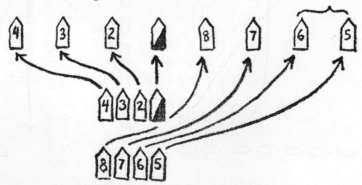

Fig. 113a. Open order drill—fours form as foragers

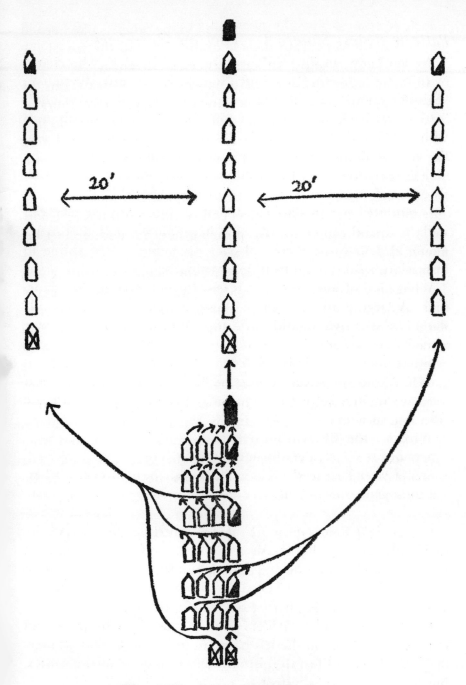

Fig. 113b. Line of squad columns

Pattern Rides: Square Dancing on Horseback

As you know, in square dances there is a "caller" who chants or calls the figures. Each dance starts with an introduction—, "Salute your partners"; "Eight hands around and circle right"; "Other way back, you're going wrong!" The dance usually ends with a "Grand Promenade." Between the introduction and the ending there is a special pattern for each dance, done by each couple in turn. Many of these country dances can be readily adapted to mounted square dancing.

Is mounted square dancing difficult? No. Anyone who can walk, trot, and canter readily, and has done enough close-order mounted drill to have control over his mount when riding in formation, will have no trouble learning it.

What kind of horse or pony is best for mounted square dancing? A large pony or a small, Western-type horse is ideal. It should be sensitive, should start, stop, and turn readily and have a good slow canter.

What kind of music is needed? Any country dance music is good. A record player with good volume is satisfactory, but outdoors or in a large arena, you may need a player with more than one speaker.

What are the different movements?

Sets in order! Riders form a set, (Fig. 114).

Salute your partners! Riders bow their heads to each other.

Salute your corners! Riders bow to the riders on the opposite side.

Circle eight hands around! Riders, turning their horses individually and simultaneously to the left, circle once around on the right hand (center of ring to their right.) Then stop again in their original places. If possible, this should be done at the slow canter; otherwise, it may be done at the trot.

Grand promenade! Riders turn to the right by pairs and circle once around on the left hand, stopping once more at their original places. This, too, is most effective done at the canter, but may be done at the trot.

Swing your partners! Riders circle around each other in a small volt. They may reach out and touch hands if they are

256

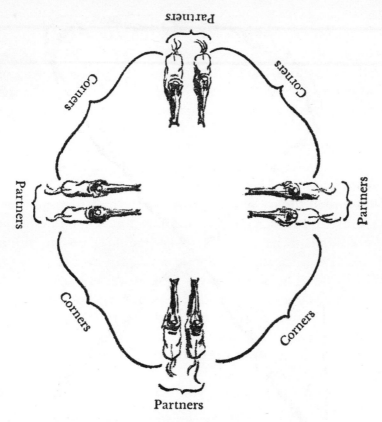

Partners

Corners

Corners

Partners

Partners

Corners

Corners

Partners

Fig. 114. A square dance set

skillful enough. Swinging while mounted is difficult; the two partners must start swinging as they approach each other, so that the horses are already in motion. Avoid dances calling for a great deal of "swinging."

Musical Rides

The most famous musical-ride team in the world is the exhibition team of the Royal Canadian Mounted Police. The Mounties are famous for the precision and smoothness with which each figure seems to dissolve into the next. Like a beautiful ballet, the line of red-coated riders on jet-black horses moves in circles, spirals, wheels, and crisscrosses, at the trot or canter. It is as though they were not individual riders at all, but parts of a gigantic living design, controlled by one master mind.

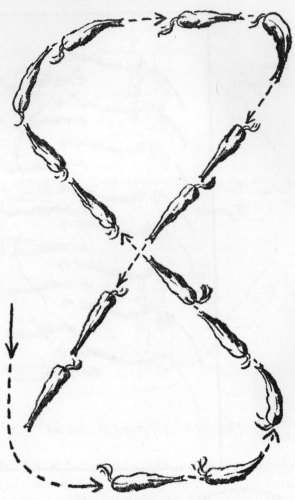

Fig. 115. "Crisscross"

How are musical rides worked out? Less-experienced riders can combine simple schooling figures such as those shown in Chapter 10. Experienced riders can do the more difficult movements shown in Fig. 116 (crossing-flanks movements), and Fig. 117a and b (the four-spoked and double-spoked wheels). Design your ride so that each figure leads into the next. Some of it may be ridden at the trot, some at the slow canter.

What type of music is suitable for musical rides? For the trotting figures, you need a cheerful, even, four-four rhythm.

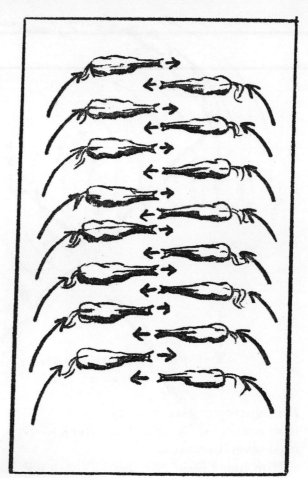

Fig. 116. Crossing flank movement

Fig. 117a. Four-spoked wheel

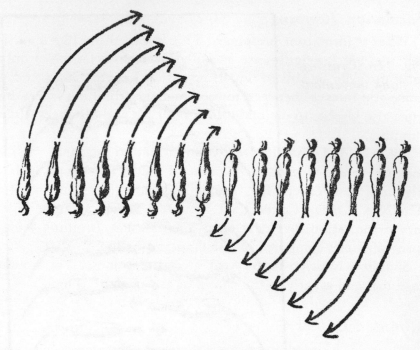

Fig. 117b. Two-spoked wheel

For figures done at the canter, use slow-rhythm waltzes. Since most musical rides take from fifteen to twenty minutes, you will need several records.

How many people are needed for a musical ride as an exhibition? Sixteen is the minimum number.

Dressage Quadrilles

What is a Dressage Quadrille? This is similar to a musical ride in that it is a memorized set of figures, but the figures are more difficult (the shoulder-in, two-track, counter-change, etc. are used), and fewer riders are needed. The execution must be very exact; the dance is usually so fitted to the music that the figures change on specific phrases or bars of the melody.

How many riders are needed for a Dressage Quadrille? Eight make a good team. In some cases four can give a good performance.

Formation Jumping

What is formation jumping? This is something like a musical ride, but the figures are executed over obstacles. Not only must the rider be able to ride in formation, keeping an exact distance and interval between himself and the adjoining riders, he must also be able to maintain these intervals and distances while jumping.

What kind of obstacles are used in formation jumping? Solid-looking, spread-type obstacles from 18 inches to 2 feet 6 inches high are best, except for very experienced riders and horses. The New Canaan Connecticut Mounted Troop, a junior military organization, has developed a Formation Jumping Ride, using obstacles composed of one-thousand balloons.

Should exhibition riders wear special costumes? Yes, simple costumes add greatly to the charm of any of these rides.

Mounted Games

There are many kinds of games which may be played on horseback. Some are simple enough for a beginner, while others are much harder. These games not only add variety to riding activities, but they do a great deal to instill boldness in riders and teach them to relax and ride automatically.

What are some good games for beginners? "Red Light" and "Scrambles" are both suitable. In Red Light, one person is It and stands at one end of the arena, facing the wall, with his back to the other players who are lined up at the opposite end. Loudly and clearly, he counts from one to ten, then says "Red Light!" and turns quickly. The other riders, meanwhile, have started forward toward him. At the words, "Red Light," they must stop. If, in turning, the person who is It sees anyone moving, he calls out the name, and the guilty rider must go back to the starting line and begin again. The first rider to reach the person who is It, touches him. All others then ride quickly back to the starting line, and the one who is It tries to catch one or more of them. The first rider caught is It for the next game.

How is Scrambles played? The riders take the track at the walk or slow trot without stirrups. Just off the track, to the inside, are stationed as many helpers on foot as there are riders. In the center stands the instructor, or another player, also on foot. When all players are moving along well, the leader blows a whistle or calls the word, "Off!" All riders jump off (the helpers stand by the horses), run to the leader, touch him, run back, and mount as quickly as they can. The rider who is mounted first with his feet in his stirrups and his reins correctly held is the winner.

What are good games for more advanced riders? One good game is "Musical Stalls." Arrange bars, as shown, to represent stalls. There should be exactly the same number of bars as there are riders, making one less stall. Notice the two barrels, one placed at each end of the arena, a little off the track. When the game starts, everybody rides on the track at a trot, going in the same direction, keeping outside the jump standards. The music starts when the players take the track. Suddenly the music stops. All riders at once try to get into a stall. One rider will be left out and must leave the ring. One of the bars is removed, and the game continues until only one player is left. Riders must enter the stalls from a specified direction and may not cut through the center or turn around and come back; while the music is going, all must ride in the same direction and keep outside the standards. Once the music has stopped, however, they may turn and go the other way and may cut in between the end stall and the standard. If two riders come into a stall at the same time, they must both go out and try again. No horse may cross a bar from one stall to another, or come out of his stall before the music starts.

Fig. 118. Musical Stalls set up for ten riders

"Musical Sacks." Empty feed sacks, one less than the number of riders, are placed on the ground, in a large circle, at equal distances from one another. When the music starts, the riders start riding in a circle around the circle of sacks. When it stops, they ride up to the sacks, jump off, and stand on a sack. A rider who fails to get a sack may reverse direction, but may not cut through the center in trying for another. As in Musical Stalls, one rider is eliminated each time, until only the winner remains. As players are put out, the sacks should be redistributed so that they are always equally spaced.

"Red Rover." One rider takes his place in the center of the field or arena. All the others are lined up at one end. The player who is It calls, "Red Rover, Red Rover, come over, come over!" All the other players then try to get from one end to the other without being tagged by the player who is It. If a rider is tagged, he joins the player in the center, and they both tag. The game continues until all except one have been caught. Mark out a boundary line at each end, about fifteen feet in from the wall or fence. Players who have passed this line are considered "safe." In this way, no rider will be forced into the fence.

Races

What are the kinds of racing games? In a "fast trotting race," riders, in groups of two or three, race at the trot over a given course. In a "slow cantering race," the riders line up at one end of the arena, and on signal take up the canter, and canter to the other end. The *last* rider to reach the end without breaking the canter is the winner. In the "sack race" riders, mounted bareback, move from one end of the arena to the other, dismount, get into a sack (one for each rider should be lying on the ground) and, leading the horse or pony, hop back to the starting line.

The "onion race," shown in Fig. 119, requires the rider to jump a low jump marked *a;* he then continues, as shown, to the post marked *b,* from which he takes an onion, and goes on to *c* for another onion. He now turns, and jumps the jump marked

263

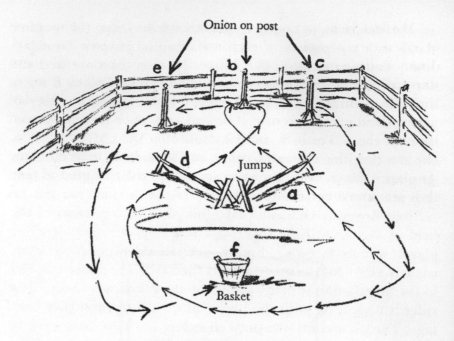

Onion on post

e   b   c

d   Jumps   a

f

Basket

Fig. 119. Onion race

d, goes on to the post marked *e,* where he gets still a third onion, then goes to the basket marked *f* into which he drops the three onions. Each rider rides the course alone with someone taking his time by stop watch. The rider who completes the course in the shortest time is the winner.

Team Games

What are team games? These are games in which teams of riders compete against each other. Polo is the most famous mounted team game. Perhaps you may never have a chance to play real polo, but you might try "broom polo," in which the players use a large soft ball and "sweep" the ball into the goal with brooms. The rules are much the same as for field hockey.

"Mounted Basketball" is played with a soft ball in a rope harness.

"Prisoner's Base" needs no equipment other than an arena marked off as shown. The playing area need not have actual marks on the ground. Jump standards can be placed as shown

264

in the diagram, to indicate the boundary lines. The game starts with the players of each team behind its own boundary line. Four, or at most, five players on each team are best and the area should not be too large. The riders of team A try to ride down through the free territory to the home territory of team B, and touch the goal. The goal is a section of fence or wall at each end. Team B scores by touching the goal of team A. Notice that the central portion of the area is marked "free ground." If an A team member goes into the free ground, and a B team member comes into it *after* the A rider has left his

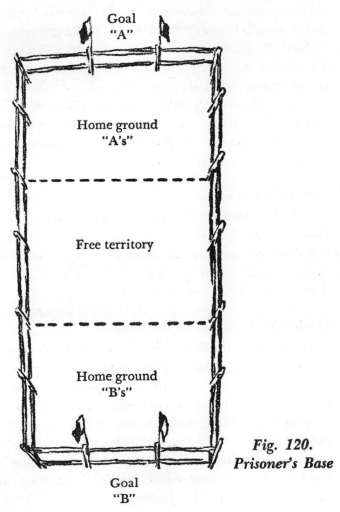

Goal
"A"

Home ground
"A's"

Free territory

Home ground
"B's"

Fig. 120.
Prisoner's Base

Goal
"B"

home territory, the B rider may tag the A rider. If a rider from one team is tagged either in the free ground or while he is behind the boundary line of the opposite team, he is a prisoner, and must remain behind the boundary line and on the home ground of the opposite team until he is freed. To free a prisoner, a member of his team must ride down and tag him without being caught himself. Any rider who either frees a prisoner or makes a goal without being caught, can return to his own home territory. He may not both make a goal and free a prisoner on the same run, and he may not tag another player until he has gone home and come out again. After ten minutes, there is a rest of five minutes; the teams exchange goals and the game goes on.

Not all games are played in an enclosed arena. In paper chases and in fox and hounds, one or more players ride off cross-country, leaving a trail of oatmeal. After giving them a few minutes "grace" (chance to get away), another group of riders follows and tries to catch them. It is better to use oatmeal than bits of newspaper, for the birds will clean it all up and the countryside will not be littered.

Monkey Drill

What is "Monkey Drill"? This is another name for Mounted Gymnastics. Any active boy or girl will enjoy learning the various ways of vaulting on and off a horse, and the other movements shown in the pictures. Just be sure your horse or pony does not mind the "monkeyshines."

Horse Shows and Gymkhanas

In certain parts of the United States, horse shows have become so popular that young people who wish to participate seriously in this type of competition, can do so every week end from May until November. The competition has become very stiff, the standards are high, and one must have a really good mount. Before entering any large horse show, you should go to watch many times. You need some good instruction and should know the rules for the different classes, the main divisions, and other technical matters.

a. Using platform to vault onto pony

b. Vaulting the pony

Fig. 121. Monkey drills

Fig. 121. (cont.)

c. Vaulting on from side into sitting position
without using the hands

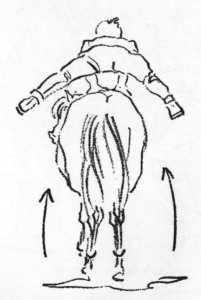

d. Vaulting pony from the rear

e. Vaulting on,
off and over galloping pony

Phase 1

Phase 2

Phase 3

How are Horse Shows classified? There are "recognized" and "unrecognized" shows. Recognized shows are run under the auspices of the American Horse Shows Association (the AHSA). They must first get permission, and then follow exactly the rules laid out by the AHSA. The judges and stewards must be qualified as such by the AHSA. Unrecognized shows are those which are not under the auspices of the AHSA. These are usually school, camp, or small local club shows. They are not required to stick to AHSA rules, but usually do to some extent.

The more important rules for showing, as well as advice on "Correct Dress," "Preparing the Horse for Showing," "Giving a Show," etc. can be found in the book *The American Horse Show*, by this author. If you plan to do any amount of showing, you should join the American Horse Shows Association.*

What is a "Gymkhana"? A Gymkhana is a competition with classes which include horsemanship, jumping competitions, and games. Many of the racing games and others described in this chapter are suitable for Gymkhanas.

"Saddling Race." The bridle and saddle for each rider are put at one end of the arena. The riders, mounted bareback with only halters on their mounts, line up at the other end. On signal, they race down, jump off, bridle and saddle their horses, mount, and race back. The rider who is back first, with his horse *correctly* saddled and bridled, is the winner.

"Bandaging Race." Each competitor is given a set of bandages, and on signal puts them on the horse as though getting him ready for vanning. Bandaging is shown and described on page 150. Sometimes two or three riders form a team for this race.

Gymkhana Jumping Competitions

"Hat Race." Riders are divided into teams of three, each team wearing a different type of headgear. A course of jumps is set up in the ring. The first team takes its place inside the arena with one member of the team on the starting line. At a whistle, he starts out. If he completes the course without a fault and within the time limit of one and a half minutes, the second mem-

* 40 East 54th Street, New York City.

ber of his team starts the course. If a team member has a refusal, the next member of his team, without waiting for him to complete the course, rides out and continues on the course at the jump at which the error was made. Even if this is the last jump on the course, as soon as he reaches the end of the course, he is replaced by the next member of his team. The team that takes the most jumps in a minute and a half is the winner. A rider who knocks down a jump keeps going, but the jump doesn't count.

Gamblers Stakes. Various jumps of different degrees of difficulty are set up around the ring. Each has a large sign telling how many points it is worth. Each rider has a minute or a minute and a half in which to take as many jumps with high points as possible. No jump may be taken more than twice.

Maze Jumping. A course such as the one in Fig. 122 is set up. On each jump a red flag or bit of ribbon is tied to one jumping standard only. The rider may take the jumps in any order he chooses, but must take each jump at least once with the red flag on his right. The rider who completes the course in the shortest time wins. Note particularly the pen jump marked *x*. This has a red flag at each corner and may be taken in one of several different ways in order to keep the red flag on the right.

Trail Riding, Cross-Country Riding

In riding on other people's property, or even along the roadside, there are a few rules of polite behavior, and several safety rules which you should know. Follow these, and you will never give anyone reason to complain against you for trespassing.

How should I conduct myself when riding on a public road? Do not obstruct traffic. Ride well on the side of the road, but keep off the grassy edge of people's property.

What should I do at crossroads? Stop completely and make sure that no cars are coming from either direction. If a group is riding together, it is wise to post road guards, as suggested earlier in this chapter, and shown in Fig. 106.

On which side of the road should I ride? On the right. Some people like to consider themselves pedestrians, and ride on the

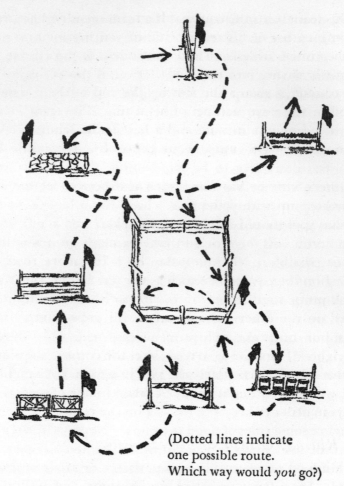

(Dotted lines indicate
one possible route.
Which way would *you* go?)

Fig. 122. Maze jumping

left, facing oncoming traffic. Many horses, however, are less bold when they see large trucks coming directly at them. They think the trucks are going to run them down and may shy suddenly off the road onto someone's lawn.

How do I go around blind corners? When you approach a corner with a high bank or shrubbery on your right, making it hard for drivers to see around it, cross to the other side of the road and go around until you have turned the corner.

In passing parked vehicles what should I do? Do not go too close. If you and your horse know the schooling figure called the leg-yield, described in Chapter 10 and shown in Fig. 91, this is a good time to use it. Pass the vehicle with the horse's hind-quarters pushed away from it so there will be no chance of his kicking it or shying into it.

How should I go up and down hills? Go slowly, especially downhill. If you are leading a line of riders, and reach the foot of a hill, continue to make your horse take short steps and progress slowly. Otherwise, your horse will get a little ahead. Since horses don't like to be left behind, those following may break into a trot before they reach the bottom of the hill in order to keep up with yours.

At what gait should I ride on a hard-surfaced road? A walk or a slow trot. Sit the trot, so that you won't get going too fast without realizing it. Never gallop on a macadam road. The pounding on the pavement will not be good for the sensitive feet and tendons of your horse.

What are the other rules of safety for cross-country riding? In riding on trails and across open fields, ride only where the footing is good. In many parts of the country there is quicksand. Rabbit or woodchuck holes are also common. As mentioned earlier, when you jump a wall or barway, make certain that the landing is safe.

What are some rules of good manners? Never walk your horse on lawns or over fields where crops are planted. Never gallop through a field where cattle, horses, sheep, or other animals are pastured. Pass slowly in order not to excite or frighten them. On overtaking a group of riders, slow your gait to theirs, ask permission to pass, and then go past carefully. When someone passes you on a narrow trail, back your horse off the path and keep him with his head toward the person who is passing. This is especially important in the hunt field where members of the hunt staff often have to get by the other riders quickly.

What are the rules for opening and shutting gates? If you find a gate shut, be sure that it is shut when you leave it. When you are with a group of riders, the leader opens the gate and either holds it until the next person takes hold of it or, if the gate will stay open by itself, swings it all the way back. Last rider through must see that the gate is securely closed, but the next to last rider should stay with him. Otherwise, his horse may try and bolt for the other horses.

What about draw bars? Draw bars which you take down, must, of course be put up again. If you jump a draw bar and damage it, report the damage to the owner and offer either to pay for it or to have it repaired.

How should I ride through low overhanging branches? Shield your face with your arms and duck low, then just push through at a walk without attempting to hold them back. Even though there may be a rider directly behind you, don't try to hold back a low branch. No one has long enough arms for that, and by trying to do it, you'll let the branch swing hard into your companion's face.

Fox Hunting, Drag Hunting, and Hunting with Harriers, Staghounds, and Bloodhounds

How did hunting with hounds originate? Hunting is a very old sport, older by far, than racing. As you learned in the first section of this book, kings and noblemen maintained their own hound packs to hunt fox, deer, wild boar, etc. Later, packs were organized in different countries. An experienced person chosen to head the organization was called the "Master." His full title today is "Master of Foxhounds," or MFH. One or two other people help him control the hounds. They are called "Whippers-in," or "Whips." The *"Kennel Master"* has charge of the hounds when they are in the kennels. Sometimes the Master does not hunt the hounds himself, but employs a professional "Huntsman."

Is there a special organization that makes the rules for hunts? Yes, this is called the Masters of Foxhounds Association. It keeps a list of all the hunts, what land they are permitted to hunt, and the names of their officers. It settles any dispute which may arise between two member hunts. Hunts belonging to this Association are called Recognized Hunts.

Can more than one Recognized Hunt use the same territory? No two hunt clubs or associations, which hunt the same game, can hunt over the same territory, but harriers (which hunt hares, and not foxes) may hunt for hare in territory used by foxhounds. The same holds true of staghounds, which hunt stag or deer.

What happens at a fox hunt? Each hunt has a card called a "fixture." This card is sent out to all members, and tells them where and at what time hounds will meet for the current month. At the given time, the Master, Huntsman, Whips, and members of the field (those people other than the hunt staff who plan to follow hounds that day), assemble at the designated spot. The Master usually allows five minutes for late comers, then he moves off at a jog trot toward the particular "covert" (brushlot) where he thinks there may be a fox. At the heels of his horse trot the hounds who have been carefully trained to follow him and not *"run riot,"* chasing cats, dogs, or rabbits. Incidentally, hounds are always counted in "couples." A Master will say that he has twelve couple (24) hounds, or twenty-five and a half couple (51) hounds out. The tails of hounds are referred to as their "sterns." A fox's tail is called a "brush," his head a "mask." Behind the hounds and Master, one on each side of the road, ride the Whips. Behind them comes the Field Master who makes sure that the riders do not break the rules.

At the chosen spot, the Master rides into the lot followed by his hounds. The members of the Field and the Field Master wait quietly on the roadside. The Whips ride around the outside of the covert, one on each side. The Master now encourages his hounds with his voice and horn to search the covert and try and smell out the fox. As soon as one hound finds the scent of a fox, he bays ("speaks," or "gives tongue") in a special voice which the Master recognizes. Indeed, he probably recognizes not only what a hound has "found," as we say, but which of the twenty or so couples has spoken. Immediately you hear an encouraging note on the horn and the words, "Hark to Rambler; hark to Rambler!" At once the other hounds make their way to the hound who has first "owned the scent," and then a glorious medley of voices joins in. Back and forth through the covert they go. The fox, meanwhile, is planning how to elude them and get into open country. Presently, there is a shout or a whistle from one of the Whips. He has seen Reynard (the fox) creep over the stone wall and lope off down the pasture. The Master or the Huntsman, calling his pack to him, leads them out to where the Whip is stationed. He sees his helper with his horse facing to the west; with his hat he is pointing in that direction. The other Whip now comes in sight. Master and Whips, accompanied by short staccato notes on the horn, encourage the hounds, who quickly pick up the scent and are off after their quarry.

The "gone away" (special short notes on the hunting horn) have told the waiting Field that the hunt is on and they follow behind the hunt staff. Sometimes there will be a long run; the fox will run boldly and fast, in which case he is called a "stiff-necked fox." Staff and Field will jump whatever obstacles are necessary, but no good horseman jumps unnecessarily. He does not know how long the day may be and wants to spare his horse. Sometimes the fox will elude his pursuers, either by running through a field of cattle or a field covered with manure, both of which "foil" (spoil or hide) the scent. Sometimes he finds an open "earth" (burrow) and takes refuge in it.

Does the fox usually get away? The fox is faster than the hounds, but has not as much staying power. However, he knows where he is planning to go, while the hounds have to guess. Because his scent is not terribly strong, if he can get five minutes ahead, the chances are he will be able to outwit the hounds.

What are the most important rules in fox hunting? You must never injure a hound. If you see a hound trying to pass you, let him go by. Never get between the Master of the Whips and the hounds. You must keep quiet at "checks." Checks occur when hounds, having lost the trail of the fox, are looking for it again. In jumping, you must be sure that the person ahead of you has jumped, landed, and gone on before you start for the obstacle. If you get a refusal, let all the people behind you pass before trying again. The rules pertaining to riding over crops and closing gates must be followed here also.

What is worn for fox hunting? The Master, his staff, and members of the Hunt Club, who have won the right to do so, wear a special Hunt Livery or Uniform. Every Hunt has its own livery. Often this consists of scarlet coats for the men and black coats with colored collars for the women. These coats are called "pink" coats, after a famous tailor named Pinke. Some Hunts, however, wear coats of other colors. Both men and women wear hard hats (especially reinforced to give protection in falls). The Hunt Staff wear hard velvet caps. Members of the Field wearing the formal hunt colors usually wear hard, high silk hats. Other members wear plain black coats and hard bowlers or derbies. Boys and girls wear hunt caps. In former times, a tax for up-keep of the hunt was imposed on any other type of hat. Farmers, over whose land the hunt rode, did not have to pay it; nor did children, nor the Hunt Staff, so all these wore velvet caps. The breeches worn are usually fawn colored, white, or canary yellow. Hunting boots have special tops: on men's boots they are ma-hogany colored, and on women's, patent leather. Altogether, the members of a hunt are very colorful and, with their glossy, well-cared-for horses, make a beautiful picture.

How long does a hunt last and how far do you go? This de-pends on the country and the conditions. In Ireland, most hunts meet at ten o'clock and often go on until four o'clock, or even later. Several different foxes will be hunted, and a number of different coverts "drawn." Altogether, Field, Staff, and hounds probably cover from twenty-five to forty miles in a day. In the United States, the hunts are not as long for there is less territory.

What is a drag hunt? This is a hunt in which something that gives out scent, generally litter from a fox's bed, is dragged along the ground by a rider. Hounds are then put on the line and follow it just as though they were after a real fox. The Staff and Field follow the same procedure as in fox hunting. When the hounds come to the end of the line, there is a juicy piece of meat called a "worry" waiting for them. Drag hunting is apt to be faster than fox hunting, for there are no checks, but it is not nearly as interesting. It is a substitute for hunting in areas where the country is too built-up for real fox hunting.

What is a bloodhound hunt? This is another substitute for fox hunting and very suitable for a young people's Hunt. Al-though it is not a recognized sport, a group of riders who enjoy riding cross-country can organize a bloodhound hunt without too much expense and have a fine time. Bloodhounds, which are the gentlest of dogs, easily learn to follow the scent of a rider on a horse. Furthermore, you need only one hound, or at most two; you do not need a pack. After your hound has been trained, the procedure is as follows:

Master, Whips, and Field, followed by the hound (or hounds), ride out together to a point from which there is open country or a variety of good trails. One of the Whips holds the hounds. One member, who is chosen to represent Reynard, now rides off, calling the hounds to follow. After four or five minutes, the hounds are released. Off they go, baying with beautiful deep voices. They will follow anywhere, through water, snow, and up and down hill. It is impossible to lose them. Since they catch the scent through the air, and not necessarily off the ground, they will often take short cuts, and you will have to ride fast to keep up. Finally Reynard hides, the hounds find him, receive their worry, have a bit of a rest, and everything starts all over again.

Suitable Riding Attire

As in swimming, skiing, and other sports, a participant needs to wear what is comfortable and will make it easy for him to do his best. In the Hunt Field and in the Horse Show, both of which are considered formal events, it is discourteous to wear other than the formal habit: black bowler or velvet cap, white stock, yellow or "tattersall" (plaid) vest, black, dark blue or oxford gray coat, white, tan, rust or canary breeches, high black English boots with or without patent leather tops. But for more casual riding we can wear less formal attire.

What kind of clothes are suitable for ordinary riding and for country shows? In winter a tweed or covert cloth "hacking" jacket with harmonizing gray, fawn, or rust breeches is suitable for ordinary riding and showing in "Hunter Seat" classes. You may wear "jodhpurs" instead of breeches if you wish, and in this case you will want low "jodhpur boots" instead of the high ones. The high ones give more support for jumping, however, and may be worn over jodhpurs for cross-country and stadium jumping. The lower boots are good for trail riding, dressage, and ordinary riding.

Instead of the intricate white stock you may prefer to wear a simple "choker" (a fitted band which buttons in back) or even a shirt with a string tie or a four-in-hand.

In summer, in the show ring you will want a coat of madras, linen, cotton, or dacron, of a light or dark color, as you prefer. For riding at home and on the trails any plainly tailored, short-sleeved, open-neck shirt will be comfortable.

In any case, it is best to wear a hard hat of some sort.

What do I wear for bareback riding? Without the stirrup leathers which necessitate protection, you can wear jeans or Levi's and any sort of footwear.

What do I need for ranch riding in the West? When in Rome you must do as the Romans do. Just as the English hunting livery is designed for a special purpose, so is the Western or cowboy costume especially suited for the conditions under which you will ride in the West. The wide hat and the neckerchief protect you from sun and dust. The low boots with high heels are intended to give you purchase on the stirrups when you rope cattle. The leather "chaps" worn over the Levi's or jeans protect your legs and thighs from cactus and other prickly plants.

13

Training the Horse or Pony

It is great fun to take a foal from the time it is born, and train it yourself. If you are going to do this, you should study the correct methods of handling and training so that you won't make mistakes.

The Foal

How soon should I start handling the new-born foal? Start from the moment it is born. New-born foals have not yet developed a fear of mankind. Most mares that have been properly handled themselves trust their owners, and do not mind having the young foal petted and handled. In fact, it is often necessary for the owner to help the newly arrived baby to find the succulent milk which his mother provides in such abundance. When the foal is born, he lies still for only a few minutes. Then he struggles to his long, wobbly legs. Usually the first try is not successful, and the second only partially so. At the third attempt, he stands, wavering like a willow switch in a breeze, but managing to maintain his balance and attempting a step toward his mother.

Although instinct tells the foal that he needs the warm milk, it does not always tell him where to find it. Sometimes a mare that has never before had a foal is as ignorant as the baby. I've seen mares that were so delighted with the new arrival that they couldn't bear to have him move back and nuzzle for the overflowing udder. Instead, they insisted on turning when the foal turned, smelling him meanwhile. Sometimes foals leave the mother entirely, and try to nurse the side of the stall door. I have even known a few mares that didn't realize that the nursing of the foal would relieve the discomfort of a full udder; they fought and kicked when the little lips searched for the nipples.

If the foal is unable to find the milk without assistance, or if the mare refuses to let him do so, you will have to help. At least two persons will be needed, and three are better. One holds the mare. The second (with the third to help), pushes the foal from behind until he is in the right position, and with the left hand under the foal's chin, guides the eager lips to the udder. Foals do not see well at birth, but they have a well-developed sense of smell. Milk a few drops onto the palm of your hand and rub it against the foal's lips. Put a little on one finger and let him suck it. As he sucks, lead his muzzle up to the udder and try to substitute the nipple for your finger. If, at the end of six hours the foal is not nursing, you had better send for the veterinary, because foals become weak very quickly. The first milk of the mare contains special vitamins and other substances which are vitally necessary for a new-born foal. Without these, he may easily die.

Will the foal be unafraid of me the second and third day, if I handled him when he was born? Yes, probably he will, though there are many exceptions to this. In any case, go into the stall several times a day during the first week, and try to get the baby accustomed both to seeing you and to having you stroke him. Never make a sudden motion, and always speak in a soothing tone of voice. Make him understand that you do not represent danger and that he has no need to fear you. By the end of the week he should be friendly, and allow you to stroke him all over. Now it is time to introduce him to a halter.

Where can I get a halter small enough for a new-born foal? All large harness and saddle companies make foal halters. If yours is a pony foal, be sure to tell the company whether he is a miniature Shetland or one of the larger varieties.

Do I keep the halter on the foal all the time? No, it is wise to keep it on only in the daytime. Be sure, too, as the foal grows, to keep adjusting the halter. Otherwise it will get tight and will rub the cheek bones, making sores that are hard to heal.

What is the next lesson that my foal must learn? Before he is three weeks old, you should teach your foal to follow on a lead. This is a hard lesson, and not a very agreeable one for the new-comer. Now, for the first time, he must learn that he cannot fight the rope, that he must obey. This is called "halter-breaking."

How do I go about halter-breaking my foal? There are several methods, but I have found the one described here the easiest and most satisfactory. In Chapter 7 are diagrams that show different methods of tying the horse. In the sketch marked 40, a ring is fixed to the wall. A rope, at one end of which a block of wood is attached, is run through the ring and clipped to the halter. This is the type of rig you need for the first step in halter-breaking. The ring must be attached near the feed manger of the mare. Beside it should be an ordinary ring to which the mare can be tied. The length of the rope used on the foal is important. It should be just long enough so that when the foal is standing with his head next to the ring, the block of wood just clears the floor of the stall.

Have your equipment ready, then tie your mare and give her a little feed in the manger. Now push the foal into position beside the mare with his head beside his ring, and snap the rope to his halter. Then step back and wait for fireworks. At first he will not know that he is tied. Then suddenly he will discover that when he wants to move away from his mother he cannot do so. He will probably lunge backward in fright. This is where the slip-type of rope helps, for the jerk that stops him is not so sudden. And when, tired out, he moves forward, the rope moves with him and there is no danger of his entangling himself.

Let him struggle against the rope for a few minutes without interfering. If he throws himself, you must be ready to unsnap the clip which is fastened to the halter. Then get him back into position and snap it on again. Since the foal's spine is delicate, it is best to prevent his throwing himself by pushing him forward from behind. This eases the tension on the halter and he will stop struggling for a moment. Never leave him tied until he has learned not to fight the rope. Always be sure that rope and halter are new and will not break. Try and soothe him in his fright by talking to him. In time he will get over his fear, and your first and hardest battle will have been won.

What is the next step in halter-breaking? Next teach the foal to walk beside the mare while you hold one end of a halter shank. Again, three people are needed. One leads the mare. One walks at the head of the foal, holding the end of the shank in the left hand, and with the right hand grasping the rope about four inches from where it snaps to the halter. The third person walks directly behind the colt, ready to urge him on. The easiest way to urge a reluctant colt forward is to push him with your body by leaning against his hindquarters. If he has been correctly handled, he will not object to this, and if he should kick, you will be too close to him to be hurt.

What do I do after the foal has learned to follow alongside the mare? He must now learn to stop and wait while the mare goes ahead a few steps, and then to catch up to her at the speed which *you* choose. Start by holding him still while your helper leads the mare a few steps. He will be excited and try to pull away. You must talk to him and calm him. Above all, don't let him succeed in pulling the rope out of your hand. When he is quiet, walk him forward. Let him stand beside the mare, and then do the same thing over again. After a lesson or so, he will learn not to struggle and will obey you. If you are not strong enough to control him, be sure to get help. It is of utmost importance that the little fellow learn from the beginning that he cannot fight with success against the tug of the rope.

What do I teach him next? The final step is to teach the foal to allow you to lead him away from the mare and bring him back again. Only a few steps are necessary at first, but be sure he gets his reward in the form of a pat, some praise, and a drink of milk when he is brought back.

At what age should a foal be completely halter-broken? By the age of three weeks the foal should know what you mean when you take hold of the halter shank (rope), and should obey you. Do not try to take him out of sight of his mother, however. To do this would be expecting too much.

What are the next lessons the foal must learn? He must learn to allow you to brush him all over with a soft brush, to comb his mane and tail, and to pick up his feet and clean them out. The first lessons in grooming should be in the stall with mare and foal both tied. Later you should teach the foal to stand in the aisle near the stall while you groom him. He should be cross-tied, as described earlier. In other words, from each side of the aisle there should be a rope which snaps to his halter, so that he cannot move more than a few inches forward, backward, or sideways.

When should the foal be weaned? Foals are usually weaned (taken away from their mothers and fed regular rations of grain and hay) at about six months. When your foal is a month old, fix up a little feed box beside the mare's bigger one. When the mare is fed, give the baby a handful of crushed oats mixed with bran. When you start using the mare again, about three weeks after the birth of the foal, leave the baby in the box stall with the door tightly closed. If you have the Dutch-type door, close both the top and bottom halves. Pay no attention to the screams of protest which you will hear. Just make sure that there are no loose ropes or jagged points of wood or metal that might hurt the foal. Do not tie him, of course. Your mare will probably nicker while you are riding her, and may perhaps try to get back to the baby, but she will settle down after a while.

Weaning time is very sad. The mare and foal must be completely separated for at least three weeks and sometimes much longer.

How much should my foal know at the end of a year? By the end of his first year, the colt (boy) or filly (girl) should come when you call him. He should follow you willingly wherever you choose to lead him, with enough confidence in you to go along even when you lead him over rough ground and into strange places. You should have taught him to go into a trailer if you have one, or to climb into a horse van. If you have no such vehicles, build a little ramp and place it in different positions and at different angles so that when the time comes to take your horse or pony to horse shows, hunts, etc., he will not be afraid to get into the van or trailer.

Your colt should enjoy being groomed, and should lift each foot and hold it up when you tell him to.

How soon do I start the actual breaking lessons? You can start "longeing" (training the horse or pony to move in a circle around the trainer at the end of a 30-foot tape) at a year and a half, provided the climate where you live permits this. Since most foals are born in the spring, trainers usually wait until the colt is two years old before beginning his formal training. Ponies mature more quickly than horses and are not so excitable, so many trainers of ponies start the longe lessons and the driving lessons at a year and a half, or even slightly sooner. The main thing to remember is that in horses the bones remain quite soft and flexible until the animal is three years old (ponies two, or two and a half), so no weight whatsoever should be put on the horse's back until that age.

What is the purpose of longeing? The purpose of teaching the horse to longe, is to voice-train him to start, stop, turn, and change gaits. Then, when the trainer mounts the animal for the first time, he will already have established a method of communicating with his pupil. Learning to balance the weight of a rider, and becoming accustomed to the feel of legs pressing on his sensitive flanks are very confusing to the colt. If he has first been taught to move, to stop, and to turn by voice commands, the trainer will not have to use his legs, hands, or whip to get control and give directions. The young animal will only have to worry about learning to balance this additional weight and accustom himself to the feel of it.

What equipment do I need for longeing? You need a 30-foot longe tape, which can be of canvas or leather. It should have a loop at one end and a snap which swivels on the other. If you cannot buy a regular longe tape, you may be able to get hold of two long driving reins which you can buckle together with the swivel-snap attached at one end. You will also need a longe whip. For best results, you need a longeing cavesson, and a "bitting rig" is very useful but not essential.

Is it hard to learn to longe a horse? It is hard at first, especially if both you and your horse are inexperienced. If possible,

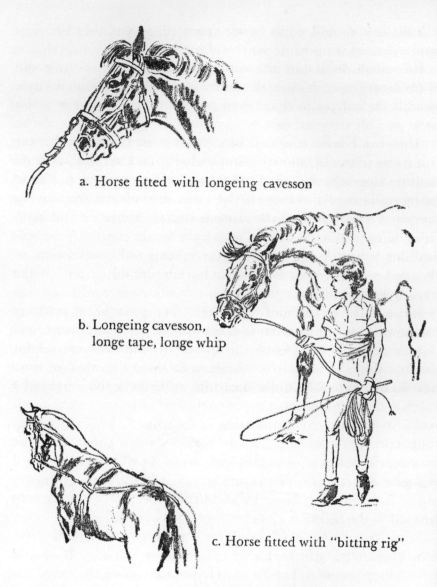

a. Horse fitted with longeing cavesson

b. Longeing cavesson,
longe tape, longe whip

c. Horse fitted with "bitting rig"

Fig. 123.

get someone who knows how to longe to help you. The main difficulty is in getting your horse to understand what you want him to do. Once he understands, you will have little trouble.

Why is it hard to get the horse to understand what you want? So far, your colt has learned that when you take hold of the halter shank, he is to walk right beside you. When you turn he turns, and when you stop he stops. Now you have to teach him that he must walk around you in a circle without having you lead him. This is very puzzling to him, naturally. At first, though he starts readily enough, as soon as you move a little away from him and stop, he will stop and face you.

How can I teach him that he mustn't come toward me? Start your first lesson as follows: Carry the whip in your left hand, the lash trailing behind you. Gather up the longeing tape in a series of loops, as shown in Fig. 124. In this way, you can release one loop at a time. Also, if the horse becomes frightened and bolts, your hand won't be caught and hurt by the tape. Now start walking your horse in a large circle, talking to him as you do so. When he is going quietly, without letting him stop, transfer your tape to your left hand, your whip to your right, and walk sideways about three feet away from him, facing the horse as shown in the picture. If he starts to come toward you, back away from him. Hold the stock of the whip out in front of you, tapping him on the nose with it if necessary, to show him that he must not do so. When he stops, start him again by leading him with

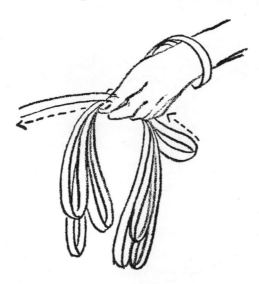

Fig. 124. Holding the longeing tape

your left hand as you tap his rump with the whip. At the same time, "cluck" with your tongue and say, "Walk." As soon as he is walking readily, let out one loop of the tape, keep him walking once around, and then say "Ho!" very sharply, at the same time stopping yourself. Before he has time to turn toward you, walk quickly up to him, praise him and pat him. Then repeat. An experienced trainer can teach the average colt to longe at the walk in about ten minutes. At the end of that time the colt will be working around him at the end of the longe, as shown in Fig. 125. Notice that the trainer does not stand exactly still but moves in a small circle, so that he is always facing the colt. The colt forms the base of a triangle, the longe forming one side of it, and the whip the other.

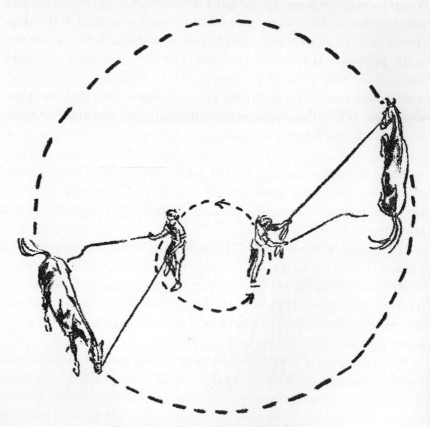

Fig. 125. How the colt is longed

When my colt walks willingly to the left should I also teach him to go to the right? Yes, as soon as he moves smoothly to the left, you must teach him to turn and go the other way. The first time lead him around, saying "Turn," and then say "Walk" again. But you will have to start all over again with the short length of tape, for he will not realize that because you stood at a distance and he walked around you to the left, he is supposed to do the same to the right.

How much am I supposed to teach my colt on the longe? In the first lesson, he should only be asked to walk, halt, turn, and walk again. During the second lesson, if he moves quietly at the walk and seems to understand, you may try a little work at the trot. Use the word "trot," changing the tone of your voice, and, if he doesn't understand, touch him with the whip. If he goes too fast, bring him right down again to the walk. A little patience is all that is needed, and before you know it, your colt will work in both directions at the walk and the trot, without excitement.

Should I teach him to canter on the longe? Yes, he must learn to canter, but only when he is well-trained at the trot. At first he won't know what you mean, and you will just have to keep urging him to trot faster and faster until he finally breaks into a canter. If you praise him so that he knows what is expected, and always use the same words and the same tone of voice for each command, you will soon find that he willingly obeys you and seems to enjoy his lessons.

How long a time should I work him on the longe at each lesson? Ten or fifteen minutes in each direction is plenty. Then give him a rubdown and a carrot as a reward for good behavior. If you want to give him two lessons a day, one in the morning and one in the afternoon, that is good also; but don't work him so long that he becomes bored.

What do I do if my colt won't stop on the longe? Longeing a "green" (inexperienced or young) horse should always be done in an enclosure of some sort. For the early lessons, work in one corner so that you have two walls as guides. Here, if your colt should rebel by bolting when he first trots or canters, you can easily stop him by walking toward the wall as he approaches it. This method is shown in Fig. 126. The colt has been working in a circle on the track as shown. Suddenly he takes it into his head to run. The trainer, leaving the center of the circle, walks toward the wall, as shown, which brings the colt right up into it and forces him to stop.

What is the purpose of the bitting rig? The bitting rig is to teach the horse to hold his head in a natural position, neither too high nor too low, and to relax his poll and jaw in stopping, instead of bracing against the feel of the rein.

How soon do I start putting a bit in my colt's mouth, instead of working him always on the cavesson? Before using a bit, train your horse to go in a simple hackamore, such as the one shown and described in Chapter 6 (Fig. 28). At the same time, you can

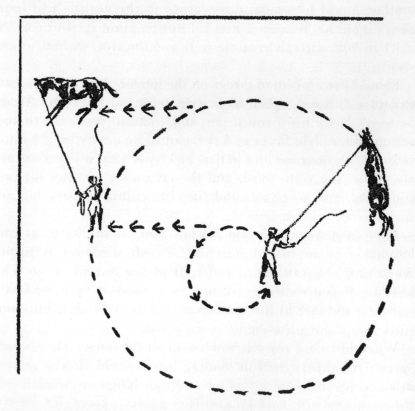

Fig. 126. Stopping the colt that tries to bolt on the longe

get him used to the feel of the saddle by putting that on him, without the stirrups. Let the reins of the hackamore lie on the seat of the saddle; if they are long enough, you can even put them behind the cantle. The reins, or the side checks used in the bitting rig, should be a little slack when the horse holds his head in a normal position; and they should be tight when he raises his head too high or pushes his nose too far out in front of him. As soon as he is working well in the hackamore, you can introduce him to the bit.

What kind of bit should I put on him first? For this purpose, there are special bits with little keys attached, but these are not really necessary. Just an ordinary, fairly thick, jointed snaffle is all you need. Since you want your horse to like the bit, you can rub a little molasses on it or wet it and sprinkle salt on it.

How should I introduce my colt to the bit for the first time? This should be done in his stall. Put rings on each side of the stall, so that you can cross-tie him as you do when you groom him in the aisle. Use a bridle without a cavesson and with no reins, and let the colt look at and smell the bit. Now slip it quietly into his mouth. At first he will try to get rid of it by pushing it with his tongue. Pay no attention, but cross-tie him so that he can't get his head down and try to get rid of it by rubbing. Then leave him for half an hour. Repeat this lesson until the colt is used to the feel of the bit and has stopped "mouthing" it. At the next longeing lesson, slip this bridle with the bit in it on under the hackamore, but have the longe tape still attached to the hackamore and not to the bit.

What is the next step in teaching the colt to answer to the bit? We want the horse to learn to bend at the poll and relax the jaw, when he feels pressure on his bars from the bit. There are several ways to teach this. Start by adjusting the bit so that it is quite low in the horse's mouth, but not so low that he can get his tongue over it. Cross-tie him as you did before, and you will probably find that the colt, feeling this new position of the bit, will start playing with it and trying to get it higher in his mouth. To do this he will bend his poll and relax his jaws.

Next, with the bit in the correct position (in an ordinary

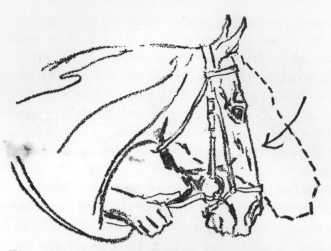

Fig. 127. Teaching horse to relax jaw and poll

bridle), take both reins in your right hand, just under his chin, and give gentle little pulls on them to coax him to relax the poll and bend his chin toward his chest. The instant he does so, relax the reins and give him a caress and a tidbit.

Do this half a dozen times, night and morning, or at the beginning and end of the longeing lesson, until he relaxes his poll and jaw, slightly wrinkling his lips, as soon as he feels the first light pressure. The final step is to attach side reins to the bit and fasten the other end of each rein to the billet straps of the saddle, as shown in Fig. 128. Have them lightly stretched and work the colt on the longe in these.

What in training comes after the longeing? The next step is driving in long reins. Put the bitting rig on the colt, or, if you have no bitting rig, try to get an old harness saddle with "terrets" through which reins are supposed to run. Attach driving reins to the bit, but do not run them through the terrets. Leave the side checks on just as though you were going to longe. Now, have someone lead the colt while you walk behind him. You will find that in a very few minutes, if you use the same commands that you used in longeing, he will learn to move out without anyone at his head, at the walk and the slow trot. At first, in

<figure>*Fig. 128. Horse fitted with side reins for longeing*</figure>

making turns, step a little to the inside of the turn and let your outside rein come against his haunches. This will help him to keep his hindquarters following the track of his forehand. Later he will turn readily without this help, and all you have to do is follow him. When he understands thoroughly what you want him to do, run the reins through the rings of the bitting or harness saddle and drive him like that.

Is it a good idea to teach a colt to drive to a cart before riding him? It is a very good idea, but you will need a proper vehicle called a "breaking cart." It must be low to the ground, with very long shafts; it must be wide between the wheels so that it doesn't tip over easily, and it must be very strong. The picture shows a homemade breaking cart made from the axle and wheels of a car. This is by far the best kind.

Is there anything special I should know about teaching my colt to drive? If your colt has been thoroughly trained on the long reins, it should not be too much trouble to teach him to pull a cart. He needs to learn how to push against the collar or breast collar, and so pull the vehicle along. He also must learn how to turn, even though the shafts seem to be telling him not to by pressing on his neck. And he should know how to lean back on

Fig. 129. Breaking cart

the breeching to keep the cart from running up into him when going downhill. All this he will learn with experience, but you must take no chances on putting him in such a position that he finds he can run away and break the cart or harness. Work in an enclosed area, and start by having one person leading the colt while you walk behind the vehicle, driving him with the long reins. Only when he has learned to start, stop, turn, etc., should you actually get into the cart. Drive only on the level and in an enclosure such as a large paddock, until you are very sure you have him under control.

When do I first start riding my colt? When he is three years old, the colt's bones will be strong enough to support your weight. A two-year-old pony colt can bear weight up to about forty pounds. To get him used to bearing your weight, start in the stall. After you have finished grooming him, lean heavily on his back. If he seems not to mind, wriggle on your stomach onto his back for a minute. This will soon show him that nothing much will happen just because of a little extra pressure on his back.

How do I go about mounting a colt in the saddle for the first time? At the end of his lesson on the longe or in the cart, bring him into the center of the paddock or schooling enclosure. Be sure that the stirrups are already set and at a comfortable length. You will also need a helper to hold the colt. Sometimes a colt will be quieter if there is another horse, with a rider, standing beside him.

Gather your reins in the normal way, and speak quietly to the colt. Now put your foot into the stirrup. If he seems restless, take it out again and hand him a bit of carrot. Repeat this until the colt stands waiting for the carrot and does not flinch. Slowly, slowly, put your weight in the stirrup and, if he shows no fear, stand in it. Unless he seems very afraid, you can settle quietly down in the saddle, immediately reaching forward and handing him a carrot, or having your helper do so. Don't stay on him, for he will find it hard to balance you. Get right off again and praise him. Repeat this several times. The next day, after his regular driving or longeing lesson, and still with a helper, mount him again, but this time have the helper lead him a few steps. Say "Walk," as though he were working on the longe, and "Ho," when you want him to stop. As soon as he is standing, dismount again and give him his reward. Gradually increase the lessons. Let another person ride alongside or ahead of you, and soon there will be no need of someone to lead you.

How do I teach my colt to obey my aids and not just my voice? As you tell him to walk, trot, etc., gently apply your legs, relaxing them as he obeys. As you say "Ho," apply your reins, using the "active" hand described in Chapter 9. Soon you will find that the voice is no longer necessary.

What should be my training goal for the first year? Do not attempt too much at first. It is better to teach your colt simple things and teach them thoroughly, leaving the more difficult things until later. At the end of the first year of training, your colt, at the age of four years, should know the following:

How to start smoothly from the halt to the walk and progress to the trot and canter, keeping each gait until told to take up the next.

How to come down from the canter to the trot, to the walk, to the halt, without resisting and with his body in a straight line on the track.

How to turn readily to right or left.

How to take either lead at the canter.

How to back up.

How to do (or be in the process of learning) the strong phases of each gait, as well as the ordinary phases. He should not have been asked to do the collected phases.

How to work willingly either alone or in company, and how to accept the ordinary noises and sights of the trail.

When should his more advanced training begin? The more advanced training, which includes the dressage movements given in Chapter 10, follows the early training, according to the way the horse responds. Do not be in a hurry. Keep working, and strive always for smoothness, flexibility, and willingness in your horse. Don't be content with abrupt or sloppy responses.

Vices and Defenses of the Horse

Whether you train your own colt, or have a horse trained by someone else, you are sure to find that at one time or another he will refuse to do what you want him to. Perhaps he has been able to get away with this with someone else. Perhaps he just doesn't understand. Perhaps you are asking too much of him. You will find below some of the most common "vices" or "defenses," as they are called, as well as the methods of dealing with them.

Rearing. A horse rears (stands on his hind legs) for one of three reasons:

Because of fright.

Because he doesn't want to do something you want him to do. (This is called rearing from vice.)

Because he has been trained to rear.

If he rears from vice, or has been trained to rear, you need not be afraid. The horse knows what he is doing and he will never go so high that he will lose his balance, provided you don't pull on his reins and throw your weight backward. If he rears from fear, that is another matter, for a frightened horse sometimes becomes hysterical and can hurt himself and you too. Rearing from fear is very rare, however. The natural instinct of a horse, when he is afraid, is to run, not to stand still and rear.

Don't be frightened and lose your head. Whatever the reason, the cure is quite simple. As soon as your horse's front feet leave the ground, lean forward, grasp a bunch of mane to keep yourself from falling backward, and apply your legs hard to get him to move forward. The minute he brings his front feet down, sit up in the saddle and slip your right rein under your toe, as shown in Fig. 130. Now pull hard, and kick with the other foot. The effect will be to cause the horse to go around and around in a tiny circle. He cannot rear, for he cannot get his head up, and he is off balance. A little of this will cure the most vicious rearer, since it immediately makes him feel completely helpless.

Bolting. Again, if your horse is running away—from vice— don't be afraid. He won't hurt himself. If he is running from fear, that is another matter. If you are calm, however, he will quickly lose his fear.

If he is running from fear, *don't* lean forward, *don't* cling with your legs, *don't* hold onto the mane or saddle, and *don't* scream! Remember that a horse that is running away is no harder to stay on than a cantering or galloping horse. Sit up straight, lean

Fig. 130. Keeping horse from rearing

back a little, speak to your horse, and use the ordinary active hand, with both hands a little high and pulling back in hard pulls, not in a steady pull. If this doesn't stop him, and you have room to turn, use the pulley-rein effect described in Fig. 70 in Chapter 9.

If your horse has developed bolting as a vice, try and get him to do it in open country, preferably uphill, and force him to keep going as fast as he can put foot to ground until he is completely worn out and cannot run another step. He must be so tired that you have to get off and lead him home. After an experience like this, he will never try it again.

Shying. Many horses will dart sideways suddenly when they see or hear something strange. You may never be able to correct this completely, but if you are a good rider, you won't care. As a matter of fact, you may enjoy this sudden motion. If your horse comes to something on the side of the road that he is afraid to pass, you will have to try different methods until you find one that works. Some horses do best if you just keep them moving while you talk to them and, with legs and voice, urge them by. Others will become calm if allowed to go up and sniff the frightening object. Sometimes you can put your horse into a shoulder-in, his head away from whatever frightens him. When you are with a companion, and something frightens your horse, let your companion go first, and the chances are your horse will follow. Even an automobile can sometimes give a horse a lead across a bridge or stream.

Tossing the Head. This is a very annoying vice, and many an unwary rider has got a split lip, bruised nose, or black eye from a horse that threw its head suddenly upward. Sometimes, but rarely, a good crack of a crop on the poll will cure this vice. Working the horse in a draw rein is more satisfactory. Fig. 131 shows how it is adjusted. The rider should use it as a punishment if the horse tosses his head, pulling so hard that his chin is brought in to his chest and held there for a moment.

Bucking. Many otherwise well-behaved animals like to give a few hearty bucks on a frosty morning, but this soon becomes a vice. Learn to feel when your horse is preparing to buck. Sit

Fig. 131. Draw-reins to girth

back in your saddle and jerk his head up suddenly, at the same time shouting at him. He cannot buck while his head is held high.

Kicking. Kicking at another horse or at a person is one of the unforgivable sins, and must be met with stern and immediate punishment. The minute the horse puts his ears back with the intention of kicking, keep a tight rein, and give him a hard cut with the whip. Some kickers can be cured by riding them between two other horses, neither of which will take any nonsense but will kick back if attacked.

It does no good to ride two kickers together. In this case, each horse figures that he can kick and swing away at the same time, thereby escaping a return kick. But if the problem horse is put between two bold companions, he won't dare to kick. Incidentally, if a kicking match should ever start between your mount and that of another rider, both of you should immediately swing your horse's heads toward each other. It does no good to kick with your legs in the hope of moving the culprits forward, but you can easily turn them so that they are in no position to hurt each other.

Kicking the Side of the Stall. If your horse repeatedly kicks the side of his stall, take a small rubber ball, attach a 12-inch length of cotton elastic to it and tie it around the horse's leg just above the hock, so that the ball hangs a little more than halfway down the leg. Now when he kicks, the ball will fly out and, swinging back, bang him on the cannon bone.

The Barn Rat. The horse that refuses to leave the stable alone, or that will not move away from his companions, is called a "barn rat." Such a horse should be worked alone for many hours until he becomes used to it. If he is too unmanageable to ride alone, start by putting him out by himself in a paddock. When he is used to this, ride him alone in the same paddock. Next lead him on foot some little distance from the barn. Give him a little feed in a pail and keep him there for a half-hour or so. The next day, take him out to the same place, give him a

Fig. 132. Correcting horse that kicks in stall

carrot, and mount him. Have a good whip with you, and be prepared to have him bolt for the stable. If he does so, use the pulley rein; bring him in short and make him stand. If he will not
move out at all, use the whip once very strongly just above or
beside the tail. If he tries to rear, use the method described in
this chapter, making him spin around and around with his nose
to your toe until he has had enough. During your lessons, make
him stop and move out, stop and move out repeatedly on command, until he moves automatically. Do not give in to him.
You must prove yourself the stronger and more stubborn or you
will never cure him.

Refusal to Stand when Mounted. Use the method described
in mounting your horse for the first time. Have several small
pieces of carrot in your pocket. Start by gathering up your reins
and giving your horse a bit of carrot. Put your toe in the stirrup
and give him another. Stand in one stirrup, reach across his
neck, and give him still another. Swing the other leg over, settle
in the saddle, and immediately give him a last bite of carrot.
Keep him standing a moment, then dismount and start over.
After twenty minutes and a half-dozen carrots, you will find that
he stands willingly.

Jumping Defenses. The most common defenses in jumping
are shying out and refusing. In shying out, the horse, without
slowing down, changes direction and avoids the jump by going
around one end of it. If you are riding a young horse, this can
be cured by letting him come up to the jump and examine it
carefully. (Be sure that the obstacle is not too high for him.)
Next, take the horse back a few paces, say 15 feet, and if he has
shied out to the left, place him as shown in Fig. 133. If he has
shied out to the right, start from the right. Start him toward
the obstacle at this angle, and, one length from it, straighten him
out so that he can jump it in the center. To correct a refusal,
provided the horse is not in a show, let him examine the obstacle
thoroughly. Then lower one end of it, if possible. Now bring
him up at the walk to within 20 feet of it. Start him at the trot,
and only when he is one stride from the obstacle, let him canter.

If the refusal occurs in the show, hold the horse facing the

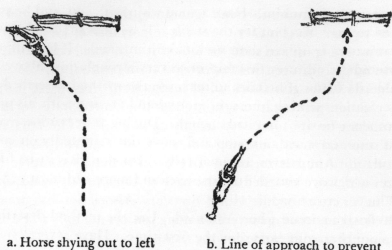

a. Horse shying out to left   b. Line of approach to prevent
                                      horse shying out to left

Fig. 133.

jump, and without allowing him to turn, back him up about
fifteen feet, then start forward at once. If you have a horse that
refuses consistently when faced with strange jumps, carry a whip,
and just as he takes his last stride and is ready to spring, give him
a sharp tap behind the saddle.

Most horses shy out and refuse because they are not yet ready
in their training to take the obstacles to which they are being
put, because they are not comfortable, or because they are bored
and sour from too much jumping. If you have rushed your
horse's training and he starts refusing, go back to much lower
jumps and don't expect so much from him. If you think he is
uncomfortable, have a veterinary check him. If he is sour, try
putting your jumps in different positions and having another
rider work with you. Follow the other or jump beside him.

Many horses and ponies that should have become satisfactory
companions and servants are so spoiled in their early years as to
be complete outlaws. Others that might have been still strong
and vigorous at twenty years or more have to be destroyed before

they are ten because, through ignorance, they were mishandled when young. So it is easy to see the importance of knowing the right way to train and care for a mount. In some communities boys and girls can get this instruction in organizations.

Do 4-H Clubs give this kind of instruction? Yes, these junior organizations with chapters throughout the United States include members who are interested in raising animals. The boys and girls often start with a young colt, steer, or lamb and raise it to maturity. Animals raised by 4-H Club members compete for prizes which are awarded on the basis of the animals' condition.

The American Saddle Horse Breeders' Association has done a great deal to encourage interest among juniors not only in raising colts but in training and showing them.

What are pony clubs? A number of years ago an organization called the *British Horse and Pony Club* was formed by the British Horse Society. Its purpose was to teach young people who owned their own mounts how best to care for them. There were many branches of the club, each one sponsored by the local hunt club. As more and more units came into existence, the country was divided into districts with a "district commissioner" to help organize and supervise the various branches within a district. There were branches of the British Club in the United States and Canada. These have been superseded by the United States Pony Club.* This is organized along the same lines as the British association, with branches in different localities, often sponsored by the local fox hunt, if there is one, and under the direction of a district commissioner.

Do these various branches ever meet in competition? Yes, there are local, regional, and national "rallies." Teams of riders are sent to these rallies, which usually last from four to six days. The competitions include cross-country riding, jumping and dressage, stable management, tests covering hunting procedures and first aid as well as general knowledge of horses. Teams are usually classified as consisting of A, B, C, and sometimes D riders. Today there are over two hundred Pony Clubs in the United

* For the name of the Pony Club nearest to you, write to Mrs. John A. Reidy, Secretary, United States Pony Club, Pleasant Street, Dover, Massachusetts

States. Riders of horses as well as ponies may join, and the club is open to anyone under twenty-one years of age.

Just watching a horse or pony gallop across a field is exciting. But to know how to raise and train one, to fit it and then to show this horse or pony yourself is a joyous experience and very often, a lifelong source of fun and satisfaction.

Glossary

aids: The rider's legs, hands, back, and the distribution of his weight are his *natural aids*. Through these he communicates with his horse and controls him. The *artificial aids* include the whip, spurs, check reins, and martingales

bight: The extra lengths of bridle reins that hang from the spot where the rider grasps the reins to the end buckles. In riding they are thrown forward and hang on the right along the horse's neck; in driving they hang straight down

blood lines: The horse's ancestry—his parents, grandparents, etc.

break: Getting a horse used to a saddle, a bridle, and the weight of the rider on his back is called "breaking" him

breed: A variety of horse, such as Thoroughbred, Saddler, Arabian, etc. Each breed has been developed for a specific purpose

brood mare: a mare kept for breeding purposes only

cast: A horse that lies down or falls down and is unable to get back on his feet without assistance is said to be "cast"

colt: A male horse or pony that is no longer being nursed by his mother and is less than six years old

combination: A horse that can be both ridden and driven

conformation: The horse's muscular and bony structure

dam: The mother of a horse or pony

dressage (*dres-sáhj*): A word borrowed from the French *dressure* that has come to mean advanced training to make the horse flexible, willing, sensitive, and strong

equitation: The art of riding

filly: A young female horse or pony that is no longer nursing

fit: To fit a horse or pony is to get him into top condition

five-gaited: A horse with the "slow-gait" and the "rack" as well as the walk, trot, and canter

"fixed" leg: When, in riding or jumping bareback, the rider carries his legs and feet as though he had stirrups—the knee bent, the ankle flexed, with the toe higher than the heel—he is said to ride with a "fixed leg"

foal: The horse or pony from birth to the time he is weaned

forehand: That part of the horse in front of the rider when he is in the saddle

forge: A horse that strikes the tip of his back shoe against the heel of his front shoe, causing a "click," at the trot is said to "forge"

foundation sire: A male horse that has the ability to pass on desirable qualities and is used to found a new breed

free-going: A word used to describe a horse that moves out freely

gait: The horse travels at the walk, trot, canter (gallop), pace, rack, running walk, amble, stepping pace, etc. These are called "gaits." The sequence in which one foot follows the other determines the gait

gelding: A horse that has been altered by surgery so that he can not be used for breeding purposes

girth: The measure around the body of the horse behind the withers and forelegs

girths: The band or strap that encircles the body of the horse to hold the saddle in place

hand: Horses and ponies are measured in hands. One hand equals four inches

hitch up: To fasten a horse to a cart or carriage

"horsemastership": Skill in training and caring for a horse, combined with correct riding techniques

lateral movement: A movement to the side

longe: To work a horse at the end of a long strap or tape, generally without a rider

mare: A female horse or pony six years old or over

near side: The left side of the horse, so called because it is nearer the rider when he mounts, leads, etc.

off side: The right side of the horse

palfrey: A small and gentle type of horse ridden by ladies in medieval days. Palfreys were chosen for their smooth gaits as well as their mild dispositions

pedigree: The list of a horse's ancestors is called his "pedigree"

"points" of a horse: Certain parts of the horse of especial importance in judging his strength and soundness (see fig. 11)

ranged in: When the rider moves in such a way that the horse's hindquarters are either pushed toward the center or travel a smaller circle than his forehand, the hindquarters are said to be "ranged in"

registered: A pure-blooded horse receives a special paper called his "pedigree" when his owner registers him with the headquarter of the particular breed. A registered show is one sponsored by the American Horse Shows Association

schooling: Generally used to mean teaching a horse to jump. This term can also mean general training

selective breeding: Developing a breed by choosing only those animals which show desirable characteristics

sire: The father of a horse or pony

sour: Used to describe a horse that is bored and irritated and refuses to continue working. Applied especially in regard to jumping

stallion: A male horse that has not been altered and can be used for breeding

stride: The distance from the point at which one foot of the horse leaves the ground to the point where that same foot is again placed on the ground

stud book: The book kept by a breeding association, listing the name and ancestry (pedigree) of each registered horse in the breed

tack: bridle, saddle, saddle-pad, stable blanket, etc.

tack up: To put the bridle and saddle on a horse

three-gaited: A word used in describing a horse that can walk, trot, and canter (gallop) but cannot do any other gait

voice-trained: A word used in describing a horse that obeys the voice of the trainer without any signals from the rider

wean: To take the foal away from the mare and prevent it from continuing to nurse

withers (or wither): top of shoulder (see Fig. 11)

weanling: A colt or filly between six months and one year of age

yearling: A colt or filly between one and two years of age

Index

[Italic page numbers denote illustrations]

Bolting, 297
Botflies, 159
Bowed tendon, 163
Braiding, 136–68
Bran, 115, 118
Breaking cart, 293, *294*
Breeding, 21–22
Bridle, 95–101, *96, 99,* 144–47, *145, 174,* 154; *see also* Bit
British Horse and Pony Club, 303
British Horse Society, 303
Broken lines, *217*
Brow-band, purpose, 97
Bucephalus, 12
Bucking, 298–99
Burs, 129
Byerly Turk, 21, *22*

C

Calico; *see* Parti-colored horse
Calks, 140
Cantering, 191–94
Capped elbow, 163–64
Capped hock, 164
Capriole, 36, *37,* 38
Care of horse or pony, 113–19
Catching the horse, 148–50, *150*
Cavaletti, 229, *229,* 232, 233, *237*
Cavalry, 12, 23–24, *172*
Cavalry knot, 126–27, *126*
Cavesson, 97, 145–46, 290
Centaur, 169
Chamberlain, General Harry D., 76
Change of hands, 208
Characteristics of breeds, American saddle horse, 30
American Shetland pony, 44
Appaloosa, 43
Arabian, 17–18
Connemara pony, 46
English Shetland pony, 43–44
Hackney pony, 44–45

Characteristics of breeds, half-breeds, 24
Lipizzaner, 34–39
Morgan, 32–34
Palomino, 42
Quarter horse, 39–40
Standardbreds, 27–28
Thoroughbreds, 23, 27
Welch pony, 45–46
Chariots, Assyrian, 11–12
Greek, 11
Charles, Archduke, of Austria, 38
Chest straps, 143
Chestnuts, 64
Chincoteague pony, 46–47
Chocolate pony, 64
Circles, 208, 210
Clipping, 134–36
Clothes, riding, 278–79
Clydesdale draft horse, 20
Coffin bone, 55
Colic, 121, 156, 158
Collected gait, 204, 206
Collection, 207
Color breeds, 40–43
Colors, Arabians, 18
Colts, 284–96
driving in long reins, 292–93
obedience training, 295
riding, 294
Commissures, 56
Communication, means of, 72
Conformation, 76–88
Connemara pony, 46, 75
Constipation, 158, 167
Contagious diseases, 156–58
Copper sulphate, 161, 168
Contes, 41
Cost, horse or pony, 93–94
Counter-change, 260
Counter-gallop, 219, 221, *221*
Courbette, 34, *36,* 38
Cow pony; *see* Stock horse

About the Author & Artist

Margaret Cabell Self is extremely well-known in the equestrian world. She is the author of nearly twenty books on horses and horsemastership, including *A World of Horses* and *Riding with Mariles*, both published by the McGraw-Hill Book Company. For over thirty years, Mrs. Self has been responsible for the training of young riders, and of riding instructors as well. Founder of the New Canaan Mounted Troop and the Silvermine School of Horsemastership, she is now advisor-consultant of the Escuela Ecuestre of San Miguel de Allende, a Mexican riding school.

After a childhood in the hunting country of Virginia, Mrs. Self married and settled in Connecticut, where she and her husband brought up four children. The Selfs now make their home on Block Island, off the coast of Rhode Island, spending their winters in Mexico.

Artist R. W. Mutch has served as a recognized judge at horse shows, including the annual show at Madison Square Garden in New York City, and is a member of the United States Equestrian Team. He studied art at the University of Virginia and now lives in New Canaan, Connecticut, with his wife and two-year-old-son, who rides a pony. Mr. Mutch was the illustrator of Mrs. Self's *Riding with Mariles*.